Cacus and Marsyas
IN ETRUSCO-ROMAN
LEGEND

Princeton Monographs in Art and Archaeology
xliv
Published for the
Department of Art and Archaeology,
Princeton University

Cacus and Marsyas
IN ETRUSCO-ROMAN LEGEND

Jocelyn Penny Small

Princeton University Press
PRINCETON, N.J.

Copyright © 1982 by Princeton University Press
Published by Princeton University Press, 41 William Street,
Princeton, New Jersey
In the United Kingdom: Princeton University Press,
Guildford, Surrey

All Rights Reserved
Library of Congress Cataloging in Publication Data will
be found on the last printed page of this book

This book has been composed in Linotron Bembo

Clothbound editions of Princeton University Press books
are printed on acid-free paper, and binding materials
are chosen for strength and durability

Printed in the United States of America by
Princeton University Press,
Princeton, New Jersey

In memory of my father

CONTENTS

ILLUSTRATIONS	ix
PREFACE	xiii
CHAPTER I. The Metamorphosis of Cacu	3
CHAPTER II. The Pictorial Evidence for the Res Gestae of Cacu	37
CHAPTER III. Greek Models and Etruscan Legends	57
CHAPTER IV. Marsyas in the Forum	68
CHAPTER V. Augury and the State	93
CHAPTER VI. Conclusion	105
APPENDIX I. Representations of Cacu	112
APPENDIX II. Misattributions to Cacus	124
APPENDIX III. Marsyas in the Forum	127
ABBREVIATIONS AND SELECTED BIBLIOGRAPHY	143
INDEX	161

ILLUSTRATIONS

following Index

PLANS

1. Rome, Augustan Era. After Coarelli, *Guida*, p. 38.
2. Palatine. After Coarelli, *Guida*, pp. 136-37.
3. Palatine, Scalae Caci and Area. After Romanelli, "Scavo," fig. 1.
4. Forum Romanum. After Müller-Karpe, pl. 2.

FIGURES

1. Cacu and the Vibennae (App. I, no. 1), London 633. After *ES* 5: pl. 127.
2. Cacu and the Vibennae (App. I, no. 1), London 633. Photograph: Courtesy of the Trustees of the British Museum.
3. Cacu and the Vibennae (App. I, no. 2), Chiusi, Tomba della Pellegrina. Photograph: Soprintendenza alle Antichità, Firenze.
4. Cacu and the Vibennae (App. I, no. 3), Siena 734. After BrK 2: pl. 119 no. 1.
5. Cacu and the Vibennae (App. I, no. 4), Florence 74233. Photograph: Soprintendenza alle Antichità, Firenze.
6. Cacu and the Vibennae (App. I, no. 5), Florence 5801. Photograph: Soprintendenza alle Antichità, Firenze.
7. Cacu(?) the Prisoner (App. I, no. 6), Berlin SK 1281. Photograph: Staatliche Museen zu Berlin, Antiken-Sammlung, Pergamon Museum.
8. Cacu(?) the Prisoner (App. I, no. 7), Florence 5777. Photograph: Soprintendenza alle Antichità, Firenze.
9. Cacu(?) the Prisoner (App. I, no. 8), Siena 730. After BrK 1: pl. 84 no. 2.
10. Cacu(?) the Prisoner (App. I, no. 8), Siena 730. Photograph: Author.

ILLUSTRATIONS

11. Cacu(?) the Prisoner (App. I, no. 9), Copenhagen, Ny Carlsberg Glyptotek H 298. Photograph: Museum.
12. Hermes and Cattle, Attic, Nikosthenes Painter, London E 815. Photograph: Courtesy of the Trustees of the British Museum.
13. Orestes and Pylades in Tauris, Apulian, Iliupersis Painter, Naples H 3223 (82113). Photograph: Soprintendenza alle Antichità delle Province di Napoli e Caserta, Napoli.
14. Musical Contest between Apollo and Marsyas, Apulian, Near the Ariadne Painter, Naples H 3231 (81392). Photograph: Soprintendenza alle Antichità delle Province di Napoli e Caserta, Napoli.
15. Musical Contest between Apollo and Marsyas, Faliscan, Berkeley 8.935. Photograph: Lowie Museum of Anthropology, University of California, Berkeley.
16. Musical Contest between Apollo and Marsyas, Attic, Marsyas Painter, Leningrad, Hermitage 1795. Photograph: Museum.
17. Musical Contest between Apollo and Marsyas, Lucanian, Brooklyn-Budapest Painter, Louvre K 519. Photograph: Museum.
18. Musical Contest between Apollo and Marsyas, Apulian, Felton Painter, Melbourne, National Gallery of Victoria 90/5. Photograph: After Trendall, "Felton," pl. 27.
19. Musical Contest between Apollo and Marsyas, Apulian, Felton Painter, Melbourne, National Gallery of Victoria 90/5. Photograph: After Trendall, "Felton," pl. 27.
20. Apollo and Marsyas, Etruscan Mirror, Rome, Museo Nazionale di Villa Giulia 12983. After *ES* 4: pl. 296.
21. Marsyas? Bound, Late Etruscan Funerary Urn, Perugia, Museo Archeologico. Photograph: Soprintendenza alle Antichità dell' Umbria, Perugia.
22. Detail of Right Panel of Anaglypha Traiani (App. III, B 1). Photograph: Deutsches Archäologisches Institut.
23. Detail of Left Panel of Anaglypha Traiani (App. III, B 1). Photograph: Deutsches Archäologisches Institut.
24. Denarii of L. Marcius Censorinus (App. III, B 2), Obverse—Apollo, Reverse—Marsyas. Photographs: American Numismatic Society.

ILLUSTRATIONS

25: (a) Aureus of A. Manlius, Reverse—Sulla; (b), (d), (e), (f) Denarii of L. Marcius Censorinus, Reverse—Marsyas; (c) Denarius Serratus of A. Postumius Albinus, Reverse—Togate Figure. Photographs: British Museum, Coin Cabinet.
26. Imperial Bronzes with Marsyas (App. III, C): (a) no. 6—Alexandria Troas; (b, c) no. 20—Neapolis; (d) no. 14—Damascus; (e, f) no. 18—Sidon; (g, h) no. 19—Tyre; (i, j) no. 15—Berytus. Photographs: Cabinet des Médailles, Bibliothèque Nationale, Paris.
27. Marsyas (App. III, B 3), Paestum, Museo Archeologico. Photograph: Prof. Nunzio Daniele.
28. Marsyas (App. III, B 4), Once Dorpat, private—G. Loeschke. Now? After Jordan, *Marsyas*, pl. III C.
29. Forum Romanum—View from Palatine. Photograph: Author.
30. Forum Romanum—View from Curia, Augustan Rostra on right; the Fig, the Olive, and the Vine on left. Photograph: Author.

PREFACE

THE passage of time fosters the development of legends. When what was once known becomes hazy, it is ripe for embellishment. The greater the separation of the teller from the event the more fabulous the account. Yet no matter how dramatic the deed, heroic the hero, or villainous the villain, a kernel of historical truth remains. This factual element not only distinguishes legend from pure myth and folktale, but also keeps the legend firmly rooted in a political sphere; for legends are told not just for entertaining or didactic purposes, but, like any propaganda, bent to meet contemporary needs. When a diversity of competing groups exists, a golden age of legends results. Such a period occurred in Etrusco-Roman Italy during the later Republic and the beginning of the Empire.

Whatever the original catalyst or catalysts, the end of the fourth century B.C. marks an increased interest in bygone events and in particular of the sixth century B.C.—a period pivotal for both Etruscans and Romans. It witnessed the height of the power of the Etruscans when they ruled Rome, as well as their expulsion and the establishment of the Roman Republic. While the characters coincide and the basic events agree, much remained open to manipulation not just once but many times. That is, prior to the beginning of the Empire Roman annalists recorded a number of highly biased accounts of rival families, while the Etruscan view can sometimes be reconstructed from their pictorial representations. Even the standard histories, such as those by Livy and Tacitus, sometimes contain stray, almost inadvertent, references that hint at situations differing from the "canonical."

Cacus is one of the few figures to appear concurrently in Roman histories and on Etruscan monuments. Although not as important as the Tarquins or those early noble Romans, nonetheless Cacus had a remarkable and indeed irksome staying power on the Palatine. Unlike other local characters he received an extended treatment in Book 8 of the *Aeneid*. His loathsome actions and half-monstrous form there contrast greatly with the Etruscan rendering of him as a fair, Apolline youth. His transformation from beauty to beast takes place over several centuries and involves a number of the major dramatis personae

PREFACE

of sixth century Rome—the Tarquins, the Vibennae, and Lars Porsenna.

The most curious aspect, however, is Cacus's association with Marsyas. If it happened only once, the connection could be considered accidental—yet another scribal error; but it not only occurs twice, it occurs in both Etruscan and Roman sources. To understand the relationship between Cacus and Marsyas requires an untangling not just of the res gestae of Cacus but also an analysis of the development of Marsyas—how and why he, like Cacus, also enjoyed a permanent and prominent landmark in the center of Rome.

Crucial evidence comes from one of the only groups of late Etruscan funerary urns securely identified as depicting an Etrusco-Roman legend. An Etruscan mirror in the British Museum with the same scene as the urns has inscriptions which clearly and indisputably label the participants as Etrusco-Roman figures: the Vibennae ambushing Cacu(s) and Artile. Although the mirror and the urns are well known and have often been published, no examination of their pictorial sources has ever been made. The model, the musical contest between Apollo and Marsyas, is likewise without dispute over its identification and equally popular in scholarship. An analysis of how the Greek prototype and the Etruscan adaptation relate to each other (Chapter III) could easily have been done in an article. Why the one became the model for the other, however, is a much more complex problem, to which the rest of the book is devoted.

The careers of Cacus and Marsyas may be likened to two balls of wool woven not just together but into a larger fabric, the legends of Rome. Consequently the unravelling of their individual strands will involve not just them but others, and similarly can only be accomplished in a particular order, not necessarily from the last stitch back to the first, but rather in a basically straightforward chronological manner. As a result this study will range far beyond the two figures to consideration of the practice of divination (Chapters I, II, IV, and V); of ancient historiography (Chapters I and II); of the topography of the Palatine (Chapter I) and the Forum Romanum (Chapter IV); of art, especially iconography and patronage (Chapters II, III, and IV); and of historical events involving Rome in the sixth and first centuries B.C. (Chapters II, IV, and V).

My terminology is standard, but a few prefatory comments may be helpful for certain words and concepts. "Etrusco-Roman" refers to those figures, legends, etc. that are neither clearly Etruscan nor fully Roman, but a mix of the two; "Italic" likewise covers what is not

PREFACE

Etruscan nor Roman nor any other specifically identifiable culture in Italy. "Divination" includes any means of foreseeing the future, of which "augury" is a particular form based on observed signs, such as birds, and "haruspicy" applies only to the examination of entrails. A "seer" may foretell the future in a number of ways; but an "augur" can do so only through sighting certain phenomena. A seer may be "prophetic," but is generally not "oracular" like "oracles" such as Apollo at Delphi or Faunus at Albunea. Finally, for clarity in describing the pictorial representations a somewhat artificial terminology will be used in distinguishing satyrs from sileni. "Silenus" will refer to the old, bald, paunchy follower of Dionysus and "satyr" to his younger counterpart.

Ancient names, words, etc. are anglicized idiosyncratically according to modern convention. Hence Vibenna not Vipinias, satyrs not satyroi. I tend to use the Greek, Etruscan, or Roman form of a particular name depending on the context. While Cacu appears on the Etruscan mirror and urns, Cacus fights Hercules in Vergil. In direct quotes the spelling of the source is preserved. Similarly all literary references are considered to be by the writer in whose works they appear unless that writer directly cites another writer by name as his source. The reference is then dated accordingly. For example, because Solinus, a second century A.D. author, says "as Gellius recorded," the passage is ascribed and dated to Gnaeus Gellius, the second century B.C. annalist. In citing ancient authors, I use the abbreviations in OCD^2 ix-xxii, except that I usually give the author's name in full. The OCD^2 also supplied the majority of dates for authors, etc.; the rest come from *RE* unless stated otherwise. Those translations, which are not my own, are generally from the *Loeb Classical Library* (*LCL*), referred to by ancient author, title, volume number, and page.

The scholarship on the subjects studied here is enormous. To do it justice would result in a Servian commentary to the text. Since I am no Vergil, I have limited my references to those works that I thought significant or found particularly helpful. A highly selected bibliography is combined with the list of abbreviations at the end of the book. In general it will be assumed that the reader can find his own way through the standard references such as *RE, ML, TDAR,* and *PDAR*. Citations of *APS, LCS,* and *RVA* follow those for *ABV* and *ARV* ^{2}, that is the page, then the number of the object thereon. Lastly, in the text the numbers and letters in parentheses after objects and quotations refer to the catalogues and lists in Appendices I through III, with the appendix given as a Roman numeral; followed by the

PREFACE

Arabic entry number for Appendices I and II and by the letter of the section and the Arabic entry number for Appendix III.

The opportunity to study the objects personally was invaluable. In particular I should like to express my gratitude to the following museums and their curators for their assistance: the Ashmolean Museum, Oxford; the British Museum, London; the Cabinet des Médailles and the Louvre, Paris; the Pergamon Museum, Berlin; the archaeological museums in Chiusi, Florence, Perugia, and Siena; and the American Numismatic Society, New York. For photographs I thank: Berkeley, Lowie Museum of Anthropology; Berlin, the Pergamon Museum; Copenhagen, the Ny Carlsberg Glyptotek; Leningrad, Museum of the Hermitage; London, the British Museum; New York, the American Numismatic Society; Paris, Cabinet des Médailles; Paris, Louvre; Perugia, Museo Archeologico; Rome, Deutsches Archaeologisches Institut; Soprintendenza alle Antichità-Firenze; and Soprintendenza alle Antichità delle Province di Napoli e Caserta-Napoli. I also very much appreciate the generous support of the Research Council of Rutgers University for the acquisition of photographs and the final preparation of the manuscript.

As ever I have benefited from discussions with my colleagues and particularly those in related fields. I especially profited from meetings with Kyle Meredith Phillips, Jr., Louise Adams Holland, and H. Anne Weis. I am very grateful to William A. P. Childs of the Department of Art and Archaeology, Princeton University for carefully shepherding the manuscript through the various stages to publication; and at Princeton University Press I thank Christine Ivusic and Marilyn Campbell.

December 1980

Cacus and Marsyas
IN ETRUSCO-ROMAN LEGEND

"Si qua sunt alia quae nos commovent, in medium proferamus, ut ipsa collatio nostrum, non Maronis, absolvat errorem."

("If there are any other passages in Vergil which trouble us, let us declare them so that, by bringing them together for our joint consideration, we may dispose of mistakes which will prove to be ours not Vergil's.")

Macrobius, *Saturnalia* 3.12.9,
translated by P. C. Davies.

· I ·

THE METAMORPHOSIS
OF CACU

The formation of Rome's legendary history took several centuries. It developed not linearly, but kaleidoscopically: as the same colored pieces in a kaleidoscope can be endlessly shaken to form new designs within the basic restrictions of the glass and pieces themselves, so each Roman period would "shake" the elements in the legends of Rome to form new patterns. As the instrument can be refined by adding new colors and shapes, so the legends were elaborated with different characters and events. The stories surrounding the figure of Cacus work in this manner.

Cacus is best known as the horrible monster in the *Aeneid* (8.184-305)[1] who grapples with Hercules over the possession of cattle which actually belong to neither, but to Geryon, a three-headed or three-bodied monster, who lives at the edge of the world, now known as Spain. Cacus, on the other hand, resides in Rome in a desolate area of the Aventine in a vast cavern. He is the half-human son of Vulcan who proves his parentage by belching forth fire and smoke, as he ravages the countryside during the time Evander rules on the Palatine. Hercules, on his return from stealing the cattle, passes through Italy, where Cacus steals the choicest of the cattle from him by the clever stratagem of dragging them backwards by their tails. Hercules recovers the cattle not through the efforts of his "superior" intelligence but by the help of the captured cows which low to the rest of the herd as he drives it by. Hercules then avenges the theft by killing Cacus. In thanks for finding the cows, Hercules himself establishes the Ara Maxima and trains the Potitii and the Pinarii in the performance of the proper ritual.

[1] The literary aspects of the passage do not affect this study. Recent commentaries on the *Aeneid* passage: Eden, pp. xxii-xxiii, 74-103; and Gransden, pp. 104-23. Specific studies of Hercules and Cacus: Bréal, pp. 1-161; Winter, pp. 171-273; Münzer, *Cacus*; Capovilla, pp. 60-83; Bayet, *Hercule*, pp. 203-33 (on pp. 206-207 he discusses the theories of Bréal, Rosen, Kuhn, Wissowa, and Preller); Kroll, pp. 389-99; Santoro, pp. 9-22; Sbordone, pp. 149-80; Bömer, "Studien," pp. 319-69; Dumézil, *Horace*, pp. 137-40; Schnepf, pp. 250-68; Bellen, pp. 23-30; Buchheit, pp. 116-33; Radke, *Götter*, pp. 75-76; Galinsky, "Cacus," pp. 18-51; Sanz Ramos, pp. 389-400; Gilmartin, pp. 41-47; Tanner, pp. 37-44; Binder; Paratore, pp. 260-82; Galinsky, *Herakles*, pp. 142ff. and 153ff.; Zarker, pp. 34-48; Pfiffig, *Religio*, pp. 23, 227, 235; Sutton, pp. 391-93.

METAMORPHOSIS OF CACU

A late fourth century Etruscan mirror from Bolsena and now in the British Museum, however, presents an entirely different view of Cacus. (App. I, no. 1; Fig. 1) In the center of the mirror between two trees two figures in almost identical poses, a youth and a young man, sit facing right with their heads slightly bowed, their feet gently crossed, and their drapery covering only their lower torsos. On the right, Cacu—the inscription appears by the crown of his head between the branches of the tree—plays a lyre, held in his left hand, with a plectrum in his right hand. He has long hair and a torque about his neck. In front, Artile—the inscription runs from top to bottom just behind his head—holds a diptych open in his hands on his lap. The letters on the diptych are not legible. In the upper middle section of the scene, a satyr or a silenus, with pointed ears and hair standing on end in true Vergilian fashion, peers over the rough rocks at the action taking place below him. Because his form readily identifies him, he alone has no accompanying inscription. On either side of Cacu and Artile two warriors, with shields and swords and in high boots, banded cuirasses, mantles, and helmets, stand poised in ambush. Because the inscriptions on the rim of the mirror name the left warrior Caile Vipinas and the right one Aule Vipinas, who are Etruscan heroes, the mirror obviously depicts an Etruscan event. Cacu's Apolline form and the diptych Artile holds have led scholars to interpret Cacu as a seer accompanied by a youthful assistant, Artile, who are both being ambushed by the Vibennae brothers.

Because this Etruscan characterization of Cacu appears to be at such variance with the better-known Vergilian monster, some scholars have either rejected the inscriptions on the mirror[2] or posited two separate figures, an Etruscan Cacu and a Roman Cacus.[3] Neither solution is correct. Cacu and Cacus not only represent the same character,[4] but the original divinatory nature of Cacu formed the basis for the transformation from a beneficent seer to a baneful monster, as a study of the chronological development of the figure of Cacu will show.

Each "classical" area, each "classical" people produced local he-

[2] For example: Levi, "Pellegrina," p. 30. Those who take this position generally support it by casting aspersions on the trustworthiness of Etruscan inscriptions. As misidentifications by the Etruscans can be found, so can they be made by the Greeks; as each Greek example is considered on its individual merits, so must each Etruscan inscription be evaluated separately.

[3] For example: Münzer, "Vibenna," pp. 599ff. and *Cacus*, pp. 113-14; and Messerschmidt, "Probleme," p. 76.

[4] Körte in *ES* 5:168; Brommer, "Caco," pp. 247-48; Pfiffig, *Religio*, p. 23; Alföldi, *SVR*, p. 186.

roes. As the individual worlds expanded, the different sets of heroes and stories came into contact with one another. The resulting conflicts were reconciled through three methods, frequently used in combination: the omission, the conflation, and the creation of characters and events. Every story retained an inviolable core, but freely permitted other less crucial elements to be altered to suit contemporary circumstances. The adaptations were not necessarily restricted to the immediate stories and figures involved, but borrowed freely from related types.[5] This process is evident in the following passage, one of the earliest extant texts about Cacus with virtually all of the basic elements of the legend already present:

> Ambiguity raised questions, because certain things were worshipped there much before Romulus. To be sure the altar, which Hercules had vowed if he found the lost cows, he dedicated to Pater Inventor after Cacus had been punished. This Cacus inhabited the place, which is called Salinae where the Porta Trigemina now stands. He, as Gellius recorded, with Megales the Phrygian as a companion, was sent as an envoy by Marsyas the king to Tarchon the Tyrrhenian, who put him in custody. He broke his bonds and went back home. Returning with greater forces, he seized the area around Vulturnus and Campania. When he dared to appropriate even those places which the laws had granted to the Arcadian, he was killed by Hercules who happened to be present. The Sabines received Megales who taught them the art of augury. Hercules himself also set up an altar to his own divinity that is held to be the greatest among the pontifices, since he had learned from Nicostrata, the mother of Evander, who was told by the prophesying of Carmenta, that he would be immortal. . . .[6]

---

[5] As these legends are studied, Joseph Fontenrose's injunction should be kept in mind. "Mythical genealogy and system-making paradoxically obscure the truth by making too sharp distinctions among mythical persons." *Python*, pp. 385-86.

[6] Ambiguitatum quaestiones excitavit, quod quaedam ibi multo ante Romulum culta sint. quippe aram Hercules, quam voverat, si amissas boves repperisset, punito Caco patri Inventori dicavit. qui Cacus habitavit locum, cui Salinae nomen est: ubi Trigemina nunc porta. hic, ut Gellius tradidit, cum a Tarchone Tyrrheno, ad quem legatus venerat missu Marsyae regis, socio Megale Phryge, custodiae foret datus, frustratus vincula et unde venerat redux, praesidiis amplioribus occupato circa Vulturnum et Campaniam regno, dum adtrectare etiam ea audet, quae concesserant in Arcadum iura, duce Hercule qui tunc forte aderat oppressus est. Megalen Sabini receperunt, disciplinam augurandi ab eo docti. suo quoque numini idem Hercules instituit aram, quae maxima apud pontifices habetur, cum se ex Nicostrate, Euandri matre, quae a vaticinio Carmentis dicta est, inmortalem conperisset.
[Solinus 1.7-10.]

Solinus, a geographical writer from the second century A.D., has used the Vergilian tradition about Hercules and Cacus as a frame for the version recorded by Gnaeus Gellius, the second century B.C. annalist.[7] If the Etruscan mirror represents an Etruscan version and Vergil's Book 8 a Roman view, then Gellius stands almost midway between the two. He looks to the Etruscans when he portrays Cacus as human, as associated with augury, as captured by the Etruscans, and as living during the time of the Tarquins; he anticipates Vergil when Cacus comes into conflict with the Arcadian, presumably Evander, and is killed by Hercules. Distinctive to Gellius are the location in Campania and the connection of Cacus with Marsyas. He makes no mention of the cattle or of Cacus's parentage. Because every one of these elements has an independent, yet interdependent, development, each must be considered first individually and then together with the others.

The Etruscan Cacu

Cacu the Man

Cacu slowly slips in status from his exalted position of seer on the Etruscan mirror, the earliest extant source. Gellius makes him an envoy of Marsyas. Cassius Hemina, another second century B.C. annalist perhaps slightly earlier than Gellius, reduces Cacu to "the slave of Evander, crafty with evil and beyond other things most thieving. . . ."[8] All these characterizations coexist in the second century B.C., because Cacu the seer appears during that period on Etruscan funerary urns (App. I, nos. 2-5; Figs. 3-6). In the following century attempts to produce an internally coherent and consistent tale change Cacus into a "shepherd . . . ferocious in strength"[9] who would by profession be interested in cattle. Next Vergil heightens the evilness of Hemina's thief and increases the bulk of Livy's shepherd by turning Cacus into a "half-man" and "monster."[10] Helping in the

---

[7] While I start the Gellius section with "hic, ut . . ." as literally stated in Solinus (n. 6 above), Peter (*HRR*², pp. 149-50, no. 7) begins it with "aram Hercules . . ." and ends it with ". . . ab eo docti." Presumably the "quoque" of the next sentence indicates that Solinus has resumed speaking. Recently see: Rawson, "Annalists," pp. 713-16.

[8] ". . . Cacus Euandri servus, nequitiae versutus et praeter cetera furacissimus . . ." *OGR* 7.7. For the entire passage and its authorship, see n. 76 below.

[9] ". . . pastor . . . ferox viribus . . ." Livy 1.7.5.

[10] *Aen.* 8.194, "semi-hominis," and 8.198, "monstro." Compare St. Augustine, *De civ. D.* 19.12, ". . . nec malus nec monstrum nec semi-homo vocaretur." He obviously had the Vergilian text at hand, as probably did Dante (*Inferno*, Canto 25.34) who took the "semi-homo" to be part-centaur. I thank James G. McGregor for the reference to Dante.

downfall was the name Cacus itself. At the same time as Cacu underwent his metamorphosis into a monster, the Romans became too well versed in Greek, with the result that they produced false etymologies. Servius states:

> We know, however, that evil is called κακός by the Greeks: at that time the Arcadians used to call him thusly. Afterwards, after the accent had been transferred [i.e. from the second to the first syllable], Cácus was said, like Ἑλένη and Hélena.[11]

Servius has merely reversed the actual process. The stress was always on the first syllable in Cácu and therefore was carried over into the pronunciation of Cácus, since Cacu has nothing to do with the Greek κακός.[12]

Significantly Cacu's decline began only after the implications of the Greek connotations of Cacus/κακός occurred to the Romans, which, in turn, possibly led to the creation, or at the very least the adoption, of Evander as his enemy; for it is not clear that Evander existed much before the second century B.C.[13]—the very period when Cacu first

---

[11] "Novimus autem malum a Graecis κακόν dici: quem ita illo tempore Arcades appellabant. postea translato accentu Cácus dictus est, ut Ἑλένη Helena." Servius, ad Aen. 8.190.

[12] Cacu is probably an Etruscan name. Ogilvie, Comm, p. 58. De Simone (p. 96) says that the Greek ending of "os" was translated into Etruscan by a final "u." One of the first scholars to recognize the false etymology of Cacus was Preuner, p. 392.

[13] No extant references to Evander date much earlier than the second century B.C., although some scholars put Evander's first appearance earlier, as Ogilvie (Comm, p. 54) does in the fourth century B.C. Dionysius (Ant. Rom. 1.79.4ff.) names Fabius Pictor, the third century B.C. annalist, as his source on the birth of Romulus and Remus. In the midst of this narrative (79.8) Dionysius puts in a contemporary aside. After he has just said, "εἰς τοῦτο τὸ χωρίον ἐλθοῦσα ἀποκρύπτεται," he comments on the landmark during his own time, "τὸ μὲν οὖν ἄλσος οὐκέτι διαμένει, τὸ δὲ ἄντρον . . . δείκνυται." At the end of this section he says, "ἦν δὲ τὸ χωρίον τῶν σὺν Εὐάνδρῳ ποτὲ οἰκισάντων αὐτὸ Ἀρκάδων ἱερὸν ὡς λέγεται." Next a new paragraph, 79.9, begins, "ὡς δὲ ἀπέστη τὸ θηρίον αἴρουσιν οἱ νομεῖς τὰ βρέφη . . ." Peter (HRR², 1:8-19, no. 5b) rightly separates Dionysius's travelogue about the Lupercal from Fabius Pictor's account, but, nonetheless, considers the sentence about Evander to be the annalist's. Yet its very position at the end of the travelogue and before the resumption of the story itself, as well as the words "ὡς λέγεται," indicate that the remark belongs to Dionysius, not to Fabius Pictor. The earliest extant references, then, date to the second century B.C.: Cincius Alimentus apud Servius, ad G. 1.10; Polybius apud Dion. Hal., Ant. Rom. 1.32; Cassius Hemina apud OGR 6; L. Coelius Antipater apud Strabo 5.3 (230); Cato apud Solinus 2.8. See also Poucet, "Pictor," p. 204. Those who accept the remark as Fabius Pictor's put Evander's debut in the third century B.C., as for example, Bayet, "Arcadisme," pp. 70-71, although in Hercule (p. 218) he does say that "la tradition d'Evandre et des Arcadiens n'ayant pu naître topographiquement qu' à Rome."

"Evander" also appears in another context in the second century B.C. Apollodorus (Bibl. 3.12.5) refers to him as a son of Priam, a version that never completely died out; for Diodorus (5.79.3) in the following century makes Evander a son of Sarpedon, and Dictys Cretensus (3.14) of the second-to-third century A.D. has him captured by

appears as κακός. Two factors influenced the genesis or espousal of Evander: the connections between Arcadia and Rome[14] and the opponent, Cacus. When the Arcadians began to settle in Magna Graecia from the sixth century B.C. on, they brought with them the idea that Greeks were founders of cities in Italy. The stories of their emigration remained general and without particular leaders until the second century B.C. Even then Gellius did not identify the "Arcadian" whose lands Cacus appropriated. Meanwhile Roman knowledge of Greece had increased to the point where latent "parallels" between Rome and Arcadia became apparent. Both shared similarly named sites, the Palatine and Pallanteum,[15] and religious rites, those associated with the Lupercalia and Pan Lykeios.[16] To impart a circumstantial reality only the figure forging the alliance between the two areas remained to be named or invented. The obvious choice would have been Pallas. Since Hesiod he had been the eponymous founder of Pallanteum in Arcadia,[17] and according to the second century B.C. historian Polybius[18] a Pallas lent his name to the Palatine. Yet he was ignored.[19] If Cacus could be κακός, what better foil could he have

---

the Greeks at Troy. Significantly Diodorus (4.21, see n. 56 below) does not know the Arcadian Evander of Rome, for Cacius alone receives Hercules.

[14] Bayet, "Arcadisme," pp. 62-143.

[15] The comparison is so stated in, for example, Varro, *Ling*. 5.53 and Dion. Hal., *Ant. Rom*. 1.31.4. Nevertheless, Varro directly and Dionysius indirectly mention that other derivations for Palatine existed. According to Kent (*LCL* Varro 1:51 n. a) "there is no convincing etymology," but Lewis and Short (p. 1291) derive the word from the Sanskrit *pala*, meaning shepherd. The latter, at the very least, reflects the fourth of Varro's suggestions: "Eundem hunc locum a pecore dictum putant quidam; itaque Naevius Balatium appellat." Ogilvie (*Comm*, p. 52, with other ancient references) believes the name derives from a pre-Indo-European root meaning rock or hill.

[16] Evander's connection with Pan in his Greek home appears to have helped foster his link with the Lupercalia, which may, in turn, have led to a confusion of Evander with Faunus, also associated with that rite. Accordingly, in another reversal of the actual sequence (cf. n. 11 above) the name and figure of Faunus were derived from Evander: "Cincius et Cassius aiunt ab Euandro Faunum deum appellatum, . . ." Cincius Alimentus (third-to-second centuries B.C.) and Cassius Hemina (second century B.C.) *apud* Servius, *ad G*. 1.10. Some modern scholars, consequently, believe the name Evander to be merely a translation of Faunus, the favoring one. See Radke, *Götter*, pp. 114, 120.

[17] Hesiod, "The Catalogues of Women and the Eoiae," no. 32 *apud* Step. Byz., s.v. "Παλλάντιον." Compare Hesiod, *Theog*., pp. 383ff. Bömer (*Komm*, p. 54) implies that Evander was associated with the Arcadian Pallanteum since the *Geryoneis* of Stesichorus in the sixth century B.C. Yet the pertinent fragment of Stesichorus quoted in Pausanias 8.3.2 merely says, "Παλλαντίου μὲν δὴ καὶ Στησίχορος ὁ Ἱμεραῖος ἐν Γηρυονηΐδι ἐποιήσατο μνήνην." Later citations connecting Evander and Pallanteum by no means permit one to interpolate Evander's existence into so early a period.

[18] Polybius *apud* Dion. Hal., *Ant. Rom*. 1.32.1.

[19] Dionysius (*Ant. Rom*. 1.32.2) clearly was concerned about this problem. Although Polybius (n. 18 above) said there was a tomb to Pallas on the Palatine, neither could Dionysius find it nor had he heard of worship of any kind being paid to Pallas. On

than the εὖ ἀνδρός? And so the Arcadian of Gellius acquired a name, Evander.[20] In fact, Cacus in the pre-Vergilian sources is κακός only when he appears with Evander.[21]

Even Vergil, followed by Propertius and Ovid,[22] did not manage entirely to suppress the humanness of Cacus. Servius in the fourth century A.D. considered that "Cacus according to fable was the son of Vulcan," but continued in the same passage: "Nevertheless the truth according to the philologists and historians maintains that this man [Cacus] was the most worthless slave of Evander and a thief."[23]

---

the other hand, he mentions that both Evander and Carmenta received public sacrifices. On the reliability of Dionysius: Andrén, "Dionysius," pp. 88-104.

[20] Rose (*Handbook*, p. 311) says, "If it [the name Evander] is pure invention, I should rather take it as meaning 'Strong-man', a not inappropriate name for the earliest settler of a city whose name suggested the Greek ῥώμη (strength)." His interpretation is based on the strict Greek definition and usage of the root "εὐανδρ-" as "physical fitness" or "manliness." It may also mean "abundance of good men and true." These definitions are from *LSJ*, p. 706. In other words, Euandros as "Good Man" is bad Greek, but good plotting. In fact, the first extant reference to both Evander and Cacus (significantly it is Roman) draws the parallel between their two natures. Cassius Hemina (*apud OGR* 6) speaks of Cacus as "nequitiae versutus et praeter cetera furacissimus" and of Evander as an "excellentissimae iustitiae vir." Later commentators were particularly fond of this contrast: Fulgentius C 25 and the fifteenth-century Coluccius Salutatus, *De Laboribus Herculis* 3.30.19, " 'Andros' enim 'homo' dicitur, 'eu' 'bonum.' " Moreover, because Evander was sometimes omitted in the late second-century B.C. and later versions, but Cacus always appeared, Evander's presence obviously depends on Cacus and not vice versa.

Because Pallas by name seemed so clearly related to the Palatine, he was retained as a relative of Evander: the grandson, according to Polybius *apud* Dion. Hal., *Ant. Rom.* 1.32.1; the son, according to Vergil, *Aen.* 8.104; or the grandfather, according to Servius, *ad Aen.* 8.51.

[21] Perhaps the most striking instance of the good Cacus appears in Diod. Sic. 4.21 (see n. 56 below). Propertius (4.9), the only surviving author to portray an evil Cacus and not to mention Evander, is clearly adapting the Vergilian characterization to his own ends. Three hundred years later, St. Augustine (*De civ. D.* 19.12) astutely remarks about the increasing blackening of Cacus's character: "Verum iste non fuerit vel, quod magis credendum est, non talis fuerit qualis poetica vanitate describitur; nisi enim nimis accusaretur Cacus, parum Hercules laudaretur." Earlier in the passage St. Augustine gives quite a touching portrayal of what life was like for the wretched Vergilian Cacus. Later commentators, such as Tiberius Claudius Donatus (*ad loc.*) and Coluccius Salutatus (*De Laboribus Herculis* 3.28 and 30), also consider the Vergilian treatment of Cacus a literary embellishment. Compare *Myth. Vat.* 3.13.1 where Cacus's theft makes him κακός and hence *malus* in opposition to the *virtus* of Hercules.

[22] Propertius (4.9) implies that Cacus was a three-headed monster, "per tria partitos qui dabat ora sonos." Ovid (*Fasti* 1.543-86) follows Vergil more closely than Propertius in the details. Cacus is merely "ferox" (550) and a "monstrum" (554) of singular frame and strength.

[23] "Cacus secundum fabulam Vulcani filius fuit, . . . veritas tamen secundum philologos et historicos hoc habet, hunc fuisse Euandri nequissimum servum ac furem." Servius, *ad Aen.* 8.190. "Historicos" probably refers to the Annalists, such as Hemina and Gellius; "philologos" may mean writers like Varro, although no mention of Cacus has survived in his extant works. *Myth. Vat.* 1.66, 2.153, and 3.13.1 make virtually the same statement as Servius.

In other words, Servius has repeated the description of Cassius Hemina. The idea that the lineage presented by Vergil was "fable" may have been reinforced by the historian, Diodorus Siculus, also writing during the first century B.C.: "Here [on the Palatine] some of the notable men, among them Cacius [sic] and Pinarius, welcomed Herakles with marked acts of hospitality and honoured him with pleasing gifts . . ."[24] This Cacus comes somewhere between the seer of the Etruscans and the envoy of Gellius. In other words, the portrayal of Cacus runs the entire gamut of possibilities from good to evil, human to monster, virtually contemporaneously.

Cacu the Seer and His Capture

While no ancient text directly associates Cacus with divination, the evidence from the Etruscan mirror (App. I, no. 1) is conclusive. There Cacu is definitely a seer, singing a prophecy which may be recorded on the diptych Artile holds. As a handsome youth with flowing locks who plays the lyre, Cacu most closely recalls Apollo. Even the setting amidst the rocky crags may resemble Delphi.

The prophetic ability of Cacus, though seemingly forgotten in later times, was never completely buried. Cacus retains a level of intelligence far greater than that to be expected from a mere monster. Cassius Hemina (*OGR*, p.6) refers to him as "clever" ("versutus"), albeit in "inequity" ("nequitiae"). In stealing the cattle, Cacus employs a gimmick which completely baffles Hercules who prevails only through brute strength. Such cunning frequently provoked mixed reactions in antiquity, and may have helped to blacken Cacu's character. Compare Hermes:

---

[24] Diod. Sic. 4.21.2. Translation from *LCL* 2.409. Although Diodorus clearly refers to a "Κάκιος," he must mean Cacus. Diodorus probably derived "Cacius" from the name Scalae Caci on the mistaken basis that the genitive Caci belonged to the group of second declension masculine nouns with the nominative singular ending in "-ius," such as *filius, fili*. Since Diodorus was writing before the Augustan period when it became common to add the "i" of the genitive to the root, i.e. *filius, filii*, he could quite naturally make this error, especially if he had generally heard the name only in the context of the Scalae. He may even have felt that "Cacus" was too close to "κακός" to be a proper name and especially for his good Cacius. On the grammatical point, see Allen and Greenough, p. 22, no. 49b. On Diodorus's knowledge of Latin, he himself says (1.4.5), "διὰ τὴν ἐπιμιξίαν τοῖς ἐν τῇ νήσῳ πολλὴν ἐμπειρίαν τῆς Ῥωμαίων διαλέκτου περιπεποιημένοι, . . ." Compare Oldfather's discussion of Diodorus's Latin in *LCL* 1.xiii-xiv.—"He knew it at least well enough for his purposes." That such errors may occur even today is shown by the reference to the "Scala Cacia" by H. E. Butler in his translation of Propertius, *LCL* 263 n. 1. Similarly, Plutarch (*Vit. Rom.* 20.4) refers to the "βαθμοὺς καλῆς ἀκτῆς," when the context indicates that the Scalae Caci were meant. On the emendation of Plutarch's text, see Flacière, "Plutarque," pp. 88-89.

METAMORPHOSIS OF CACU

For then she [Maia] bare a son, of many shifts, blandly cunning, a robber, a cattle driver, a bringer of dreams, a watcher by night, a thief at the gates, one who was soon to show forth wonderful deeds among the deathless gods. . . . [Yet] your father got you to be a great worry to mortal men and deathless gods.[25]

As Hermes was a "bringer of dreams," Cacus was a seer. Hermes steals the cattle of Apollo in the same manner as Cacus removes those of Hercules. Both not only hide the beasts in a cave, but when accosted about the theft reply glibly.

Then Hermes answered him [Apollo] with crafty words: "Son of Leto, what harsh words are these you have spoken? And is it cattle of the field you are come here to seek? I have not seen them: . . . Am I like a cattle-lifter? . . . This is no task for me: . . . I care for sleep, and milk of my mother's breast . . ."[26]

Cacus in Dionysius of Halicarnassus tries to stall Hercules by switching the blame onto the victim:

But Cacus stood before the door, and when Hercules inquired after the cattle, denied that he had seen them, and when the other desired to search the cave, would not suffer him to do so, but called upon his neighbours for assistance, complaining of the violence offered to him by the stranger.[27]

The same close relation between the two figures also exists in the pictorial tradition. A fifth century red-figure kylix, found in Etruria

[25] καὶ τότ' ἐγείνατο παῖδα πολύτροπον, αἱμυλομήτην,
ληιστῆρ', ἐλατῆρα βοῶν, ἡγήτορ' ὀνείρων,
νυκτὸς ὀπωπητῆρα, πυληδόκον, ὃς τάχ' ἔμελλεν
ἀμφανέειν κλυτὰ ἔργα μετ' ἀθανάτοισι θεοῖσιν. . . .
ἔρρε πάλιν· μεγάλην σε πατὴρ ἐφύτευσε μέριμναν
θνητοῖς ἀνθρώποισι καὶ ἀθανάτοισι θεοῖσι.
["Homeric Hymn to Hermes," 13-16 and 160-61. Translation from *LCL* 365, 375. Compare Brown, *Hermes*, especially pp. 69-105, 148-55.]

[26] Τὸν δ' Ἑρμῆς μύθοισιν ἀμείβετο κερδαλέοισι·
Λητοΐδη τίνα τοῦτον ἀπηνέα μῦθον ἔειπας
καὶ βοῦς ἀγραύλους διζήμενος ἐνθάδ' ἱκάνεις;
οὐκ ἴδον, . . .
265 οὐδὲ βοῶν ἐλατῆρι . . . ἔοικα,
οὐδ' ἐμὸν ἔργον τοῦτο, . . .
ὕπνος ἐμοί γε μέμηλε καὶ ἡμετέρης γάλα μητρός,
σπάργανά . . .
["Homeric Hymn to Hermes," 260ff. Translation from *LCL* 383.]

[27] τοῦ δὲ Κάκου πρὸ τῆς θύρας ἑστῶτος καὶ οὔτ' ἰδεῖν τὰς βοῦς φάσκοντος ἐρομένῳ οὔτ' ἐρευνᾶσθαι ἐπιτρέποντος αἰτουμένῳ τούς τε πλησίον ὡς δεινὰ πάσχοι ὑπὸ τοῦ ξένου ἐπιβοῶντος, . . .
[Dion. Hal., *Ant. Rom.* 1.39.3. Translation from *LCL* 1.127.]

at Vulci,[28] renders Hermes seated on a rock, on the left, and playing a lyre in a pose remarkably similar to Cacu on the mirror from the next century (Fig. 12). Accordingly, Hermes and Cacus resemble each other not just in the deed they perpetrated, but also in their very personalities, the hallmark of which was cleverness—a reminiscence in the case of Cacus of his previous position as a seer, since only Cacus, of all the classical cattle thieves, steals cattle in the same way Hermes does.[29]

Beyond the one deed and the character necessary to accomplish it, Hermes and Cacus had entirely different adventures. That is, the two other stories known about Cacus both involve his capture—an indignity never suffered by Hermes. The Etruscan mirror and the related urns (App. I, nos. 1-5) clearly show an ambush. Cacu was a seer, and ambushes of seers for their knowledge were a hazard of the occupation. For example, Ovid tells that Numa captured Picus and Faunus in a grove under the Aventine by getting them drunk in a story modelled on the capture of Silenus by Midas.[30] Proteus, on the other hand, was violently ambushed.[31] The Etruscan representations, then, fit one of the typologies for a private seer:[32] to obtain a prophecy, the inquirer knows he must ambush or otherwise trick *and* make the seer a prisoner before the seer will speak. The idea that Cacus as a seer was prone to being captured may have influenced the tale of Gellius, for there Cacus, though an envoy ("legatus") and presumably sacrosanct, was imprisoned. Let it suffice merely to note for now that divination obviously forms an underlying theme of the passage with the specific mention of "the art of augury" which Megales, significantly the companion of Cacus, taught to the Sabines.

[28] London E 815 by the Nikosthenes Painter. *ARV*², p. 125 no. 15; Yalouris, pp. 175-76 (the basic study of the vase representations); Blatter, pl. 40 fig. 2; he (p. 128) notes that after the early classical period interest in Hermes the cattle thief died out.

[29] In fact, it may be that the striking resemblances between Cacus and Hermes helped to influence the transformation of Cacus into a cattle thief, because it must be remembered that it is Cacu the Etruscan seer, not Cacus the Roman thief, who corresponds in the pictorial tradition to Hermes. Note that the two have frequently been compared in their modus operandi for accomplishing the theft of the cattle (e.g. Eden, pp. 78, 81), but they have not been related in their shared literary and iconographical imagery before. For the other thieves of Hercules' cattle, see n. 87 below.

[30] Picus and Faunus: Ovid, *Fasti* 3.285ff.; Bömer, *Komm*, pp. 165-66. Silenus: Herodotus 8.138; Xenophon, *Anabasis* 1.2.13; Rose, *Handbook*, pp. 157, 163 n. 62, 298, and 318.

[31] He was captured by Menelaus and Aristaeus in Homer, *Odyssey* 4.385ff. and Vergil, *Georgics* 4.386ff. respectively.

[32] Public oracles, such as Delphi, would be approached openly for consultation, the requirements of which depended on the nature of the oracle. Private seers, however, were notorious for their desire and ability to avoid capture. This deviousness also appears in the later Cacus's theft of the cattle.

METAMORPHOSIS OF CACU

The Floruit of Cacu

The mirror (App. I, no. 1) offers specific information about the date of Cacu when it identifies his ambushers as Aulus and Caeles Vibennae. The two men are attested in the literary and pictorial tradition, as well as in inscriptions on vases. While the sources do not entirely coincide, there is a consensus on the century. According to the literary and pictorial information, the Vibennae were involved in two major undertakings in addition to the ambush of Cacu: (1) the settlement of the Caelian and the Capitolium in Rome and (2) raids around Rome.[33]

Each brother was associated with a hill in Rome: Caeles with the Caelian and Aulus with the Capitolium. Whichever king added the Caelian hill to the urbs of Rome determines when Caeles lived—from the time of Romulus in the second half of the eighth century B.C. to that of Tarquinius Priscus in the first quarter of the sixth century B.C. Varro says that "the Caelian Hill [was] named from Caeles Vibenna, a noble Tuscan leader, who is said to have come with his band in help for Romulus against king Tatius";[34] while Tacitus states, perhaps more honestly:

> ... [the hill] soon called "Caelian" after Caeles Vibenna, who, as a leader of an Etruscan group, after he had brought aid had received this site from Tarquinius Priscus—or some other king gave [it]; for the writers disagree on this.[35]

Since Varro does refer to Caeles as a "Tuscan leader" and the Etruscans were most active in the area during the rule of the Tarquins, Tacitus's date in the sixth century B.C. seems more likely, and is roughly corroborated by the sources on Aulus and the Temple of Jupiter Capitolinus. Arnobius preserves the most complete account:

> What man is there who does not know that the Capitol of the imperial people is the tomb of Olus [*sic*] Vulcentanus? Who is there, I say, who does not know that from the place where its foundations were being laid there rolled out a human head bur-

---

[33] The discussion here concerns only the date of the Vibennae, not an interpretation of what they did with whom—a subject far beyond the present scope.

[34] "... Caelius mons a Caele Vibenna, Tusco duce nobili, qui cum sua manu dicitur Romulo venisse auxilio contra Tatium regem." Varro, *Ling.* 5.46. Dionysius (*Ant. Rom.* 2.36.2) agrees.

[35] "... montem ... mox Caelium apellitatum a Caele Vibenna, qui dux gentis Etruscae cum auxilium tulisset sedem eam acceperat a Tarquinio Prisco, seu quis alius regum dedit: nam scriptores in eo dissentiunt." Tacitus, *Ann.* 4.65. Perhaps most importantly both Varro and Tacitus agree that there was an extensive Etruscan settlement in the area. Compare Gelsomino, pp. 108-112.

ied not very long before, either by itself without the other parts, as some say, or together with the other members? Now, if you demand that this be attested by the witness of authors, Sammonicus, Granius, Valerianus, and Fabius will declare to you whose son Aulus was . . . and the great city, the worshipper of all divinities, did not blush, when it gave a name to the temple, to name it the "Capitolium" from the head [caput] of Olus rather than use a Jovian name.[36]

Although Arnobius lived around A.D. 295, he bases his story on four sources, of whom Fabius Pictor from the end of the third century B.C. is the earliest. Since the foundations of the Temple of Jupiter Capitolinus were laid during the reign of Tarquinius Superbus and Aulus had been buried recently, Aulus should have lived in the second half of the sixth century B.C.[37]

Not only the time Aulus lived, but also the city he came from, are confirmed by the evidence from the François Tomb. Like the mirror it dates to the late fourth century B.C., and its location in Vulci puts it in the same general region as the find-spot for the mirror. The tomb contains a fresco which portrays five pairs of labelled figures.[38]

---

[36] . . . regnatoris in populi Capitolio qui est hominum qui ignoret Oli esse sepulchrum Vulcentani? quis est, inquam, qui non sciat ex fundaminum sedibus caput hominis evolutum non ante plurimum temporis aut solum sine partibus ceteris—hoc enim quidam ferunt—aut cum membris omnibus humationis officia sortitum? quod si planum fieri testimoniis postulatis auctorum, Sammonicus Granius Valerianus vobis et Fabius indicabunt, cuius Aulus fuerit filius, . . . nec erubuit civitas maxima et numinum cunctorum cultrix, cum vocabulum templo daret, ex Oli capite Capitolium quam ex nomine Iovio nuncupare.
[Arnobius, *Adv. Nat.* 6.7. McCracken, translator, pp. 458-59 and notes on pp. 590-92.]
"Olus" is another form for "Aulus" which also appears in the Latin text. See Lewis and Short, p. 1263, s.v. "Olus." On the identity of the two: Alföldi, *ERL*, pp. 216-20, with other ancient references and a discussion of Etruscan gems (pl. XIII.1-14) possibly depicting this scene. Valerianus may be the second-century B.C. annalist Valerius Antias. McCracken, p. 591 n. 61; and Ogilvie, *Comm*, pp. 211-12.

[37] According to tradition, for example Livy 1.55, the Temple of Jupiter Optimus Maximus was vowed by Tarquinius Priscus, but built by Tarquinius Superbus. Some sources, for example Isiodorus, *Etym.* 15.2.31, maintain that Tarquinius Priscus laid the foundations and hence experienced the prodigy. The literary sources are collected in Lugli, *FTVUR*, vol. 6, pt. 2, pp. 104-109.
Heurgon ("Coupe," p. 525) considers the Tomba Cucumella in Vulci a cenotaph or heroon to Aulus. Hus (*Statuaire*, pp. 137-38 and *Vulci*, p. 106) dates the structure to 560-550 B.C. in accordance with the earlier chronology.

[38] The scene runs along the long wall opposite the Sacrifice of the Trojan Captives and wraps around the two side walls. Scholars are divided into two groups, "unitarians" and "separatists," over the question as to whether the scene with Marce Camtlnas killing Cneve Tarchu(nies) Rumach belongs with Macstrna's freeing of Caile. For the opposing views, see especially Körte, "Wandgemälde," pp. 57-80 (unitarian); Messerschmidt, *Vulci*, pp. 137-52 (separatist); and for unitarianism from the historian's

In the first group Macstrna frees Caile Vipinas from his bonds, while in the fourth group Aule Vipinas stabs Venthi Caule Plsachs in the gullet. According to a speech of Claudius the Emperor to the Senate in A.D. 48, "Servius Tullius, if we follow our own, was born from the captive Ocrisia, if [we follow] the Etruscans, [he was] once the most faithful friend of Caeles Vibenna and his companion in every adventure . . . in Etruscan his name was Mastarna."[39] This equation of Servius with Mastarna would place the Vibennae in the middle of the sixth century B.C.[40] A bucchero cup from Veii dated to the mid-sixth century B.C. provides further confirmation. On its foot is inscribed: "mine muluv[an]ece vipiiennas—Aulus Vibenna dedicated me."[41] In other words, a real Aulus Vibenna stands behind the legends preserved in the literary and pictorial sources.

Thus Cacu must have been alive during, and probably in the second half of, the sixth century B.C. Gellius indirectly supports this conclusion. While his references to Hercules and the Arcadian place Cacus in the heroic age of the thirteenth century B.C.,[42] the "political" situation he describes reflects the sixth century. Only at that time did the Etruscans wrest virtually complete control of Campania, as Gellius implies when he has Cacu seize "the area around Vulturnus and Campania." Already by the following century the Etruscans were

---

view, Momigliano, pp. 85-86 n. 30 (with extensive bibliography). On the date of the tomb, to the fourth century B.C.: Cristofani, "Vulci," pp. 186-219, with bibliography on pp. 186-87. Compare Hus, *Vulci*, pp. 103-106, 124-25, and 192 (with bibliography), and pl. 16.

[39] ". . . insertus Servius Tullius, si nostros sequimur, captiva natus Ocresia, si Tuscos, Caeli quondam Vivennae sodalis fidelissimus omnisque eius casus comes . . . Tusce Mastarna ei nomen erat . . ." *CIL* 13.1668. On the speech, see Momigliano, pp. 10-16, 84-85 n. 28 (with bibliography).

[40] Traditionally Servius Tullius ruled Rome from 578-535 B.C. Even though a number of scholars do not accept Claudius's identification of Mastarna, all their suggestions (Lars Porsenna, the Etruscan equivalent of Magister, or a separate figure) still retain a date in the sixth century B.C. Recently see: Radke, "Vibenna," pp. 2454-57 (with literary references and a summary of the scholarship); idem, "Etrurien," pp. 45-48; Ridley, "Enigma," pp. 147-77; Gantz, "Tarquin," pp. 549-53; and Coarelli, "Comizio," pp. 237-38.

[41] Translated by Heurgon, "Coupe," p. 517. The cup is in the Villa Giulia Museum. For a recent illustration: Pallottino, *Etr*, pl. XII left (discussion on p. 152).

An Etruscan red-figure kylix from Vulci, in the Musée Rodin, Paris (Inv. Tc.980, formerly Inv. 1943) and dated to ca. 450 B.C., is also inscribed with the name of Aulus Vibenna ("avles v[i]pinas?"). Heurgon's ("Coupe," pp. 517-25 and 527-28 figs. 1-3) interpretation of the inscription as an example of γραμματικὰ ἐκπώματα precludes any contradiction of the evidence from the sixth century bucchero vase. *EVP* pp. 3, 25-27, and pl. IV figs. 1-3. To the bibliography given by Heurgon, "Coupe," p. 517 n. 4, add: Pallottino, "Iscrizione," p. 399—a discussion of both inscriptions with the conclusion that an Etruscan Vipina family was active in the fifth century B.C.

[42] Here the traditional dates given by Dionysius (*Ant. Rom.* 1.63 and 74) are used.

The Roman Cacus

The Palatine and Its Augural Inhabitants

forced to begin to relinquish these holdings and to retreat north.[43] No more than two centuries after the deaths of Cacu and Aulus, the Etruscans heroized their exploits.

According to tradition the Palatine was the site of the oldest settlements in Rome. Such a choice was topographically logical. On the east bank of the Tiber a low, flat, albeit swampy, area, the later Fora Boarium and Romanum connected three hills: the Capitoline, the Palatine, and the Aventine (Plan 1). As the smallest hill in Rome, the Capitoline was an impracticable site for the early settlers. The Aventine and the Palatine shared the advantages of great height and of an area large enough for settlement, but the Palatine alone possessed natural fortifications. While the Aventine slopes gently to its summit, the Palatine offers steep cliffs on three sides and an easily defensible, narrow entrance across the brow of the Velia on the north. Consequently, both tradition and archaeology agree that the southwestern crest, the Germalus, which faced the Tiber, became the site for the first inhabitants (Plan 2).[44] There the Romans located the figures, the events, and the monuments most closely associated with the founding of Rome: the Lupercal and the Ficus Ruminalis, the turgurium Faustuli, the casa Romuli, Roma quadrata, the mundus, the auguratorium, the curia Saliorum, and the Scalae Caci. Except for the Scalae Caci, these monuments refer to Romulus. The cave of the Lupercal, where Romulus and Remus were suckled by the wolf beneath the Ficus Ruminalis, stands at the foot of the Palatine. The other landmarks are all located at the head of or near the Scalae Caci and fall into two categories, dwellings and augury. Romulus grew up in and took the augury for founding Rome from the hut of Faustulus or the house of Romulus, as it was more generally called after its most famous occupant.[45] Alternate traditions call the site for these first

---

[43] On the Etruscan presence in Campania, see among others: Johannovsky, pp. 420-23; and Scullard, *Cities*, pp. 188-97. For the full discussion of the historical aspects of the Gellius passage see Chapter II.

[44] For the ancient tradition, among others, Dion. Hal., *Ant. Rom.* 1.31 and Plutarch, *Vit. Rom.* 1. For the archaeological evidence, *PDAR* 2:163, with extensive bibliography. For the clearest plans and good photographs: Romanelli, "Scavo," cols. 201-330.

[45] Dion. Hal., *Ant. Rom.* 1.79.11, with a description of its appearance during his lifetime. The nomenclature and buildings may be more confused than implied in my discussion. (1) The tugurium Faustuli may be a separate building: Solinus 1.18; Not.

auspices either the auguratorium[46] or Roma quadrata;[47] its center may have been the mundus, a trench which received the first offerings.[48] In the conflict over either who should rule or where the site should be Romulus and Remus created the model for the ritual for establishing cities. Romulus prevailed. After his death the *lituus* he used to take the auspices was preserved in the curia Saliorum.[49]

Reg. X; Dio Cassius *apud* Zonaras 7.3; and Hieron., preface in Libr. Didymi de Spiritu Sancto 2.105. (2) There were two casae Romuli. The second stood on the Capitoline: Livy 5.53.8; Vitruvius 2.1.5; Conon, *Narr.* 48; and Seneca, *Controv.* 2.1.4. Because both buildings were preserved at least as late as the first century A.D., they were frequently included in literary itineraries, such as those of Vergil, *Aeneid* 8 and Propertius 4.1. (3) An aedes Romuli may or may not be the same as the casa Romuli: Varro, *Ling.* 5.54. On the casa Romuli in general: *PDAR* 2:163; Palmer, *ACR*, pp. 86ff. (on the relation between the augural *templum* and the casa Romuli) and p. 89 n. 3 (on hut construction). On the excavations of the huts on the Germalus: Gjerstad, *ER*, 3:48-62 and 4:45-49.

[46] The auguratorium was an augural area on the Palatine according to the Constantinian Regionary Catalogue (Regio X) and Mirabilia 28. An inscription, *CIL* 6:976, says that Hadrian restored it. It may be either the place from which Romulus took the auspices before founding Rome or the curia Saliorum (see n. 49 below). If the former, the remains of a small building between the Temple of Magna Mater and the House of Livia may be the auguratorium. *TDAR*, p. 61 and *PDAR* 1:163 and fig. 176. According to Coarelli (*Guida*, p. 140), however, the building is probably a sanctuary of Juno Sospita, which Ovid (*Fasti* 2.55-56) placed next to the Temple of Magna Mater. Note that Coarelli incorrectly refers to the auguratorium as the auguraculum. The two, though similar in function, were not the same. Auguracula stood on the Quirinal and the Capitoline.

[47] Varro *apud* Solinus 1.17; Plutarch, *Vit. Rom.* 9.4; Dio Cassius I *apud* Tzetzes *ad* Lycophron, *Alex.* 1232. The term *Roma quadrata* was applied to: (a) the city Romulus founded, as in the text here, and (b) the shrine which held sacred objects associated with the foundation of that city. The latter was also located on the Palatine, probably in the area of the Temple of Apollo Palatinus. *TDAR*, pp. 448-49. Scott, "ERTrad," p. 54 (especially for an analysis of the literary sources). Basanoff, *Pomerium* with a plan showing *Roma quadrata* according to Varro; Dion. Hal., *Ant. Rom.* 1.80; and Tacitus, *Ann.* 12.24. Palmer, *ACR*, pp. 26-34 (on its composition and division of land). Rykwert, pp. 97-99, 117, 125.

[48] The mundus was a trench into which, "ἀπαρχαί τε πάντων, . . . ἀπετέθησαν ἐνταῦθα. καὶ τέλος, ἐξ ἧς ἀφῖκτο γῆς ἕκαστος ὀλίγην κομίζων μοῖραν, ἔβαλλον εἰς ταῦτα καὶ συνεμίγνυον. . . . εἶτα ὥσπερ κύκλον κέντρῳ περιέγραψαν τὴν πόλιν." Plutarch, *Vit. Rom.* 11.1-2. Problems arise over its location—in the Forum Romanum or on the Palatine—and its nature. Recently Coarelli ("Ara," pp. 358-73) and Verzar (pp. 378-98) have identified it with the Umbilicus in the Forum Romanum. On the Palatine various cisterns in the area at the head of the Scalae Caci have been suggested. Because the mundus may have functioned in more than one way, it was subject even in antiquity to much confusion. The Plutarch passage implies that it worked almost like a modern time-capsule placed in the first foundation stone of modern buildings. Rykwert (pp. 58-59, 97-98, 117, 121-29, and 161) believes that it represented the original, central hearth. *TDAR*, pp. 346-47; Weinstock, "Mundus," pp. 111-23 (the basic study); Dumézil, *ARR*, pp. 350-53; Catalano, "Aspetti," pp. 462-64; Magdelain, "Pomerium."

[49] For the dispute over the rule, among others, Livy 1.6.1 and Ovid, *Fasti* 4.812. Because Romulus, as the founder of Rome, had to be well versed in the religious practices necessary for properly founding a city or the city would not prosper, his

METAMORPHOSIS OF CACU

The only incongruous element in this hallowed area appears to be the Scalae Caci.[50] While today it is common to name streets after famous personages, it was not so in antiquity. Roman streets tended to be named after the direction of their route, such as the Viae Ostiensis or Praenestina; their function, such as the Sacra Via or the Via Triumphalis; or their builder, such as the Via Appia.[51] Specific places, such as the Saxum Tarpeium or the Lacus Curtius, were called after the person whose most important deed occurred at the spot.[52] Of these four possible explanations for the name of the Scalae Caci, a designation of their function can be immediately eliminated since Cacus is a proper name.[53] Likewise, none of the ancient evidence makes Cacus a builder; he is either a seer or a thief. The fourth category may apply only in the loose sense that the name, Scalae Caci, may imply that Cacus did do something on the Palatine. The solution lies in the nature of the Steps and the area as well as in the original character of Cacus himself.

The Scalae Caci provided indirect access from the Forum Boarium and hence the Tiber to the summit of the Palatine[54] where stood the hut of Faustulus and the house of Romulus. In fact, the area at the

---

association with augury is extremely strong. For example: Cicero, *Div.* 1.48 (107) and 2.38 (80), simply calls both Romulus and Remus "augures"; Propertius, 4.6.43, says "murorum Romulus augur"; and Plutarch, *Vit. Cam.* 32.5, similarly refers to Romulus as "μαντικώτατος."

On the curia Saliorum: Cicero, *Div.* 1.18 (30-31); Plutarch, *Vit. Rom.* 22 and *Vit. Cam.* 32.4-5. According to Nash (*PDAR* 1:163) the curia Saliorum may possibly be the same as the auguratorium. On the lituus: Rykwert, pp. 208-209 n. 32.

The sacred cornel tree, which stood in a special enclosure by the house of Romulus, is the only "legendary" monument not discussed in the text, because the Romans themselves seemed not to have attached much significance to it. According to Plutarch (*Vit. Rom.* 20.5-6) Romulus hurled a spear, whose shaft was made of cornelwood, from the Aventine to the Palatine in a trial of strength. It took root where it landed and came to symbolize the flourishing of Rome. Nonetheless, when it died during repairs at the top of the Scalae Caci at the time of Julius Caesar, it was not replanted.

[50] The name is mentioned in Solinus 1.18.

[51] Radke, *Viae*, pp. 8-15, 78ff.; Allen and Greenough, pp. 150-51, no. 249. So also for the gates of Rome: Holland, *Janus*, p. 115 n. 35.

[52] Saxum Tarpeium: *PDAR* 2:409-10; and Ogilvie, *Comm*, pp. 74-75. Lacus Curtius: *PDAR* 1:542-44; and Ogilvie, *Comm*, pp. 75-77. On the names of Steps in Rome: *TDAR*, pp. 465-67, s.v. "Scalae..."

[53] While it may be possible to translate Scalae Caci as "Steps of Evil," like the Κακαὶ Σκάλαι between Corinth and Megara, it is not likely. Although it is not known when the Steps first received their name, the connection of Cacus with them appears to be old, in which case it should reflect the seer Cacu who had no association per se with evil.

[54] Excavation has revealed cuttings for steps along the east wall of the "Staircase"— the practicable solution for the steep gradient of the slope. The base of the Scalae Caci may have ended at the Porta Romanula on the Clivus Victoriae from which another path provided direct access to the Forum Boarium. *TDAR*, p. 466 and *PDAR* 2:299-300.

head of the Scalae Caci always remained at least semi-residential even during the Empire when Augustus and later emperors lived there.[55] Because houses naturally have staircases leading to them, the nomenclature of Scalae might have seemed apposite, even though the original huts were certainly not of palatial grandeur. Cacus would then have lived in the settlement at the top of the hill. Diodorus Siculus supports this conclusion:

> . . . at this time [when Hercules was going back to Greece with the cattle of Geryon] certain people of the vicinity had their homes on the Palatine Hill, as it is now called, and formed an altogether inconsiderable city. Here some of the notable men, among them Cacius and Pinarius, welcomed Heracles with marked acts of hospitality and honored him with pleasing gifts; and memorials of these men abide in Rome to the present day. . . . and as for Cacius, there is a passage on the Palatine which leads downward, furnished with a stairway of stone, and is called after him the "Steps of Cacius," and it lies near the original house of Cacius . . .[56]

Three points are crucial: Cacius is a notable man; he lives on the Palatine; a stone staircase leads to his home. Since the characterization fits the Cacus of the second century B.C. and earlier, his residence

---

[55] The choice of this section of the Palatine for the homes of those ruling Rome could not have been accidental; it must have always reflected the traditions about the foundation and first ruler(s) of Rome even before Augustus consciously drew the parallel by maintaining his home there, as Vergil (*Aen.* 8.363) well knew when he called Evander's humble home a "regia." During the Republican period, according to Coarelli (*Guida*, pp. 136-37), it was "un quartiere residenziale della classe dirigente romana . . ." with examples cited. In the Empire not only Livia and Augustus built homes there, but so also did Tiberius, Domitian, and Septimius Severus.

[56] τότε δὲ τινες τῶν ἐγχωρίων κατῴκουν ἐν τῷ νῦν καλουμένῳ Παλατίῳ, μικρὰν παντελῶς πόλιν οἰκοῦντες. ἐν ταύτῃ δὲ τῶν ἐπιφανῶν ὄντες ἀνδρῶν Κάκιος καὶ Πινάριος ἐδέξαντο τὸν Ἡρακλέα ξενίοις ἀξιολόγοις καὶ δωρεαῖς κεχαρισμέναις ἐτίμησαν· καὶ τούτων τῶν ἀνδρῶν ὑπομνήματα μέχρι τῶνδε τῶν καιρῶν διαμένει κατὰ τὴν Ῥώμην. . . . τοῦ δὲ Κακίου ἐν τῷ Παλατίῳ κατάβασίς ἐστιν ἔχουσα λιθίνην κλίμακα τὴν ὀνομαζομένην ἀπ' ἐκείνου Κακίαν, οὖσαν πλησίον τῆς τότε γενομένης οἰκίας τοῦ Κακίου.

[Diod Sic. 4.21. Translation from *LCL* 2.409.]

For the use of Cacius, see n. 24 above. This passage has frequently been attributed to Timaios. While the characterization of Cacus as a notable man fits the third century B.C., the attribution is dubious. Only at the very end of the chapter does Diodorus mention Timaios. He says, "καὶ περὶ μὲν τῶν ἐν Φλέγρᾳ φονευθέντων γιγάντων τοιαῦτα μυθολογοῦσί τινες, οἷς καὶ Τίμαιος ὁ συγγραφεὺς ἠκολούθησεν." In other words, Diodorus acknowledges Timaios only for the episode of Hercules against the Giants. Timaios may still be the source for the passage on Cacus, but, in the absence of direct evidence, it is better to take a cautious view and merely date the passage to the period when Diodorus was actually writing, 60-30 B.C. As Timaios and the oldest source on Cacus: Wissowa, "Cacus," p. 1166.

on the Palatine is no surprise; the idea that the Scalae Caci specifically went to his home supplements the information on the early Cacus.[57] The Greek of the last words quoted is important: "τῆς τότε γενομένης οἰκίας τοῦ Κακίου," literally "the house of Cacius which existed at that time." In other words, Diodorus has recorded what he actually saw:[58] the stone staircase and where it went, but not the actual dwelling, which unlike the casa Romuli no longer existed in the first century B.C. Recent excavation, however, has uncovered remains of post-holes for a hut precisely where Diodorus says they should be—at the very top of the staircase (Plan 3).[59] The "Steps" were, then, named after the building to which they *led*, like the first group of Roman roads such as the Via Ostiensis. Furthermore, the location of Cacus in that particular area of the Palatine was justified by his original profession as a seer, for at the head of the Scalae Caci the only landmarks other than residences were those connected with augury—Roma quadrata, the mundus, the auguratorium, and the curia Saliorum. Thus, although Cacus may not have necessarily performed

[57] An extremely corrupt passage in Festus, *Romam* (L 328), possibly corroborates Diodorus. "historiae Cumanae compositor, . . . quorum subiecti qui fuerint ‡caeximparum‡ viri, unicarumque virium imperio montem Palatium, in quo frequentissimi consederint, apellavisse a viribus regentis Valentiam . . ." Niebuhr restored the ἅπαξ of "caeximparum" with "Caci improbi." Cacus is then a leader of a group of men who resided on the Palatine, a situation similar to that in Diodorus and perhaps like the settlement of Caeles Vibenna on the Caelian. Festus attributes this information to the "historiae Cumanae compositor," another ἅπαξ. Some scholars accept the reading as is and date such a history to the beginning of the fourth century B.C., while others restore "historiae cummunis," a work written by Q. Lutatius Catulus, who was an annalist active at the turn of the second century B.C. The problems do not even end here. Whatever work it was, it was epitomized by Verrius Flaccus, an Augustan freedman, who was epitomized by Festus in the late second century A.D., who was epitomized by Paulus Diaconus of the eighth century A.D. Because Flaccus, Festus, and Paulus lived after Cacus became κακός, any one of them, if not Niebuhr himself, could have added the characterization of "improbus" to the original source without changing the basic content of the passage. Compare: Bayet, *Hercule*, pp. 151ff.; Alföldi, *ERL*, pp. 56-58; and Opelt, "Roma," pp. 50ff.

[58] Remember that Diodorus says in the passage that "memorials of these men abide in Rome to the present day." In 1.4.1-2 he speaks not just of living in Rome, but also of the necessity to:
ἵνα τῶν ἀναγκαιοτάτων καὶ πλείστων μερῶν αὐτόπται γενηθῶμεν· πολλὰ γὰρ παρὰ τὰς ἀγνοίας τῶν τόπων διήμαρτον οὐχ οἱ τυχόντες τῶν συγγραφέων, ἀλλά τινες καὶ τῶν τῇ δόξῃ πεπρωτευκότων. ἀφορμὴ δὲ πρὸς τὴν ἐπιβολὴν ταύτην ἐχρησάμεθα . . . τῇ ἐν Ῥώμῃ χορηγίᾳ τῶν πρὸς τὴν ὑποκειμένην ὑπόθεσιν ἀνηκόντων.
Diodorus's modus operandi remains valid to this day. On the research facilities available in Rome: Marshall, "Library," pp. 252-64.

[59] Romanelli, "Scavo," cols. 203-204 with figs. 1-3. He notes that the holes may possibly be for pozzetti burials, but more likely are for huts. Arthur Schneider (p. 163) also postulated a casa Caci in the same area on the basis of the idea of Scalae, but without the supporting material, both literary and archaeological, presented here.

a specific deed in this area—the cattle theft generally takes place on the Aventine—his practice of prophecy there was sufficiently important to lend his name to the steps by which he could be reached for consultation.[60] The presence of Cacus on the Palatine among landmarks closely associated with augury and the foundation of Rome no longer seems inappropriate.[61]

Like Cacus and Romulus, the two other legendary inhabitants of that section on the Palatine, Evander and Faunus, were also associated with divination. Evander's mother, no matter what her name, was renowned for her oracular expertise, the knowledge of which she generously shared with her son.[62] Faunus, on the other hand, presided over the incubation oracle at Albunea[63] and, as mentioned previously, because of his prophetic knowledge was captured along with Picus by Numa. Each of these oracular figures practiced a different kind of divination. Romulus watched birds; Faunus prophesied during the sleep of the inquirer; Evander's mother sang her re-

---

[60] This interpretation of this area of the Palatine fits well with one of Palmer's (*ACR*, p. 89) conclusions about the Argei: "Only the Palatine Region in this itinerary shows no survivor of augury, although the Palatine aedes Romuli, casa Romuli and tugurium Faustuli point to similar foundations." No longer does the anomaly exist. Note that according to Solinus 1.18—"ea [Roma quadrata] incipit a silva quae est in area Apollinis, et ad supercilium scalarum Caci habet terminum, ubi tugurium fuit Faustuli"—the area was also augurally hallowed as one of the corners of *Roma quadrata*.

[61] There may have been two other "landmarks" associated with Cacus in Rome: the Atrium Caci, in the *Notitia* and *Curiosium* under Regio VIII (Forum Romanum); and the Cacum, another name for the Forum Boarium, perhaps indicating a vicus Caci in the *Cosmographia* (*Geogr. Lat. Min.*, ed. Reise, p. 83). The former has never been identified and the latter is dubious. Neither affect the present inquiry. *TDAR*, pp. 56 and 87.

[62] Evander's mother was called: (1) Nicostrata by, e.g., L. Coelius Antipater *apud* Strabo 5.3 (230)—the earliest extant mention of his mother made during the same period as Evander's own first appearance; (2) Carmenta by, e.g., Dion. Hal., *Ant. Rom.* 1.31 and Vergil, *Aen.* 8.399; and (3) Themis by Plutarch, *Quaest. Rom.* 56. She generally imparts helpful information to her son, such as the coming apotheosis of Hercules (Strabo 5.3 [230]), and the site for the Arcadian settlement in Rome (Dion. Hal., *Ant. Rom.* 1.31). Ogilvie (*Comm*, p. 59) considers Carmenta's motherhood of Evander "a late manipulation."

[63] This oracle was consulted by Latinus (Vergil, *Aen.* 7.81-106) and Numa (Ovid, *Fasti* 4.649-72), although Faunus sometimes is called a prophet without specifying his type or the location where he practices, as in Plutarch, *Quaest. Rom.* 20. See Palmer, *Religion*, chap. 3, especially pp. 80-89 and 146-49.

Fontenrose (*Python*, p. 341 n. 31) believes that "Since the crime [Cacus's theft of Hercules' cattle] was committed during his [Hercules'] sleep, it may be significant that Faunus, Cacus's counterpart, was considered a nightmare demon and called Incubus." By no means can Cacus and Faunus be so equated. Cacu was a lyre-strumming seer (App. I, nos. 1-5) entirely dissimilar to Faunus in form and practice. The theft during sleep may reflect the temporal setting in the parallel story of the theft of Hercules' mares in Herodotus 4.9—although, on purely practical grounds, night has always provided the most popular time for such activities.

sponses; and Cacu appears to have accompanied his prophesies on the lyre. Consequently, the four must have come into conflict with each other over the right to practice their individual form of divination in this area. This rivalry constitutes a part of the basis for the legends about the *ius hospitii* and cattle-stealing.

Ius hospitii

By the first century B.C. the sequence of Rome's ruler-founders and inhabitants had been established. Dionysius, for example, described three waves of invaders and two groups who merely settled in the area: the Aborigines under Faunus, the Pelasgians, and the Arcadians under Evander who received both Hercules with his followers and Aeneas with the remnants of the Trojans.[64] Even after this cosmopolitan gathering, Rome had to wait four centuries for Romulus to make the "actual" foundation. Remarkably by the time of Dionysius all previous hostilities had been resolved. Faunus graciously receives Evander and even allocates territory to him. Evander, in turn, becomes the great entertainer who enjoys regaling later guests, such as Aeneas, with tales of his earlier and more prominent visitors, such as Hercules. Romulus, born too late, seems to avoid such encounters, peaceful or otherwise.[65] Cacu remains the only irksome character. The situation was not always thus.

In the fourth century B.C. Derkyllos described a somewhat chillier reception for visitors than that related by first century B.C. writers:

> When Hercules was driving through Italy the cattle of Geryon, he was entertained by king Faunus, the son of Mercury, who was wont to sacrifice his guests to the god that was his father. But when he attacked Hercules, he was slain.[66]

---

[64] Dionysius, *Ant. Rom.* 1.60ff., provides one of the fullest lists of settlers. Compare also Plutarch, *Vit. Rom.* 1, and Festus, s.v. *Romam* L 326, 328. Because only the groups that produced specific, named leaders associated with the Palatine concern the present inquiry, the Pelasgians are eliminated from discussion. Note, however, that since Hesiod (*Catalogues of Women and Eoiae* 31-32 apud Strabo 5.2.4 [221] and Steph. Byz., s.v. Παλλάντιον) the Pelasgians were not only identified with the Arcadians, but also related to Pallas (and hence, much later, to Evander) who was the grandson of Pelasgus.

[65] Romulus may, however, have indirectly enjoyed a harmonious relationship with Evander, because Faustulus, the shepherd who reared him and Remus, was of Arcadian descent according to Dionysius, *Ant. Rom.* 1.84 3. Although the Rape of the Sabine Women, e.g. Livy 1.9, may be one of the best examples of the abuse of the *ius hospitii*, it does not truly fit the story-pattern under consideration, because it focuses on the Sabines, not on the first and augural settlers of the Palatine, and because its plot-mechanism depends on an invitation to neighbors, not travellers or emigrants.

[66] ΗΡΑΚΛΗΣ τὰς Γηρυόνου βοῦς ἐλαύνων δι' Ἰταλίας ἐπεξενώθη Φαύνῳ βασιλεῖ, ὃς ἦν Ἑρμοῦ παῖς καὶ τοὺς ξένους τῷ γεννήσαντι ἔθυεν· ἐπι-

METAMORPHOSIS OF CACU

Servius explains why:

> Among our ancestors foreigners used to be seldom received, unless they held the right of hospitality [ius hospitii]; for it was uncertain with what intent they came. Wherefore even Hercules at first was not received by Evander; afterwards indeed when he had said that he was the son of Jove and had proven his worth by the death of Cacus, he was both received and honored for his divinity.[67]

The principle of the *ius hospitii* underlies all the encounters on the Palatine, for it refers to the formal relationship established between two heroes from different places.[68] Faunus and Evander are both rulers receiving a foreign dignitary, Hercules. Likewise, Evander entertains Anchises, the representative of the Trojans, and later his son, Aeneas.[69] Cacus also fits in this category, as the Gellius passage shows. When Tarchon flouts the *ius hospitii* by making Cacus, the "legatus" of Marsyas, a prisoner, Cacus justifiably retaliates by leading forces

---

χειρήσας δὲ τῷ Ἡρακλεῖ ἀνῃρέθη· ὡς Δέρκυλλος ἐν τρίτῳ Ἰταλικῶν.
[Plutarch, *Moralia: Parallela Graeca et Romana* 38 (315 C). Translation from *LCL* 4.313.]

[67] apud maiores *nostros* raro advenae suscipiebantur, nisi haberent ius hospitii; incertum enim erat quo animo venirent. unde etiam Hercules primo non est ab Euandro susceptus; postea vero cum se et Iovis filium dixisset et morte Caci virtutem suam probasset, et susceptus et pro numine habitus est.
[Servius, *ad Aen.* 8.269.]
Virtually the same are *Myth. Vat.* 1.69 and 3.13.7. Although Servius is of the late fourth century A.D., Evander's original rebuff of Hercules is plausible. Hercules often met with opposition on his return from Spain, albeit most frequently in the form of cattle thieves. Perhaps the earliest extant example of this type, but not localized at Rome, belongs to Hecataeus *apud* Steph. Byz., s.v. Σολοῦς (FGrHist 1 F 77): "πόλις Σικελίας, ὡς Ἑκαταῖος ἐν Εὐρώπηι. ἐκλήθη δὲ ἀπὸ Σολοῦντος κακοξένου, ὃν ἀνεῖλεν Ἡρακλῆς." Hercules himself was not above such antics. He kills Iphitos, his guest, and steals his mares in Homer, *Od.* 21.22-30 and Diod. Sic. 4.31.

[68] The best-known example is the encounter between Glaukos and Diomedes, Homer, *Il.* 6.119-236 and especially 215ff. Because their fathers were guest-friends, so too must they be. As a celebration of that relationship they exchange armor and vow not to fight each other. See also: Wagenvoort, *Dynamism*, pp. 144ff., with n. 3 on p. 145 for a summary of modern theory; Ogilvie, *Comm*, p. 690; Gauthier, pp. 13-19; Bolchazy, *passim*; and Hiltbrunner, pp. 443-46.

[69] Vergil (*Aen.* 8.154ff.) is the first to have Evander receive Aeneas and Anchises. The story probably indicates that Vergil knew Evander the son of Priam (n. 13 above). That is, one Evander with a Trojan lineage makes another Evander a likely ally of Trojans, such as Anchises and Aeneas.
Servius (*ad Aen.* 8.345) preserves the details of another tale, merely alluded to by Vergil (*Aen.* 8.345-46), about Evander's *hospitium* and the necessity of obeying the prescripts established for such receptions. Because a certain Argus coveted the rule of his host, Evander, Evander's allies killed Argus; but, ". . . cui Evander et sepulchrum fecit et locum sacravit, non quod ille merebatur, sed hospitalitatis causa. bene autem in hac re Evander inmoratur et docet causas, ne apud hospitem veniat in suspitionem."

to seize the area around Vulturnus and Campania; when Cacus, however, then "dared to appropriate even those places which the laws [iura] had granted to the Arcadian," he rightly was killed.

Cacus himself appears as a host in Diodorus (4.21), Propertius (4.9.7), and Dionysius. In the first instance, "Cacius," a noble man, "welcomed Heracles with marked acts of hospitality . . . ;" in the second case, Cacus was a "disloyal host" ("infido hospite"). Likewise, Dionysius's euhemeristic version of the conflict between Hercules and Cacus describes Cacus as "an exceedingly barbarous chieftain reigning over a savage people . . . established in the fastnesses."[70]

If Cacus, like Faunus and Evander, fills the role of leader and host, then the idea of his possession of a house on the Palatine at the head of the Scalae Caci among the stately homes of Romulus and Augustus becomes reinforced. Thus, all the legendary figures (Faunus, Evander, Cacus, and Romulus) who lived there not only shared the two characteristics of sovereignty and divination, but also fought over the right to practice both.

Cattle-Stealing

As the *ius hospitii* naturally underlies stories about visitors to and usurpers of the settlement on the Palatine, so cattle inherently became the other focus for the legends of that area. It is an ancient and modern commonplace that cattle formed one of the major economic bases of the earliest communities.[71] Rome preserves that fact in the names given to various areas[72] as well as in archaeological remains. The region of the Palatine where Romulus, Cacus, and Evander lived had a cattle enclosure dating to the Iron Age; burials from the same period included cattle bones.[73] Since the earliest settlements were restricted to the hilltops, so also would the cattle. As the communities expanded and came into direct contact with each other, pasture for

---

[70] "δυνάστην τινὰ κομιδῇ βάρβαρον καὶ ἀνθρώπων ἀνημέρων ἄρχοντα, . . . ἐρυμνοῖς χωρίοις ἐπικαθήμενον . . ." Dion. Hal., *Ant. Rom.* 1.42.2. Translation from *LCL* 1.137. Similarly, Gellius (n. 6 above) may have rationalized Cacus the stealer of cattle as Cacus the appropriator of territory.

[71] In antiquity, for example: Varro, *Ling.* 5.17 (92) and 5.19 (95); Pausanias 4.36.3. In modern scholarship: Gjerstad, *ER*, 6:32, 42; Ogilvie, *Comm*, p. 31; and Lincoln, pp. 62-63.

[72] The following places, for example, have names related to cattle: Forum Boarium, Porta Mugonia, and perhaps the Palatine itself. Varro, *Ling.* 5.32 (146) and 5.34 (164); and n. 15 above respectively.

[73] Propertius (4.9.3) places Evander's cattle there. For the cattle enclosure just to the west of the top of the Scalae Caci, see Romanelli, "Scavo," col. 212. For the burials, see n. 44 above.

and possession of cattle would be contested. The legends reflect this background. For example:

> When Romulus and Remus were about eighteen years of age, they had some dispute about the pasture with Numitor's herdsmen, whose herds were quartered on the Aventine hill, which is over against the Palatine. They frequently accused one another either of grazing the meadow-land that did not belong to them or of monopolizing that which belonged to both in common, or of whatever the matter chanced to be. From this wrangling they had recourse sometimes to blows and then to arms.[74]

Even those founders on the Palatine, who did not actually themselves indulge in cattle-raiding, retained an association with cattle in general. Faunus was worshipped as a god of flocks, while Evander emigrated with his "exiled kine."[75]

Thus Hercules' presence in Rome with the cattle of Geryon was not mythically necessary to bring cattle to the area; rather because Hercules came with cattle, the Romans were able with little effort to adopt him into their pattern of legends. In fact, Cacus, the quintessential raider and stock opponent of Hercules in the first century B.C. and later, appears earlier to have faced a different foe. The *Origo Gentis Romanae* preserves Cassius Hemina's account:

> At the time when [Evander] was ruling, by chance a certain Recaranus, of Greek origin, a shepherd of huge frame and great strength, who, excelling others in form and courage, was called a Hercules, came to this place. While his herd were grazing about the Albula [Tiber], Cacus, the slave of Evander, crafty with evil and beyond other things most thieving, stole the cattle of the guest (hospitis) Recaranus and, lest there be any trace, dragged

---

[74] ἐπεὶ δὲ ἀμφὶ τὰ ὀκτωκαίδεκα ἔτη γεγονότες ἦσαν ἀμφίλογόν τι περὶ τῆς νομῆς αὐτοῖς γίνεται πρὸς τοὺς Νεμέτορος βουκόλους, οἳ περὶ τὸ Αὐεντῖνον ὄρος ἀντικρὺ τοῦ Παλλαντίου κείμενον εἶχον τὰς βουστάσεις. ἠτιῶντο δέ ἀλλήλους ἑκάτεροι θαμινὰ ἢ τὴν μὴ προσήκουσαν ὀργάδα κατανέμειν ἢ τὴν κοινὴν μόνους διακρατεῖν ἢ ὅ τι δήποτε τύχοι. ἐκ δὲ τῆς ἁψιμαχίας ταύτης ἐγένοντο πληγαί ποτε διὰ χειρῶν, εἶτα δι' ὅπλων.
[Dion. Hal., *Ant. Rom.* 1.79.12. Translation from *LCL* 1.271.]
Compare Livy 1.5.4 and Plutarch, *Vit. Rom.* 7.1.

[75] "Profugae boves," Propertius 4.1.4. Faunus: for instance, Horace, *Carm.* 3.18. Compare Fowler, *Festivals*, pp. 256–65 and Dumézil, *ARR*, pp. 344–46. Cacus, like the others on the Palatine, may also once have owned his own cattle, since Livy (1.7.5), among others, calls him a shepherd (*pastor*). According to Alföldi (*SVR*, p. 121) in the early periods cattle-raiding was a demonstration of the ability and a privilege of the nobility, while Brown (*Hermes*, p. 5) considers it to be a "public enterprise" in Homer.

them backwards into the cave. After the neighboring regions had been explored and all the hiding-places examined in this way, Recaranus despaired that he would find them. Nevertheless he bore the loss philosophically and decided to leave the area. But indeed when Evander, a man of excellent justice, found out what had happened, he gave the slave for punishment (servum noxae dedit) and had the cattle returned. Then Recaranus dedicated an altar to the Inventor Pater at the foot of the Aventine and called it Maxima. . . . These things Cassius wrote in his first book.[76]

Already by the middle of the second century B.C. the entire plot of the raid had been established. While a foreigner stopping at Rome is entertained by the ruler, a local inhabitant steals the guest's grazing cattle by dragging them backwards into a cave. The guest unsuccessfully at first seeks his lost property, but upon his inevitable recovery of it dedicates an altar in thanks. The only major deviation from the basic plot to occur later is the explicit death of Cacus, for "servum noxae dedit" is a legal formula governing the responsibility of masters (*domini*) for thefts committed by their slaves. Restitution of stolen property or delivery of the slave to the wronged person was the usual punishment.[77] Since the cattle are returned to Recaranus and no mention is made of Cacus's death, presumably Cacus—only in this version—survived the encounter after appropriate chastisement by Evander.

Because the action became fixed earlier than the actors, the event

---

[76] Eo regnante forte Recaranus quidam, Graecae originis, ingentis corporis et magnarum virium pastor, qui erat forma et virtute ceteris antecellens, Hercules appellatus, eodem venit. Cumque armenta eius circa flumen Albulam pascerentur, Cacus Euandri servus, nequitiae versutus et praeter cetera furacissimus, Recarani hospitis boves surripuit ac, ne quod esset indicium, aversas in speluncam attraxit. Cumque Recaranus vicinis regionibus peragratis scrutatisque omnibus eiuscemodi latebris desperasset inventurum, utcumque aequo animo dispendium ferens, excedere his finibus constituterat. At vero Euander, excellentissimae iustitiae vir, postquam rem uti acta erat, comperit, servum noxae dedit bovesque restitui fecit. Tum Recaranus sub Aventino Inventori Patri aram dedicavit appellavitque Maximam. . . . Haec Cassius libro primo.
[*OGR* 7.6-7.]
Paragraph 6 is entirely devoted to Cacus, and the first sentence of the next paragraph attributes that story to Cassius Hemina. Peter (*HRR*²) does not include the passage among Hemina's fragments, but Rawson ("Annalists," pp. 694-95) does. The use of Albula, an early name for the Tiber (Lewis and Short, p. 80 s.v. "Albula"), may be an indication of a date in the second century B.C. for the passage. Compare Vergil, *Aen.* 8.331-32, "a quo post Itali fluvium cognomine Thybrim/diximus; amisit verum vetus Albula nomen."

[77] Law of XII Tables, XII.2 *apud* Gaius, *Inst.* 4.75-76. Crook, pp. 169, 182-83. Jolowicz and Nicholas, p. 173.

obviously was more important to the Romans than its perpetrators, who were invariably typecast. The cattle-owner, whoever he is and whatever he does, must be a strongman of limited intelligence.[78] Consequently, Recaranus, otherwise unknown, "excelling others in form and courage was called a Hercules."[79] Servius records a version of Verrius Flaccus, the Augustan freedman, who explains "that Garanus was a shepherd of great strength, who crushed Cacus, and indeed all those of great strength were called Hercules among the ancients."[80] Garanus, like Recaranus, appears in the ancient sources only once and is also a shepherd, as is to be expected for a possessor of cattle. Unlike Recaranus, he does kill Cacus. By the time of Vergil Hercules, by his sheer brute force, his obtuseness, and his possession of Geryon's cattle, has so assumed the role of protagonist that all other contenders for the honor of killing Cacus virtually disappear. As Servius says, "Clearly the Greeks as well as the Romans agree about Cacus having been killed by Hercules . . ."[81]

Although Hercules, according to the literary evidence, does not seem to have had a connection with Cacus until the second century B.C.,[82] his arrival in Rome goes back to at least as early as the late sixth century B.C.; for Pliny, citing Varro, speaks of a cult statue of

---

[78] Even in Vergil's account, perhaps the most laudatory of those extant, Hercules cannot discover the cattle all by himself. Brown (*Hermes*, p. 7) opposes the brawny robber Hercules with the cunning thief Hermes, and makes the additional distinction (pp. 6-7) between theft as "appropriation by stealth" and robbery as "open and forcible appropriation." Later Brown (p. 85) points out that in the Homeric period a robbery such as Hercules' was not viewed as a crime. That is, Hercules could nobly steal the cattle of Geryon, but Cacus could only ignominiously remove them in turn from Hercules.

[79] Despite the paucity of ancient information Recaranus has been the subject of much scholarly speculation, particularly about his "origins." Among others, Piganiol ("Hercule," pp. 1261-63) considers Recaranus as related to χάρανος and thereby to κοίρανος and hence finally to Kronos and Quirinus.

[80] ". . . solus Verrius Flaccus dicit Garanum fuisse pastorem magnarum virium, qui Cacum adflixit, omnes autem magnarum virium apud veteres Hercules dictos." Servius, *ad Aen*. 8.203. Bayet ("Funéraire," pp. 75-77) maintains that Garanus is another form for Geryon, who substitutes for Hercules in Italy where the two are allied and confused with each other. Gagé ("Dieu," pp. 113-18) believes the names Garanus and Recaranus are related to Carna and hence an augural-sacrificial tradition which passed from Etruria to Rome. Höfer ("Tarvos," pp. 128-32) and Heichelheim ("Nymphai," pp. 1592-96) connect Garanus to the Celtic deity Tarvos Trigaranos.

[81] "sane de Caco interempto ab Hercule tam Graeci quam Romani consentiunt . . ." Servius, *ad Aen*. 8.203. There is a tendency among scholars to consider both Recaranus and Garanus as equivalents of Hercules. The point is not that the same figure (Hercules) performs the same deed under different names, but that there were different figures who came to be absorbed and certainly eclipsed by one figure.

[82] The earliest extant reference to Cacus and Hercules is that of Gellius (n. 6 above). Sutton (pp. 391-93) may not accept the passage, which she does not mention, and so dates the "creation" of the encounter to the Augustan period.

Hercules made by Vulca from Veii which still existed in the first century A.D.[83] Sometime during the fifth century B.C. the private cult of Hercules as a god of commerce was established at the Ara Maxima and superintended by the Potitii and the Pinarii.[84] Again, the institution of this worship as a result of the recovery of the cattle from Cacus is not testified before the second century B.C., when the Romans became interested in explaining seemingly anomalous practices in their religion and in documenting their "history." The Greek Herakles seems never to have been fully assimilated into the Roman culture. He demonstrates his Greekness by the form of his worship at the Ara Maxima[85] and by his continuing status as a visitor, never a settler, in Rome.

Because of his labors Hercules turned into a world traveller par excellence. In particular the quest for Geryon's cattle became the standard way to account for his presence and worship in Italy. At first circumscribed in area, the journey lengthened and the stopovers increased as the boundaries of the known world expanded and more areas desired the honor of a visit from Hercules. These encounters occur only on Hercules' return to Argos after his theft of Geryon's cattle, and almost invariably involve the same incident, a theft of the cattle from Hercules. By the time of Hecataeus, ca. 500 B.C., the second stealing of the cattle had become an integral part of the legend.[86] The identity of the thief, if not his ultimate demise at Hercules' hands, however, varies considerably. In fact, Fontenrose has counted twenty-one perpetrators and believes there may be more. They live all over the Mediterranean world—from France to Asia Minor to Italy.[87] In other words, when the story of Hercules and Geryon's

[83] Pliny, *HN* 35.45 (157). According to recent scholarship Hercules reached Rome via the Greeks and Magna Graecia, not through Etruria. Le Bonniec, "Hercules," pp. 302-303. Bayet (*Hercule*, pp. 178-82) similarly traces the spread of the tale of Hercules and his cattle from the south to the north. E. Richardson ("Gods," pp. 128-29) puts Hercle's arrival in Etruria in the second half of the sixth century B.C.

[84] Ogilvie, *Comm*, pp. 56, 60-61, and 656-57. The origin of the cult at the Ara Maxima and the related problem of the possible connections between Hercules and Melqart lie outside the present scope.

[85] Livy (1.7.3), among others, comments that Hercules' worship at the Ara Maxima differs from Roman practice. Ogilvie (*Comm*, p. 57) mentions three Greek aspects of the rite: the head of the one sacrificing was uncovered, but wreathed with laurel, and women were excluded. Also see Bayet, *Hercule*, pp. 297ff.

[86] Hecataeus *apud* Steph. Byz., s.v. Μοτύη (*FGrHist* 1 F 76): "Μοτύη· πόλις Σικελίας ἀπὸ Μοτύης γυναικὸς μηνυσάσης Ἡρακλεῖ τοὺς ἐλάσαντας τοὺς αὐτοῦ βοῦς. Ἑκαταῖος Εὐρώπηι."

[87] Fontenrose, *Python*, pp. 334-46 and 338 with n. 27, a list of all the figures Hercules encountered. The second theft occurs in Scythia (Herod. 4.8) and in Liguria in the Alps (Apollod., *Bibl.* 2.5.10), as two disparate examples. It is interesting to note that Hercules never "loses" his cattle in Etruria. Although the Etruscans knew the story of

cattle came into contact with a specific place, a local figure was invariably fitted to the Procrustean mold of thief. The defeat of the local boy in later versions came to redound to the credit of his home town in two ways: the area was rid of a great nuisance and the local inhabitants began to worship Hercules, as well as frequently to claim that they were the first to recognize his divinity.[88] Only in Italy, however, does the tale of Hercules and the cattle of Geryon become entwined with the motif of the *ius hospitii*.[89] Consequently, when Hercules passes through Italy, he obviously has to stop in Rome where the most dramatic cattle theft is finally and firmly localized.

The Aventine

At the same time as Cacus became a thief, Rome with its complex local traditions succeeded more than any other place in adapting Hercules' visit to its own needs. On the one hand, the theft forms merely the prelude to the establishment of the Ara Maxima;[90] on the other hand, it provides the means to unite a number of disparate and possibly contradictory figural and topographical elements. For the most part, the characters involved have already been discussed, but a consideration of their sphere of action in Rome has been confined to the Palatine. Yet each of them is also linked with the neighboring hill, the Aventine. Near the Porta Trigemina at the foot of the Aventine by the Tiber stood an altar to Evander, a temple to Hercules Invictus, and according to Vergil the home of Cacus. Bona Dea, the wife of Faunus, had her sanctuary on the Aventine, which perhaps accounts

---

Hercules and Geryon, as shown by the Greek vases with that scene found in Etruria, no extant Etruscan objects depict both figures together. Bayet, *Herclé*, pp. 98-102. E. Richardson, "Gods," p. 129 (on Geryon in Etruria).

[88] This honor was shared by such diverse cities as Rome (already discussed), Marathon (Pausanias 1.15.3), and Agyrium (only Diod. Sic. 4.24., because Diodorus came from there—1.4.4).

[89] For example, in South Italy Locros graciously receives Hercules, while Latinus, his son-in-law, steals the cattle, which results in the deaths of both Latinus and Locros (Conon 3 *apud* Photius, *Bibl*. 186.131b); but in Liguria Hercules, as usual, kills the thieves, Ialebion and Dercynus (Apollod., *Bibl*. 2.5.10). The guest-friendship motif with Hercules as the perennial sponger, like the second theft, also enjoys an independent existence. For example, in Egypt Busiris, compared by Plutarch to Faunus before he gives the Derkyllos account (n. 66 above), tries unsuccessfully to slay Hercules, as does Lityerses when Hercules visits Phrygia during the time when he was serving Omphale (Servius, *ad Ecl*. 8.68).

[90] An alternate tradition has Hercules dedicate an altar to Iuppiter Inventor in gratitude for finding the cattle: Cassius Hemina *apud OGR* 7.6 (". . . appellavitque Maximam . . ."); Dion. Hal., *Ant. Rom*. 1.32; Ovid, *Fasti* 1.579-80; and Solinus 1.7. This altar stood in the same general area at the foot of the Aventine near the Porta Trigemina, as the other landmarks to be discussed, but it has not been excavated.

for Numa's capture of Faunus on that hill.[91] Finally, Romulus is associated with the Aventine through his brother, Remus.

As the cattle raid and the theft obeyed certain rules, so the Aventine always performed the same role no matter who the actors were. The episode about Romulus and Remus taking the auspices before founding Rome clearly delineates that function:

> Since the brothers were twins, and respect for their age could not determine between them, it was agreed that the gods who had those places in their protection should choose by augury who should give the new city its name, who should govern it when built. Romulus took the Palatine for his augural quarter, Remus the Aventine. Remus is said to have been the first to receive an augury, from the flight of six vultures. The omen had been already reported when twice that number appeared to Romulus. Thereupon each was saluted king by his own followers, the one party laying claim to the honour from priority, the other from the number of the birds. They then engaged in a battle of words and, angry taunts leading to bloodshed, Remus was struck down in the affray.[92]

The hill each brother chooses determines who will prevail: the winner will be on the Palatine, the loser on the Aventine. In other words, the two hills echo the rivalry between the two brothers.[93]

---

[91] Lyngby (pp. 75-96) studies the Porta Trigemina, and dates its construction or refurbishment to 190 B.C. (pp. 91-94). Evander's altar has not been securely identified (*TDAR*, p. 204). On the temple to Hercules Invictus, Macrobius (*Sat*. 3.6.10) says "Romae autem Victoris Herculis aedes duae sunt, una ad portam Trigeminam altera in foro Boario." While both buildings are in the general area studied here, the one near the Porta Trigemina, still unidentified (*TDAR*, p. 254), is the one specifically under consideration. On the sanctuary of Bona Dea, see: Merlin, pp. 43-45 and plan at end of book; *TDAR*, p. 85. Bona Dea may be the wife of Faunus, as in Plutarch, *Rom. Quaest.* 20; or the daughter of Faunus, as in Varro *apud* Macrobius, *Sat.* 1.12.27.

[92] Quoniam gemini essent nec aetatis verecundia discrimen facere posset, ut dii, quorum tutelae ea loca essent, auguriis legerent, qui nomen novae urbi daret, qui conditam imperio regeret, Palatium Romulus, Remus Aventinum ad inaugurandum templa capiunt. Priori Remo augurium venisse fertur, sex vultures, iamque nuntiato augurio cum duplex numerus Romulo se ostendisset, utrumque regem sua multitudo consalutaverat: tempore illi praecepto, at hi numero avium regnum trahebant. Inde cum altercatione congressi certamine irarum ad caedem vertuntur; ibi in turba ictus Remus cecidit.
[Livy 1.6.4-7.2. Translation from *LCL* 1.25.]

[93] An alternate, and probably earlier, version also put Romulus on the Aventine, as Ennius *apud* Cicero, *Div*. 1.48 (107). By the latter part of the first century B.C. the positions appear to have been established as Livy states. On the earlier tradition: Skutsch, "Enniana," pp. 252-67; and Ogilvie, *Comm*, p. 55. As Romulus built his city on the Palatine, so Remus was to have built Remoria where he was eventually buried by Romulus. On its location: Merlin, pp. 108-109, 262, 265; *TDAR*, pp. 447-48. Faus-

The Aventine also had other advantages. Its propinquity to the Palatine and its frontage on the Tiber made it a better receiving ground for visitors coming up the Tiber than the other hills. Secondly because the Aventine lay outside the *pomerium* or official boundary of Rome until the time of Claudius,[94] it remained comparatively free of earlier figures and therefore had the space to accommodate later arrivals such as Cacus. Further evidence of the manipulation of tradition may be reflected in the fact that Cacus had no specific and fixed site on the Aventine, as he had on the Palatine with the Scalae Caci.

Consequently, Vergil followed tradition and exhibited a thorough familiarity with local topography when he moved Cacus to the Aventine in order to leave Evander supreme on the Palatine.[95] Curiously enough Evander never acquired his own "landmark" on the Palatine. Instead his altar by the Aventine must have been an added argument in favor of Cacus's relocation by the Porta Trigemina. There Cacus could continue to face the same enemies, Hercules and Evander, whom he had fought on the Palatine.

Vergil and the Palatine

Like his selection of the Aventine as the new home for Cacus, Vergil's motive for the transference was also logical. The usual explanation maintains that Vergil wished to keep the site of the future Rome untainted by so baneful a creature as his Cacus. On one level that sentiment may be true. Yet it ignores the significance of the parentage Vergil gives to Cacus and the import of Augustus's build-

---

tulus similarly opposed his brother Faustinus, who lived on the Aventine (Dion. Hal., *Ant. Rom.* 1.84.3). As might be expected, Titus Tatius had his tomb there (Varro, *Ling.* 5.152).

The relationship between the two hills may reflect geographical reality. That is, as discussed on page 16, the Aventine had certain natural features which made it a logical alternative for the first settlement, but these physical aspects, when compared to those of the Palatine, were insufficient to attract early occupation.

[94] ". . . erat Aventinum antea, sicuti diximus, extra pomerium exclusum, post auctore divo Claudio receptum et intra pomerii fines observatum." Aulus Gellius, *NA* 13.14.7.

[95] Compare Aulus Gellius (*NA* 5.12.13), "Propterea Vergilium quoque aiunt, multae antiquitatis hominem sine ostentationis studio peritum, . . ." Vergil appears to have been the first to transfer Cacus to the Aventine. Propertius (4.9) took the new location for Cacus and used it to introduce the story of the encounter between Bona Dea and Hercules. While Bona Dea at first bests Hercules by denying him water to slake his thirst, in the end he puts the Aventine resident in her place by denying women the right to participate in the ceremonies at the Ara Maxima. Note that in line 9 Propertius refers to Cacus as "incola" which Camps (IV.137) defines as "often used of one who is resident in a place without being originally native to it." In other words, Propertius, like Vergil, is well aware that Cacus came from the Palatine.

ing program on the Palatine in the area around the head of the Scalae Caci.

Until Vergil the surviving literary sources remained silent about Cacus's background. In the *Aeneid*, however, Cacus possesses a father appropriate to his character of the κακός and, like his father, spews forth fire and smoke. As Vergil was free to relocate Cacus, but only on the Aventine, so he worked creatively within established conventions when endowing him with a father; for Cacus had a sister who played a crucial part in the Vergilian genealogy. Servius in the fourth century A.D. records that: "His sister of the same name betrayed him [Cacus]: whereupon she merited even a *sacellum*, in which she used to be honored by the Vestal Virgins [or] by an eternal fire like Vesta."[96] Lactantius, writing in the third/fourth centuries A.D., provides the only other major extant reference to Cacus's sister: "Caca, who disclosed the theft of the cattle to Hercules, is also worshipped; she secured divinity because she betrayed her brother."[97] These late remembrances of a Caca must depend on an old and true tradition, otherwise the information would be gratuitous. Cacus, having survived so well seemingly without a sister, does not suddenly need to acquire one during the late Empire, nor would authors from that period *sua sponte* create a new divinity to usurp an old one's prerogatives. Not only did a Caca who was guardian of the hearth exist, but, paradoxically, it is Vergil who proves it; for, when searching for a father appropriate to Cacus in his fallen status, he selected the one and only figure who could be both father and role-model. As Caca, the hearth-goddess, could have been a daughter of Vulcan, so her brother would have shared the same parent.[98] With one stroke

[96] "Hunc soror sua eiusdem nominis prodidit: unde etiam sacellum meruit, in quo ei per virgines Vestae sacrificabatur [aut] in quo ei pervigili igne sicut vestae sacrificabatur." Servius, *ad Aen.* 8.190. The manuscripts preserve both readings. Virtually the same are *Myth. Vat.* 2.153 and 3.13.1, which both follow the first version.

[97] "Colitur et Caca, quae Herculi fecit indicium de furto boum, divinitatem consecuta quia prodidit fratrem, . . ." Lactantius, *Div. Inst.* 1.20.36. Compare Coluccius Salutatus, *De laboribus Herculis* 3.30.6: "Habet autem sororem nomine Cacam, que germani sui dicitur indicatrix. Idem enim compositum complexionem generat atque maliciam complexionis, a qua proditur Cacus, quoniam malicia hominis sue complexionis signum est."

The passages emphasize the betrayal, which was based on a combination of the tales about Hercules and Geryon with those concerning the Vestal Virgins. As early as the *Tale of Geryon* by Hecataeus, ca. 500 B.C., a woman, Motya, revealed where the thief had hidden the cattle (n. 86 above). Several Vestals exhibited a similar faithlessness. Tarpeia, for example (Livy 1.11.5-9), revealed to the Sabines how to capture the Capitoline. Thus Caca, like a Vestal, could be a betrayer; but her reward of divinity most likely came from the tale of Hercules, for Tarpeia was killed by the Sabines.

[98] Juturna and Turnus, as divine sister and mortal brother, resemble Caca and Cacus. They are not a bisexual deity like Pales; nor do they represent the female and male

METAMORPHOSIS OF CACU

Vergil demonstrated his incredibly extensive knowledge of early Rome and his ability to preserve that knowledge, at the same time as he seemingly obscured it.

In the same way even the cave in which Vergil places Cacus fits not only a monster and a son of Vulcan, but also a seer.[99] Italic oracular centers tended to be in wild, nonresidential areas, such as caves and woods. Numa, for example, was accustomed to meet the goddess Egeria in such a cave,[100] while Faunus had an oracle in "the groves of Albunea, which greatest of woods rang with a holy fountain and dark breathed a savage vapor."[101] As Cacus's cunning could be used against him, so could his dwelling reinforce the portrayal of him as evil.[102] The seers who prophesy from such places frequently

aspects of the same function like Pomona/Pomo and Libera/Liber. Juturna was a water nymph, and Turnus was the leader of the Rutulians against Aeneas. Similarly the sibling relationship between Caca and Cacus led to a shared parentage, but not necessarily to expertise in the same area: Caca becomes a goddess of fire; Cacus was a seer and sometime thief, whose pyrotechnic displays in the *Aeneid* merely demonstrate an inherited talent, not a god's domain. Wissowa (*Religion*, p. 161) considers Cacus and Caca an old pair of divinities who already had receded before the fixing of the calendar. Frazer (*Fasti* 2:207-208) unnecessarily surmises that Cacus was originally the husband of Caca. According to Galinsky ("Cacus," pp. 36-37) Vergil consciously parallels Turnus/Juturna and Cacus/Caca by the association of both Turnus and Cacus with fire.

Because of his father Cacus has frequently been interpreted by modern scholars as a god of fire and hence related to Caeculus, another son of Vulcan and the legendary founder of Praeneste. The theory maintains that the name Caeculus is a diminutive of Cacus. Yet linguistically the diphthong "ae" does not contract to a long "a," on which see De Simone, pp. 24-25 with extensive bibliography and discussion. Nowhere do the ancient sources link the two figures; instead, they always view them as distinct entities operating in separate spheres, as their unrelated etymologies for both names demonstrate. While Cacus was associated with κακός, Caeculus was derived from "caecus" (blind) because of his strange birth from fire, for which see Cato *apud* Servius, *ad Aen.* 7.681 and Servius, *ad Aen.* 7.678. Like the later Cacus, he was known as a thief, but of what booty has not survived (Servius, *ad Aen.* 7.678). For Cacus as a god of fire and related to Caeculus: Schneider, p. 163; Brelich, *Tre*, pp. 34-43; and Radke, *Götter*, pp. 75-76 and 282ff.

[99] In fact, Vergil directly preserves the relationship of seer, cave, and Vulcan when he refers to Vulcan as "haud vatum ignarus venturique inscius aevi." *Aen.* 8.627, and 420 for the cave.

[100] For instance, Dion. Hal., *Ant. Rom.* 2.61 where their meeting and its setting is compared to that between Minos and Zeus on Crete. Similar caves appear to have been associated with early oracles on Greece and Crete. Parke, *Oracles*, pp. 26-27.

[101] ". . . lucosque sub alta/. . . Albunea, nemorum quae maxima sacro/fonte sonat saevamque exhalat opaca mephitim." Vergil, *Aen.* 7.82-84.

[102] Again, Vergil plays with tradition and the status quo. While Cacus's original home on the Palatine was presumably a house, similar to that of Romulus still preserved in Vergil's day, its location just above the Palatine caves, alongside of which ran the Scalae, lets Vergil juggle Cacus into a cave.

Because of Cacus's new home and his father some scholars have incorrectly interpreted Cacus as a chthonic demon. Fontenrose, *Python*, p. 342; Reeker, pp. 146-51; Eden, p. 77.

show the effects of their underground living. For instance, the Cumaean Sibyl who lives "in a remote area, an enormous cave . . . the huge side of the Euboean cliff hewn out into a cave . . ." became a savage old hag.[103]

Finally, the genealogical and topographical relationships Vergil has arranged refer symbolically to Augustus. At the same time as Vergil manipulated Cacus, Augustus had accomplished the same result physically on the Palatine. At the head of and to the east of the Scalae Caci, he built a temple to Apollo Palatinus and another to Vesta.[104] In the temple to Apollo he placed the Sibylline Books.[105] Because this new temple to Apollo became the oracular repository for Rome, Cacus the seer, no longer needed on the Palatine, could be demoted to the Aventine. Likewise Vesta replaced Caca, in a sense, twice: first in the regal period and then during the Augustan era. The cult of Vesta probably did not belong to the earliest phase of Rome, as the location of her temple not within the original *pomerium* of the Palatine, but in the slightly later settlement of the Forum Romanum, shows. Tradition agrees with this archaeological evidence when it attributes the importation of her cult to Rome by Numa.[106] Nonetheless, the first settlement must have had a central hearth with a perpetual fire. Caca would have presided over that function until Augustus put Vesta on the Palatine.[107] Together, Cacus and Caca, living on the Palatine, would have governed the two most important spheres of life in early Rome: divination, necessary for the foundation itself and for most every other human activity; and fire, essential for existence.[108]

---

[103] ". . . secreta . . . antrum immane, . . . Excisim Euboicae latus ingens rupis in antrum, . . ." Vergil, *Aen.* 6.10, 42. Likewise, ". . . insanam vatem . . . rupe sub ima . . ." (*ibid.* 3.443). The Sibyl is called "horrendae" (*ibid.* 6.10) and "anum" and "vivacis" (Ovid, *Fasti* 4.158 and 875 respectively).

[104] On Augustus's building program: Carettoni, "Problemi," pp. 55-75. According to Becker (pp. 123-24) the fight between Cacus and Hercules is a mythical rendering of the Augustan battle at Actium, depicted on the shield of Achilles in *Aeneid* 8.671-713.

[105] Vergil, *Aen.* 6.72; Tibullus 2.5.17; Suetonius, *Aug.* 31.1; Servius, *ad Aen.* 6.72.

[106] For example, Livy 1.20 (Ogilvie, *Comm*, pp. 97-98) and Ovid, *Fasti* 6.258ff. There was another tradition (e.g. Plutarch, *Vit. Rom.* 22.1-2) that the cult dated to Romulus, which the location of the temple in the Forum Romanum (Rykwert, pp. 99-106) makes unlikely. According to Altheim (*Religion*, pp. 140-43) Vesta was not a "primitive Italian deity."

[107] The round *aedicula* to Vesta in the house of Augustus on the Palatine was dedicated by the emperor on 28, April 12 B.C. The structure has not been located, and even the exact nature of Vesta's commemoration on the Palatine remains unclear. Only her presence, which is uncontested, matters for my argument. *PDAR* 2:511-13. Guarducci, "Enea," pp. 73-118. Hommel, "Vesta," pp. 397-420.

[108] After the auspices for the foundation of Rome were taken, the mundus (cf. n. 48 above) was made with an altar set on top for the fire of the new hearth (Ovid, *Fasti* 4.821-25). In other words, the presence of a Cacus as seer/augur and a Caca as guard-

METAMORPHOSIS OF CACU

Conclusion

Over a period of approximately seven hundred years the legends of Cacu developed. At no time was there just one dominant version. Even Vergil with his masterful characterization of the malevolent Cacus did not manage to quell variants. Only by analyzing the extant sources within their chronological framework can the scholar understand Roman legends which remained in a constant state of flux from the very beginnings of Rome through the late Empire. Their incredible adaptability accounts for their survival and their remarkable preservation of things past. At the same time a limited number of patterns was consistently used, and long-established rules unwaveringly obeyed.

Cacu began his career as a seer living in Rome on the Palatine at the head of the Scalae Caci. Slowly and not always smoothly he evolved into the Roman cattle thief and monster, a son of Vulcan. While he adjusted to new, and often Greek, arrivals in Rome, the stationary landmarks maintained an unvarying stance. That is, the same deeds were always performed around them, even if the personnel changed. The Palatine, the Aventine, and the Forum Boarium provided the setting for two kinds of encounter: guest-friendship (the *ius hospitii*) and cattle raids. Underlying both actions was the foundation of Rome with its augural traditions. This background led to a series of augur-seer/rulers: Cacus, Faunus, Evander, and Romulus. At the same time the contemporary political situation in Rome affected who was received, the Etruscan Vibennae, the Greek Hercules, the Arcadian Evander, and the Trojan Aeneas, and how these figures were treated.

One problem in a sense still remains unresolved—the precise origins of Cacus. While it is clear that Cacu is the Etruscan form of the Latin Cacus, it is not at all clear how thoroughly Etruscan he is. That is, Cacus is never called Etruscan in any of the extant sources. Instead

---

ian of the hearth is essential to perform the first two rites in the foundation of Rome. There may have been a similar association between Hestia and Apollo at Delphi: Fauth, pp. 1118-19; Hommel, "Vesta," pp. 399ff.

Schneider (pp. 163-65) pursued an extremely similar line of reasoning to that presented here about the worship and location of Caca. He saw the cults of the ruler (*Regia*) and the hearth (Vesta) as inseparable. Hence, on the one hand, Augustus had to have Vesta situated near his house on the Palatine, and, on the other hand, the casa Romuli, the oldest *regia*, must have also had a cult of the hearth, that is a casa Cacae. The wandering of the cult of the hearth from the Palatine to the Forum Romanum he rightly likened to that of the Ficus Ruminalis. Ovid also emphasizes the virtually triadic association of ruler-, hearth-goddess, and augur-god, when he speaks of the new arrangement on the Palatine: "Phoebus habet partem, Vestae pars altera cessit; quod superest illis, tertius ipse [Augustus] tenet . . . aeternos tres." *Fasti*, 4.951-52, 954.

there appears to be a fair degree of unanimity that he resided in Rome, be it on the Palatine or the Aventine, before the arrival of the succession of settlers. In other words, Cacus, as a figure native to Rome, may well be pre-Roman and pre-Etruscan and hence generically Italic.[109] Varro describes the situation well: "... some of these names have roots in both languages [Greek and Sabine], like trees which have sprung up on the boundary line and creep about in both fields."[110]

Despite the mistiness of Cacus's ultimate "nationality," he does appear comparatively discrete in his actions. To the Etruscans he was primarily a seer and a figure of good; to the Romans he became an increasingly nefarious character—perhaps even due to too much "Etruscophilia" on his part. Both characterizations—seer and thief—coexisted in the second century B.C. The metamorphosis of Cacu was not complete until the next century, but even then intimations of his grander past have remained for the scholar to shake his kaleidoscope to see.

[109] For example, Radke, *Götter*, pp. 75-76.
[110] "... e quis nonnulla nomina in utraque lingua habent radices, ut arbores quae in confinio natae in utroque agro serpunt." Varro, *Ling*. 5.74. Translation from *LCL* 1.71, 73.

· II ·

THE PICTORIAL EVIDENCE FOR THE RES GESTAE OF CACU

Not until the fourth century B.C. did the Etruscans and the Romans become markedly interested in their legendary past. In the François Tomb in Vulci the Etrusco-Roman story of the freeing of Caeles Vibenna becomes the equal of the Greek tale of the sacrifice of the Trojan captives by Achilles.[1] As the Greeks used their heroic tradition to symbolize contemporary events,[2] so the Etruscans drew upon their own legendary background to refer to their current political situation. The François Tomb preserves a pictorial view of the increasing encroachment of Rome on Etruria: the sacrifice may poignantly capture Tarquinia's unsuccessful war with Rome;[3] the liberation may express the desire for ultimate success by recalling a time and an event when Etruscans overcame Romans. Within this context the Etruscans, and also the Romans, began to expand their scope in both art and literature from isolated deeds to more complete documentation of their heroes' careers. Not surprisingly the earliest evidence for Cacu appears during this period,[4] and significantly it forms part of the cycle about the Vibennae brothers. Although Cacu has demonstrated his ability to persist through the ages, as a seer he is limited to being a participant in the dramas of others rather than a subject of his own independent cycle; for seers are invariably consulted about undertakings of great magnitude, but rarely do they initiate action. Consequently, if Cacu and the Vibennae lived during the same period, as they did, then they should encounter each other, as they do. Only a mirror from Bolsena (App. I, no. 1) and four urns from Chiusi (App. I, nos. 2-5) record that meeting.[5] An analysis of these objects and a comparison with another legend about an Etruscan seer will establish the basic sequence of events, if not the details, which,

[1] See Chapter I n. 38.
[2] Among others, Thomas, *Mythos, passim.*
[3] Gagé, "Tarquinies," pp. 79-122.
[4] On the misattributions of pieces, dated earlier than the fourth century B.C., see Appendix II.
[5] At the end of each entry in the catalogue of Appendix I is a bibliography, as complete as possible, to the previous scholarship. Here only the major theories will be cited to give an idea of the range of interpretations.

in turn, will help clarify the passage from Gellius, preserved in Solinus.

The Objects

The Roman seizure of an Etruscan soothsayer during the war with Veii at the beginning of the fourth century B.C. provides a model. In Livy's account:

> ... [A Roman soldier] enticed the seer to a conference. And when they had walked a little way apart from the friends of both, unarmed and fearing nothing, the stalwart young Roman laid hold of the feeble old man in the sight of them all, and despite an unavailing hubbub raised by the Etruscans, bore him off to his own fellows.... When the Fathers questioned him what it was he had meant about the Alban Lake, he answered that the gods must surely have been incensed at the people of Veii on the day when they put it into his mind to reveal the destruction destined to befall his native city; and so what he had then uttered under divine inspiration, he could not now unsay and recall.... Thus then it was written in the books of fate, thus handed down in the lore of the Etruscans, that when the Alban water should overflow, if then the Romans should duly draw it off, they would be given the victory over the Veientes.[6]

The artisans of the urns have condensed a parallel sequence of events into single frames comprising the moment of the surprise attack with the immediate reaction of the "hubbub raised by the Etruscans."

Yet the urns differ in one major respect from the story about the seer from Veii: while that seer was forced to reveal the Etruscans'

---

[6] ... ad conloquium vatem elicuit. Cumque progressi ambo a suis longius essent inermes sine ullo metu, praevalens iuvenis Romanus senem infirmum in conspectu omnium raptum nequiquam tumultuantibus Etruscis ad suos transtulit. ... sciscitantibus quidnam id esset quod de lacu Albano docuisset, respondit profecto iratos deos Veienti populo illo fuisse die quo sibi eam mentem obiecissent ut excidium patriae fatale proderet. Itaque quae tum cecinerit divino spiritu instinctus, ea se nec ut indicta sint revocare posse. ... Sic igitur libris fatalibus, sic disciplina Etrusca traditum esse, quando aqua Albana abundasset, tum si eam Romanus rite emisisset victoriam de Veientibus dari; ...
[Livy 5.15.7-11. Translation from *LCL* 3.55.]
On the relation between the two stories about seers, see Bayet in Bayet and Baillet, *Tite-Live*, pp. 128-34. Why Bayet (p. 131) refers to the Veii episode as "plus pur" than that of Cacu and the Vibennae is not clear. Compare Ruch, "Devin," pp. 333-50. In the *Little Iliad* Odysseus similarly captures the Trojan seer, Helenus, during the Trojan War to learn that Troy could not be taken unless Philoctetes were present, for which see Apollod., *Epit.* 5.9.

secret, Cacu will never prophesy to the Vibennae. The Hellenistic Etruscan artists followed certain principles in constructing a scene to make it comprehensible.[7] They represented the one moment that would explicitly or implicitly reveal the denouement. For example, the absence of effective defenders on the urns with the matricide of Alcmaeon indicates Eriphyle's impending death;[8] likewise, the presence of Aphrodite in scenes with the recognition of Paris deters the brothers of Paris from killing him.[9] On the urns with Cacu the course of the fray is clearest on no. 4 (Fig. 5), the highest in quality of the group. Nowhere does a sword point murderously at someone; Caeles not only restrains the warrior to his right, but in turn is held back by that figure. Furthermore, Artile does not mourn on this urn; he merely extends his right hand toward the rescuer beside Caeles. In the midst of the melee, the composure of Cacu, nonetheless, presents a sharp contrast to the rest of the scene. He leans back in a relaxed pose with his right hand over his head. Indeed, on none of the examples is he visibly upset at the surrounding fracas. On nos. 3 and 5 (Figs. 4, 6), which depict moments slightly previous to that on no. 4, he has just noticed that something untoward is happening (no. 3) and so ceases to play (no. 5). The end of the fray is least clear on nos. 1 and 2 (Figs. 1-3), which are limited to the four central actors who never actually fight with each other. Nonetheless, the attitudes of the two about to be ambushed—the absolute serenity of both Cacu and Artile on no. 1[10] and the calm of Cacu on no. 2—mean that the two were

---

[7] I have been studying this aspect of late Etruscan funerary urns in a series of articles: "Aeneas," "Matricide," and "Lucretia."

[8] Small, "Matricide," pp. 132-35 and 143-44 with plates 17-18 (Florence 5741, 78480, and no number from the Tomba Inghirami, Volterra; and Cortona AE1025AM respectively). BrK 2:pls. 26-27 nos. 1-4 (Cortona AE1025AM; Florence, from the Tomba Inghirami, 78480 and 5741 respectively).

[9] Small, "Lucretia," p. 354; and "Matricide," pp. 134-35 and pl. 21 fig. 2 (after BrK 1:pl. 13 no. 28, Volterra 227).

[10] The interpretation of the action of Artile on no. 1 has been disputed. According to Alföldi (*ERL*, p. 229) and Bloch (*Prodiges*, p. 104) he is writing down the prophecy that Cacu sings. Petersen ("Vibenna," p. 43) maintains that Artile is singing. Robert ("Cacus," p. 79) believes that he is reading the prophecy. If Artile were recording the prophecy, surely he would have a stylus. Compare the figure with stylus and diptych on the right on three mirrors, briefly discussed in Appendix II, 5. Instead the position of Artile's diptych implies that each tablet is supported by one of his hands. Whether or not Artile is singing is difficult to ascertain from the mirror, for all the figures have their mouths closed, as is common for many representations of singing or talking figures in classical art. Since it does not seem likely that prophecies were sung (or perhaps chanted) as duets, if one of the two is singing, it should be Cacu as the elder, more important figure and lyrist. Also see discussion below. Note that Livy speaks of the seer from Veii as "cecinit" (5.15.4) and "cecinerit" (5.15.10). On the nature of diptychs: Posner, *Archives*, pp. 162-64.

not unsuspecting victims.[11] Cacu knew throughout the attack not only that he and Artile would not be captured by the Vibennae, but also that, as a result, he would not have to reveal his prophecy to the enemy.[12] Because Artile was not an accomplished seer (note his youth) and presumably not aware of Cacu's information about the course of the ambush, he is visibly upset about the attack on nos. 2, 3, and 5; but by no. 4, the last in the extant sequence, he realizes that all will turn out well.[13]

The idea that the Vibennae fail to accomplish their objective,[14] the capture of Cacu, may at first seem odd for a representation made by Etruscans for an Etruscan market, particularly when Cacu, the center of attention, has strong ties to Rome. The explanation for this reversal lies in the origin of the objects. Since they come only from the area of Chiusi,[15] they must depict a local tale about Etruscans against Etruscans. Artile identifies the circumstances. His name in Etruscan means "Little Arnth" which aptly describes the youth with Cacu on the mirror. While Arnth is a common Etruscan praenomen, only one likely candidate exists who was associated with Chiusi during the time the Vibennae lived: Arruns, for that is the Latin form of Arnth, the son of Lars Porsenna, king of Chiusi in the second half of the

---

[11] Otto Brendel (*EtrArt*, p. 416) suggests that the Vibennae are eavesdropping on Cacu to hear his prophecy. On the basis of no. 1 alone the Vibennae's next action is unclear. Since the urns (nos. 2-5) do show a fight, the Vibennae on no. 1 should be understood as listening for a little, probably in hopes of learning additional information, before commencing the attack. The artist of the late fourth century B.C. tended to choose quieter and earlier moments in an episode than the artist of the later Hellenistic period, as this group of objects demonstrates.

[12] Compare Chapter I, p. 12.

[13] Körte (BrK 2:257 and *ES*, 5:170-71) says that the Vibennae capture Cacu to prevent him from delivering a message to Tarchon, their enemy. Petersen ("Vibenna," p. 44) maintains that the Vibennae were mercenaries of Tarchon. He places the action at night, because he believes that Artile on no. 5, whom he identifies as a servant, is asleep. Sleeping figures on Etruscan urns, however, do not rest their heads on one hand, which is a pose of sadness (sorrow or mourning), but generally lie flat with their heads on pillows and their eyes shut, like the ineffective guard of Eriphyle on urns with the matricide of Alcmaeon (e.g., Florence 5741 and 78480, for which see n. 8 above).

[14] Thimme (I, pp. 104-106 n. 57), for example, contends that just because the Vibennae are heroes they would not be depicted as villains; they are therefore defenders of Cacu, as the relaxed attitude and fearlessness of the central group, especially on no. 1, is supposed to show. Münzer ("Vibenna," pp. 602-603) similarly considers the Vibennae national heroes, but in his view as mercenaries of Cacu.

[15] All the urns (nos. 2-5) come from Chiusi. The mirror, however, was found in Bolsena, which, according to tradition, was at one time ruled by Lars Porsenna: "vetus fama Etruriae est inpetratum, Volsinios, urbem de populatis agris subeunte monstro quod vocavere Oltam, evocatum a Porsina suo rege" (Pliny, *HN* 2.54 [140]). Whether modern Bolsena is the ancient Volsinii does not matter for the present purpose—only that the area was once within the Chiusine orbit is important.

sixth century B.C.[16] In fact, of the objects in this group two have survived with inscriptions naming their owners; and, in both cases, they relate to Porsenna and his son. Surely it is not coincidental that the praenomen of the man in no. 4 is Arnth, while the one in no. 2 is the son of a Larth, the Etruscan form of Lars.[17] Thus the two men by the selection of the ambush of Artile and Cacu for their casks must be recalling an exploit of their own ancestors and namesakes.

Although little is known about Arruns, the son of Lars Porsenna, beyond his death at the Battle of Aricia, the date of the battle in ca. 506/504 B.C. does make it possible for him, as a youth, to have had an encounter with the Vibennae.[18] The presence of Cacu places the scene on the Palatine, his home, which accords with the fact that Porsenna controlled Rome during the period prior to the engagement at Aricia.[19] While the mirror and the urns provide no indication of a precise setting, the two trees against a craggy landscape on no. 1 make a plausible location for a seer and especially Cacu who lived on the Palatine with its rough terrain and caves.[20] Probably due to the different nature and shape of the areas to be decorated, the urns omit the cliffs, but, except for no. 4, do retain the left tree. Instead of the right tree, a horse rears its head on nos. 2 and 3, but is controlled by Aulus on no. 4 and by a rescuer on no. 5. The Vibennae, and perhaps also the rescuers, came on horseback to Cacu's grove.[21] In other words,

[16] Heurgon (*Vie*, p. 283), among others, presents the progression from Artile to Arnth to Arruns, but not the identification of this Artile with Arruns, the son of Lars Porsenna. The other known Arruns are: (1) the fourth-century Chiusine "tutor" who provoked the Gallic invasion (Dion. Hal., *Ant. Rom.* 13.10-12; Livy 5.33); (2) the first century seer ("vates") from Luca in Lucan I.584ff.; and (3) Arruns Veltymnus, the recorder of Vegoia's prophecy, for whom see discussion and n. 31 below.

[17] For the inscriptions, see Appendix I, nos. 2 and 4. The "al" suffix of Larthal is a genitive ending (Cristofani, *Etrusco*, pp. 61-62). For Lars and Larth, Lewis and Short, p. 1036, s.v. "Lar."

[18] The two basic accounts for the battle are Livy 2.14.5-9 and Dion. Hal., *Ant. Rom.* 5.36, for which see discussion below. Ogilvie (*Comm*, p. 269), e.g., puts the battle in 506 B.C., but Heurgon (*Rome*, p. 157) places it in 504 B.C. See also Alföldi, *ERL*, pp. 47-84. On the floruit of the Vibennae, see Chapter I, pp. 13-16. I particularly wish to thank Timothy N. Gantz for his comments on the "historical" aspects of this and the following section on the Gellius passage.

[19] Tacitus, *Hist.* 3.72.1: ". . . quam [sedem Iovis Optimi Maximi] non Porsenna dedita urbe neque Galli capta temerare potuissent, . . ." Pliny, *HN* 34.39 (139): "In foedere, quod expulsis regibus populo Romano dedit Porsina, nominatim comprehensum invenimus, ne ferro nisi in agri cultu uteretur."

[20] See Chapter I, p. 33. The satyr on no. 1, who surveys the proceedings from a high vantage point, is naturally at home in the sylvan surroundings. The setting on the mirror has been considered a grotto by Piganiol (*Jeux*, p. 42).

[21] Petersen ("Vibenna," p. 44) believes that the horse belongs to Cacu and Artile who are supposed to be travelling together. The single horse, as well as the interpretation offered here, make that idea unlikely. Compare n. 22 below.

the mirror and the urns confound absolute chronological accuracy when they juxtapose the Vibennae and Artile in a setting that implies the decade previous to the Battle of Aricia. The Etruscan artists, however, were interested not so much in strict historical verity, as in a *plausible* interpretation of their legendary past.

Artile cannot be an inquirer of Cacu[22] because of his age on no. 1,[23] as well as the way he sits beside the seer, bowing his head as he follows the text of the prophecy recorded on the diptych held in his lap. Artile is instead a pupil of the seer in a manner resembling that described by Cicero:

> . . . in the days of our forefathers, it was wisely decreed by the Senate, when its power was in full vigour, that, of the sons of the chief men, six should be handed over to each of the Etruscan tribes for the study of divination, in order that so important a profession should not, on account of the poverty of its members, be withdrawn from the influence of religion, and converted into a means of mercenary gain.[24]

The emphasis on "the sons of the chief men," whether they are Roman or Etruscan,[25] fits Artile, the son of a king. The concern for the "poverty of its members" was probably not nearly as important as the retention of the control of prophecy by the "chief men."[26] Since it was probably common knowledge that Artile had been entrusted by his father to Cacu for formal instruction in the art of divination, it seems possible that the Vibennae planned not only to ambush Cacu

---

[22] Robert ("Cacus," p. 82) interpreted the yoke with vases, placed between Artile and Cacu on nos. 4 and 5, as the baggage of a traveller, and hence concluded that Artile journeyed by the horse on nos. 2-5 to consult Cacu. The "extra" figure next to Cacu on no. 5 is a servant of Artile because of his position near the yoke. On no. 4 either Artile toted his own baggage or the servant is "off-stage." Nonetheless, since no. 1 has no yoke with vases and nos. 2 and 3 each have only an isolated vase, it is possible that the vases and also the yoke functioned as space-fillers which could belong to such a scene without necessarily adding to the meaning.

[23] On the urns (nos. 2-5) Artile alone always has the short, close cropped hair of a youth—particularly clear on nos. 2 and 4—in contradistinction to the other figures.

[24] . . . bene apud maiores nostros senatus tum, cum florebat imperium, decrevit, ut de principum filiis sex singulis Etruriae populis in disciplinam traderentur, ne ars tanta propter tenuitatem hominum a religionis auctoritate abduceretur ad mercedem atque quaestum.
[Cicero, *Div*. 1.41.42. Translation from *LCL* 323.]
Heurgon (*Vie*, p. 286) says the passage refers to a *senatus consultum* of the second century B.C.

[25] See *LCL* 322 n. 2 and Pease, *Comm*, p. 259, who believes the "*filiis*" must be Etruscans. He also cites Val. Max. 1.1.1 and Cicero, *Leg*. 2.7.21 in comparison.

[26] The control of augury is discussed at length in Chapter V.

but also to capture Artile, for the possession of the son of their enemy as a hostage would have added immensely to their bargaining power.[27]

The Vibennae may have had a third objective for their ambush: the seizure of Cacu not just for an immediate military gain, but for the possession of his "complete" *libri*, since it was an Etruscan practice to collect their prophecies in books, like the "libri fatales" of the seer from Veii.[28] Furthermore, as the passage from Cicero implies, "each of the Etruscan tribes," i.e. cities, had their own form of the *disciplina etrusca*. As Tarquinia had its "Tages, who had sung the 'discipline' of extispicy, which the *lucumones* ruling Etruria at that time had written down,"[29] so Chiusi claimed the nymph Vegoia, whose revelations were similarly recorded in *libri*.[30] In other words, the diptych Artile holds should be an excerpt from such writings. His association with Cacu—note that Cacu appropriately sings like Tages—indicates another facet of Chiusi's prophetic tradition. In fact, the recorder of Vegoia's revelations about *limitatio* was a namesake of Artile—Arruns Veltymnus, whose date and origin unfortunately remain unclear.[31] At the very least a tradition existed in Etruria that divination was frequently performed by an Arruns.[32] In any case, Porsenna would naturally strive to guard the *libri* Artile holds as closely as Rome did the Sibylline Books in later years. Hence Cacu and Artile are so promptly rescued on nos. 3-5.

This group of objects (nos. 1-5), then, establishes Cacu's practice of divination among the Etruscans. His pupil, Artile, connects him to Lars Porsenna. In addition these objects offer a rarely preserved

---

[27] Robert ("Cacus," p. 84) has a similar, but not identical, interpretation. Artile is the main subject of the representations whom Cacus protects from the Vibennae by the sanctity of his personage.

[28] For example, Cicero, *Div.* 1.33 (72): ". . . Etruscorum . . . et haruspicini et fulgurales et rituales libri."

[29] ". . . Tages, qui disciplinam cecinerit exstispicii, quam lucumones tum Etruriae potentes exscripserunt." Censorinus, *D.N.* 4.13.

[30] "Qui libri [Sibyllini] in templo Apollonis servabantur, nec ipsi tantum, sed et Marciorum et Begoes [Vegoiae] nymphae, quae artem scripserat fulguritarum apud Tuscos." Servius, *ad Aen.* 6.72. For extant texts, Thulin, *Script*, pp. 12-21; Weinstock, "Vegoia," p. 579; Heurgon, "Vegoia," pp. 41-46; Pfiffig, "Prophezeiung," pp. 55-64; Harris, *Rome*, pp. 31-40; Torelli, *Elogia*, p. 132; Turcan, pp. 1009-1019.

[31] The major identifications of Veltymnus range from a haruspex from Chiusi (Heurgon, "Vegoia," pp. 41-42) or Perugia (Torelli, *Elogia*, p. 132) of the second (Weinstock, "Vegoia," p. 579) or first (Heurgon, "Vegoia," p. 42) century B.C. to an equation with the Etruscan god Vortumnus (Pfiffig, "Prophezeiung," pp. 58-59).

[32] In n. 16 above only the first Arruns, who is a guardian ("tutor" in Livy 5.33.3), is not associated with prophecy in some form or another. Furthermore, the dwarf, helping Vel Satie to take the auspices in the François Tomb, is labelled "Arnza" (*CIE* 5277) which also means "Little Arnth" (Müller-Deecke 1:447).

RES GESTAE OF CACU

Etruscan view of an Etruscan legendary event with an interesting sidelight on Etruscan divinatory customs.

The Account of Gellius

While a general chronological sequence and certain details about the participants can be ascertained, the absence of literary sources precludes a determination of the specific cause of the Vibennae's ambush. The information, however, that Arruns, the son of Lars Porsenna, was involved with Cacus does help elucidate the passage of Gnaeus Gellius about Cacus, for it intertwines historical events with mythological episodes.

"Historical" Aspects

First, consider a traditional account of the Battle of Aricia, preserved in Dionysius of Halicarnassus:

> In their [Spurius Larcius and Titus Herminius] consulship Arruns, the son of Porsena, king of the Tyrrhenians, died while besieging the city of Aricia for the second year. For as soon as peace was made with the Romans, he got from his father one half of the army and led an expedition against the Aricians, with a view of establishing a dominion of his own. When he had all but taken their city, aid came to the Aricians from Antium, Tusculum, and Cumae in Campania; nevertheless, arraying his small army against a superior force, he put most of them to flight and drove them back to the city. But he was defeated by the Cumaeans under the command of Aristodemus, surnamed the Effeminate, and lost his life, and the Tyrrhenian army, no longer making a stand after his death, turned to flight.... many more dispersing themselves about the country, fled into the fields of the Romans.... These, some of them half dead, the Romans brought from the fields into the city.... many of them, induced by ... kindly services, no longer felt any desire to return home but wished to remain with their benefactors. To these the senate gave, as a place in the city for building houses, the valley which extends between the Palatine and Capitoline.... In consequence of which ... the Romans ... give the name of "Vicus Tuscus" or "the habitation of the Tyrrhenians," to the thoroughfare that leads from the Forum to the Circus Maximus.[33]

---

[33] ἐπὶ τούτων Ἄρρους ὁ Πορσίνου τοῦ Τυρρηνῶν βασιλέως υἱὸς τὴν Ἀρικηνῶν πόλιν δεύτερον ἔτος ἤδη πολιορκῶν ἐτελεύτησεν. εὐθὺς γὰρ

RES GESTAE OF CACU

Two comments are necessary before comparing Dionysius to Gellius. Although Dionysius did not believe that Porsenna had taken Rome, his reference to the reception of the Tuscan wounded by the Romans probably signifies that Porsenna still controlled Rome and had been using it as his base for the attack south. In any event, Dionysius does put the battle after Porsenna's assault on Rome when he says "For as soon as peace was made with the Romans, . . ." His record of the outcome of the battle and the decisive role of Aristodemus are generally accepted.[34]

Gellius says, to repeat:

> He [Cacus], . . . with Megales the Phrygian as a companion, was sent as an envoy by Marsyas the king to Tarchon the Tyrrhenian, who put him in custody. He broke his bonds and went back home. Returning with greater forces, he seized the area around Vulturnus and Campania. When he dared to appropriate even those places which the laws had granted to the Arcadian, he was killed by Hercules who happened to be present. The Sabines received Megales who taught them the art of augury.[35]

If the passage is stripped of the names for its characters, the action can be seen to parallel that in Dionysius. The assault proceeds successfully until a new leader for the defenders joins battle and kills the attacking commander. The mention of Campania puts the battle in the proper area; and Volturnus makes it Aricia:

> . . . a remarkable prodigy appeared. . . . The rivers, namely, which ran near their [the barbarian] camp, one of which is called

---

ἅμα τῷ γενέσθαι τὰς Ῥωμαίων σπονδὰς τὴν ἡμίσειαν τῆς στρατιᾶς μοῖραν παρὰ τοῦ πατρὸς λαβὼν ἐστράτευσεν ἐπὶ τοὺς Ἀρικηνοὺς ἰδίαν κατασκευαζόμενος ἀρχὴν καὶ μικροῦ δεήσας τὴν πόλιν ἑλεῖν, ἐλθούσης τοῖς Ἀρικηνοῖς ἐπικουρίας ἔκ τε Ἀντίου καὶ Τύσκλου καὶ τῆς Καμπανίδος Κύμης, παραταξάμενος ἐλάττονι δυνάμει πρὸς μείζονα τοὺς μὲν ἄλλους ἐτρέψατο καὶ μέχρι τῆς πόλεως ἤλασεν, ὑπὸ δὲ Κυμαίων, οὓς ἦγεν Ἀριστόδημος ὁ Μαλακὸς ἐπικαλούμενος, νικηθεὶς ἀποθνήσκει, καὶ ἡ στρατιὰ τῶν Τυρρηνῶν μετὰ τὴν ἐκείνου τελευτὴν οὐκέτι ὑπομείνασα τρέπεται πρὸς φυγήν. . . . ἄλλοι δὲ πλείους σκεδασθέντες ἀνὰ τὴν χώραν εἰς τοὺς ἀγροὺς τῶν Ῥωμαίων . . . κατέφυγον. . . . οὓς ἐκ τῶν ἀγρῶν οἱ Ῥωμαῖοι κατακομίζοντες εἰς τὴν πόλιν . . . ὥστε πολλοὺς αὐτῶν ταῖς χάρισι ταύταις ὑπαχθέντας μηκέτι τῆς οἴκαδε ἀφίξεως πόθον ἔχειν, ἀλλὰ παρὰ τοῖς εὐεργέταις σφῶν βούλεσθαι καταμένειν· οἷς ἔδωκεν ἡ βουλὴ χῶρον τῆς πόλεως, ἔνθα οἰκήσεις ἔμελλον κατασκεύσασθαι, τὸν μεταξὺ τοῦ τε Παλατίου καὶ τοῦ Καπιτωλίου . . . ὅθεν Τυρρηνῶν οἴκησις ὑπὸ Ῥωμαίων καλεῖται κατὰ τὴν ἐπιχώριον διάλεκτον ἡ φέρουσα δίοδος ἀπὸ τῆς ἀγορᾶς ἐπὶ τὸν μέγαν ἱππόδρομον.
[Dion. Hal., *Ant. Rom.* 5.36. Translation from *LCL* 3.103, 105.]

[34] For example, Ogilvie, *Comm*, p. 269 and Heurgon, *Rome*, p. 157.
[35] For the Latin text, see Chapter I n. 6.

the Volturnus and the other the Glanis, abandoning their natural course, turned their streams backwards and for a long time continued to run up from their mouths toward their sources. The Cumaeans, being informed of this prodigy, were then at last encouraged to engage with the barbarians.[36]

This prodigy, however, occurred during the first battle of Aricia in 524 B.C. Gellius has telescoped the two engagements between the Etruscans and the Cumaeans into one.[37] An Arcadian closely joined to Hercules must mean Evander and consequently an oblique reference to an attack on Rome, which should be the Rome of Porsenna in order to agree with the political situation at the time of the second battle at Aricia. Hence, Cacus, a natural enemy of Evander and one also associated with Porsenna according to the analysis of the mirror and the urns, becomes a plausible insertion. Cacus's role as the head of an army might seem incongruous for a seer, but seers for obvious reasons accompanied armies and as a result frequently fought in battles, as Amphiaraus did at Thebes. Moreover, one tradition did consider Cacus a leader of men. Diodorus refers to Cacus as one of "the notable men" and Dionysius, somewhat less flatteringly, describes Cacus as "an exceedingly barbarian chieftain reigning over a savage people."[38]

The killing of Cacus by Hercules may reflect not only the standard version of the end of Cacus, barely established by the time of Gellius, but also the special death awarded to fighting seers. That is, although seers, when captured, are not subject to murder by their strong-armed inquirers, as mortals they eventually have to die. When Cacus leads men and himself fights in battle, he sacrifices the sanctity of his personage like Amphiaraus, who was swallowed up by the earth.[39] Cacus in his final combat confronts a worthy opponent, the hero-god Hercules. At the same time, Hercules performs the same role as Ar-

---

[36] ... τέρας γίνεται θαυμαστόν. ... οἱ γὰρ παρὰ τὰ στρατόπεδα ῥέοντες αὐτῶν ποταμοί, Οὐολτοῦρνος ὄνομα θατέρῳ, τῷδ' ἑτέρῳ Γλάνις, ἀφέντες τὰς κατὰ φύσιν ὁδοὺς ἀνέστρεψαν τὰ νάματα καὶ μέχρι πολλοῦ διετέλεσαν ἀπὸ τῶν στομάτων ἀναχωροῦντες ἐπὶ τὰς πηγάς. τοῦτο καταμαθόντες οἱ Κυμαῖοι τότε ἐθάρρησαν ὁμόσε τοῖς βαρβάροις χωρεῖν.
[Dion. Hal., *Ant. Rom.* 7.3.2-4. Translation from *LCL* 4.153.]

[37] Some scholars have also considered the two battles as one, against whom, with citations pro and con, see Alföldi, *ERL*, p. 71.

[38] "... τῶν ἐπιφανῶν ὄντες ἀνδρῶν Κάκιος ..." Diod. Sic. 4.21. "... Κάκον, δυνάστην τινὰ κομιδῇ βάρβαρον καὶ ἀνθρώπων ἀνημέρων ἄρχοντα ..." Dion. Hal., *Ant. Rom.* 1.42.2. Translation from *LCL* 1.137.

[39] For example, Apollod., *Bibl.* 3.6.8. See also Small, *Studies*, chap. 3 for references to representations in Greek and Etruscan art.

istodemus at the actual battle when at the last moment he slays Arruns, the leader of the attacking forces, and so ends the conflict.

Because of the political context Tarchon must stand for Tarquinius Superbus who, according to the traditional accounts, sought the aid of Lars Porsenna to restore him to his throne in Rome. After the second battle of Aricia, Porsenna, valuing his association with Rome more highly than that with Tarquinius, abandoned the deposed king who then fled to Cumae for refuge.[40] Recent scholarship, however, maintains that Porsenna probably never supported Tarquinius and that Tarquinius must have immediately allied himself with Aristodemus at Cumae. Instead of restoring Tarquinius, Porsenna had taken possession of Rome.[41] It is not just that this situation must be reflected in the Gellius passage, but it is the only situation that can explain the strange appearance of a Tarquin in Campania. It may even be significant that he is merely labelled "the Tyrrhenian," for he was no longer a king. During his occupation of Rome Porsenna must have had dealings with the Tarquins who must have tried to oust him. Servius briefly alludes to such an attack: ". . . after the city had been besieged by the Tarquins and after a truce had been made between Porsenna and the Romans . . ."[42] In any case, Gellius seems to refer to the failure of one particular attempt at negotiation between the two Etruscan rulers which resulted in a major war.

Mythological Aspects

The use of the general name Tarchon, rather than Tarquinius, enables Gellius to retain a full cast of mythological figures who could have lived at the same time as Hercules; for a Tarchon was the legendary founder of Tarquinia and other Etruscan cities, and, more important, sometimes the amanuensis of the revelations of Tages.[43] Since Cacus was himself a seer, the passage may reflect, in addition to the political situation, a dispute over divination. On the historical level the Tarquins had notoriously bad relations with seers. Tarqui-

[40] For a traditional account, Livy 2.9-15.

[41] For sources, n. 19 above. For discussion, Ogilvie, *Comm*, pp. 269-70.

[42] ". . . obsessa urbe a Tarquiniis inter Porsennam et Romanos factis indutiis, . . ." Servius, *ad Aen*. 11.134. On the general enmity between Porsenna and Tarquinius, see Plut., *Vit. Publicola* 18-19. Particularly important here is the mediating role between Tarquinius and Porsenna played by Arruns in 18, and Arruns's rescue of the Roman maidens ambushed by the men of Tarquinius in 19. In both cases, the events make excellent sense with Porsenna already based in Rome and consequently repelling the attempts of Tarquinius to regain the throne.

[43] Tarchon is credited with founding Tarquinia (Strabo 5.2.1), Pisa (Servius, *ad Aen*. 10.179), and Mantua (*ibid*. 10.198). For Tarchon as a recorder of Tages' revelations, see Lydus, *de ostentis*, prooemium 2-3.

nius Priscus was opposed by the augur Attus Navius;[44] and Tarquinius Superbus, specifically, nearly destroyed the opportunity to purchase the Sibylline Books.[45] Thus the mythological Tarchon logically represents another facet of the same conflict. By his imprisonment of Cacus did he hope to squelch an unfavorable and rival seer or prevent the spread of augural knowledge? The latter seems more probable, for it alone explains why Marsyas appears and Megales "taught [the Sabines] the art of augury."

Since Marsyas, as will be seen, was also involved with augury, and was associated with Cacus, he could plausibly be included among the protagonists. Equally significant, on the historical level, he could play the role of king, and hence be the equivalent of Lars Porsenna; for elsewhere Gellius speaks of Marsyas as the king of the Lydians who founded Archippe.[46] Its location on Lake Fucino probably reinforced the choice, because a more local, contained war—common enough in truth—may have seemed more believable to Gellius than an incursion from the more distant Etruria. Once Marsyas with his eastern origin made an appearance, a "Phrygian" in the guise of Megales could easily follow, since the dual function he performs of companion to Cacus and disseminator of augury had to be filled by someone;[47] for the Sabines, notwithstanding their traditional religious piety, were apparently almost devoid of any distinctive, native augural learning.[48] Moreover, the reception of Megales by the Sabines fits the general pattern in Dionysius, since the surviving invaders "turned to flight . . . dispersing themselves about the country, . . ." In addition to the Romans mentioned by Dionysius, the Sabines, by propinquity, could also have welcomed the defeated as happens in Gellius. At the same time Megales appears to be very much like what Arruns, the pupil of Cacus on nos. 1-5, might have been when grown—a companion ("socio") of Cacus and a trained augur, capable of teaching others.

[44] For example, Livy 1.36.

[45] For example, Dion. Hal., *Ant. Rom.* 4.62. Also compare Tarquin and the prodigy of the head connected with the foundation of the Temple of Jupiter Capitolinus (Chapter I n. 36).

[46] Pliny, *HN* 3.12 (108): "Gellianus auctor est lacu Fucino haustum Marsorum oppidum Archippe, conditum a Marsya duce Lydorum; . . ." Solinus 2.6: "Archippen a Marsya rege Lydorum, quod hiatu terrae haustum dissolutum est in lacum Fucinum."

[47] Gellius does not appear to distinguish clearly between Lydian and Phrygian, on which see Chapter IV n. 30. His use of "socio" for Megales may be significant, since it means "ally," not just companion, which may define the relationship between Cacus and Artile. That is, Cacus comes ultimately from Rome, Artile from Chiusi; in a joint military endeavor they would be "socii."

[48] Their main contribution to augury appears to be the *sodales Titii*, on which see Catalano 360 and 562.

At this point a contradiction arises. Unlike the other figures in Gellius, who are all mythological and therefore may be simply equated with their later historical counterparts because they did not coexist, Cacus bridges the two levels. He belongs to the period of the foundation of Rome and to the sixth century B.C. As a result, in Gellius Cacus apparently performs the part of Arruns, the son of Porsenna, although as a contemporary of Arruns and Porsenna he should represent himself. That is, Gellius seems to have reversed the roles of Cacus and Arruns. Cacus should have been the teacher of augury as he was in the general sense on nos. 1-5, and Arruns should have been called by his own name or even Megales, if the narrative were to be internally consistent. Dionysius indirectly offers the best, if not the only, explanation in his description of Gellius's research methods:

> ... the most illustrious was Gelon ... who had lately succeeded to the tyranny of Hippocrates—not Dionysius of Syracuse, as Licinius and Gellius and many others of the Roman historians have stated, without having made any careful investigation of the dates involved, as the facts show of themselves, but rashly relating the first account that offered itself.[49]

Since this comment of Dionysius happens to form part of his introductory remarks about the battle at Aricia, it should not be surprising that Gellius garbled and/or misunderstood other aspects of the events and figures associated with that battle.

Thus by grafting together two distinct themes—the Etruscan invasion of Campania and the spread of augury—Gellius has obscured both. He has increased the confusion by drawing his characters from both events. That is, he has peopled his narrative with figures with whom he was familiar and who could fit the roles rather than with the entire cast of "original" characters from either one of the two tales. On the historical level the passage may be read as follows. Marsyas (Lars Porsenna) sent Cacus (Arruns Porsenna?) as an envoy ("legatus") with Megales (Cacu?) to Tarchon (Tarquinius Superbus) who violated the right of ambassadors by imprisoning Cacus.[50] Ca-

---

[49] ... ἐπιφανέστατος δὲ Γέλων ... νεωστὶ τὴν Ἱπποκράτους τυραννίδα παρειληφώς, οὐχὶ Διονύσιος ὁ Συρακούσιος, ὡς Λικίννιος γέγραφε καὶ Γέλλιος καὶ ἄλλοι συχνοὶ τῶν Ῥωμαίων συγγραφέων οὐθὲν ἐξητακότες τῶν περὶ τοὺς χρόνους ἀκριβῶς, ὡς αὐτὸ δηλοῖ τοὔργον, ἀλλ' εἰκῇ τὸ προστυχὸν ἀποφαινόμενοι.
[Dion. Hal., *Ant. Rom.* 7.1.4. Translation from *LCL* 4.147.]

[50] Cicero, *Verr.* 2.1.33 (85): "Etenim nomen legati eius modi esse debet quod non modo inter sociorum iura sed etiam inter hostium tela incolume versetur." On Lars Porsenna and Fidenae: Gagé, "Diplomates," pp. 237-76. Note that Bayet (*Hercule*, p. 221) suggests that Tarchon is a substitute for the Vibennae, and hence the entire epi-

cus escaped home to Rome, where Porsenna was based, gathered forces, and attacked Campania. The fortuitous arrival of Hercules (Aristodemus) turned the tide of battle in Tarchon's favor with the death of Cacus.[51] Other augural aspects of the passage, particularly the kinds of augury/divination involved and the relationship between Cacus and Marsyas, will be considered in Chapters IV and VI. It is only necessary to note here that an augural subject exists in the story, as the association of four out of five of the protagonists with one form or another of divination shows. Hercules alone has no explicit prophetic powers.

Cacu? the Prisoner

The Gellius passage forms the basis for an interpretation of a second group of urns (App. I, nos. 6-9; Figs. 7-11).[52] While they closely resemble the type of Cacu ambushed by the Vibennae in the choice of figures and the composition, two major changes separate it from nos. 1-5: the added nude woman on the left and the action (nos. 7-9 only) which no longer shows an ambush, but a man being taken prisoner. Several minor alterations also distinguish the second group: the absence of trees; the addition of an altar on no. 7; the increased age of "Artile"; only one attacking "brother"; and, except for no. 6, no lyre for "Cacu." Although the scene, despite these crucial differences from nos. 1-5, has sometimes been incorrectly identified as having the same subject (the ambush of Artile), more frequently it has been interpreted as Orestes and Pylades in Tauris;[53] but both the variations from the standard iconography used for that episode and the sequence of events portrayed on the urns remove them from the sphere of Orestes and his exploits.

Euripides' play, "Iphigenia in Tauris," brings Orestes and Pylades, at Apollo's urging, to Tauris where, unbeknownst to them, Iphigenia

---

sode is the same as on nos. 1-5. Over and above the interpretation presented here, the hypothesis does not work, for Cacus as a seer could have suffered more than one ambush.

[51] Elizabeth Rawson ("Annalists," pp. 715-16) also accepts the Solinus passage as genuinely Gellius, but she believes the narrative to be about the relationships between the early kingdoms, founded when Italy was first settled by people from Asia Minor, among whom would, of course, be Marsyas and his followers (see n. 46 above).

[52] A much abbreviated and unrevised version of this section appears in Small, "Cacu Imprisoned."

[53] Most interpretations as Orestes and Pylades in Tauris depend on the first major publication of these urns in BrK 1:106-12. Both Hamburg (*Urnas*, pp. 37-39) and Levi ("Pellegrina," p. 30) agree that all the urns (nos. 2-9) form one coherent group, but differ in that Hamburg considers the subject to be Artile, while Levi maintains it is Orestes.

is a priestess of Artemis. Thoas, the king of the island, has ruled that all foreigners who enter his realm must be sacrificed to Artemis. Orestes and Pylades are captured and led to Iphigenia whom they immediately recognize, but who herself fails to identify them. During her questioning of them before the sacrifice is performed, she makes an arrangement that, if Pylades will deliver a letter to her brother, she will sacrifice only his companion. Before she actually gives the letter to Pylades, however, she learns who they are. Together the three plot a successful escape from the clutches of Thoas.

Closest in figural type to the urns is a fourth century Apulian volute-krater by the Iliupersis Painter, now in Naples. (Fig. 13).[54] The three protagonists are labelled. Leaning on a staff, Pylades stands on the left with his right hand resting on his head. Orestes with bowed head takes the center of the scene, as he sits on an altar. To the right Iphigenia, elaborately draped, gestures to Orestes with her right hand. In her left hand, she holds the key to the temple of Artemis.[55] On the far right a fully draped woman approaches. The oinochoe she carries in her right hand and the tray she balances on her head with her left hand identify her as a temple servant. Above and behind a rise in the ground stands the temple of Artemis. To the left of it sit Artemis, who holds two spears, and Apollo, who turns back to look at her. The painter has chosen the moment when Iphigenia has not yet recognized Orestes, but is still inquiring about the fate of the Greeks (Eur. *IT* 517ff.).

On the urns (nos. 7-9) the nude woman leaning on a column on the left has been interpreted as Iphigenia with Pylades sitting in sorrow on the altar beside Orestes. This scene, however, differs significantly in several details from the vase painting. "Orestes" is still bound, yet he holds the "letter." According to Euripides (*IT* 468-69), as soon as Orestes and Pylades came within the temple precinct, Iphigenia ordered them to be freed from their shackles. Moreover, the whole point of the story depends on Iphigenia's recognition of Orestes *before* she ever delivers the letter, and even then it is to Pylades and not to Orestes. In fact, the vase representations which select the moment of near-delivery always show Iphigenia still holding the letter. It never passes to Pylades.[56] Furthermore, the so-called Iphi-

---

[54] Naples H 3223 (Inv. 82113). Trendall-Webster, p. 92 no. III 3.28 (with photograph and bibliography). See also n. 55 below.

[55] Note that the drawing of this vase in *MonInst* II: 43, frequently reproduced in later studies, does not include Iphigenia's key which was depicted in white paint, as photographs clearly show.

[56] For a list of the vases with Orestes in Tauris: Brommer, *Vasen*[3] pp. 453-54. For other objects with the same scene: Brommer, *Denk* 3:327-30. In later depictions in

genia on the urns for the first time lacks not only the temple key but her clothes. Iphigenia, as a temple priestess, would not, even and perhaps especially, be rendered without drapery on late Etruscan funerary urns.[57] Finally, the Iphigenia and the Pylades of the urns are dejected, while only Orestes is downcast on the Naples vase.

Instead nos. 7-9 show the imprisoning of only one man whose fate is lamented by both the nude woman and the nude man on the left. Like nos. 2-5, each urn of this series selects a slightly different moment within the one action. On no. 7, the first of the three, the prisoner still holds a folded diptych (compare Artile on no. 3), as his hands are about to be bound. By no. 9 the binding has been completed, but the diptych has been omitted. On no. 8 the captor removes the prisoner's sword before leading him fully bound off to the right. Because the nude woman on the left on this, the last, urn in the sequence, has the diptych, it must have been passed to her by the prisoner rather than vice versa.[58] Her royal garb (elaborate crossed bands, necklace, and tiara) sets her apart from the usual Etruscan demon; yet her nudity precludes a wealthy matron or a queen. She

Roman painting and on sarcophagi, an earlier moment in the confrontation between Iphigenia and Orestes and Pylades is chosen than on the South Italian vases which are more comparable in episode and iconography to the urns. In the Roman examples, the two men, still bound, are being or have just been led into Iphigenia's presence (Eur. *IT* 468-69). For a complete survey of the artistic tradition: Phillipart, pp. 5-33. Schefold in *LAW*, s.v. "Iphigenie," gives recent bibliography.

[57] Compare the sacrifice of Iphigenia on late Etruscan funerary urns, see BrK 1:pls. 35–47. While Iphigenia most frequently appears almost overdressed (chiton and voluminous himation), occasionally she is depicted with a discreetly bared breast (e.g. BrK 1:pl. 47 no. 25 Florence 5754) or breasts (e.g. BrK 1:pl. 36 no. 4 Perugia, Necropoli Palazzone, and BrK 1:pl. 40 no. 10 Villa Giulia 50311), which probably indicates vulnerability rather than loose moral standards (I thank Larissa Bonfante for this suggestion). Never does or would Iphigenia be represented in total nudity. Helen presents a slightly different character. As her famed beauty was the raison d'être for all her woes, her body was more likely to be displayed. Even then only two urns (BrK 1:pl. 17 no. 1 Volterra 257 and BrK 2:pl. 8 no. "a" Berlin 1285) have survived with her in half to three-quarter nudity; on the Berlin urn in fact she has just been rudely awakened and pulled into an upright position which causes her covers to fall away from her body. In other words, even in Helen's case a physical "mishap" explains her nudity. See also Small, "Matricide," p. 139 with n. 133.

[58] Hamburg (*Urnas*, pp. 38-39) has misinterpreted no. 8 when she claims that the prisoner is being liberated by the nude man on the right. He does not cut him free from his bonds, as Mastarna in the François Tomb clearly slices through the rope tying Caeles's hands. The empty sheath Mastarna holds belongs to the sword he himself is using, while the extra sheathed sword will be given to Caeles; on no. 8 the nude man removes the sword, still sheathed, from Cacu. Nor can the sequence of the urns be reversed (i.e. 9, 8, 7) to portray successive moments in the freeing of a prisoner, for then the nude woman and the "Artile" figure would be "happy," not mourning. Moreover, it would be odd for the prisoner suddenly to acquire the diptych on no. 7, the last urn in the proposed sequence. I thank Laura Jean Siegel for that observation.

must be a divinity.[59] Because of her mourning attitude she is probably related to the prisoner as mother, sister, or wife.[60] While no. 7 locates the scene in a sanctuary with an altar and perhaps a temple attendant (the second added woman on the far left),[61] nos. 8-9 apparently take place outside, as the horse(s) indicate(s). No. 9, with its fully armed warrior on the right and the fallen woman to the right of the center, implies that the prisoner was seized after a violent scuffle.

While the action can be established from just the friezes, giving the figures names and identifying the circumstances are no simple matter. The diptych appears to be the crucial element, particularly since it is valuable enough to be passed from the prisoner to the divine woman. It can be either a letter, like Iphigenia's on the vases, or a recorded prophecy, like Artile's. In either case these urns *could* illustrate the imprisonment of Cacus by Tarchon as Gellius recounts, since the Chiusine artists were obviously interested in Cacus as shown by nos. 1-5. If a letter, it could be a diplomatic communication, such as those carried by the envoys of Tarquinius Superbus to Rome;[62] the scenes would then reflect the political situation Gellius describes. If an oracular diptych, then the urns may represent another episode about Chiusi and the control of the *disciplina etrusca*, to which Gellius alludes.

In either event, Cacu would be the prisoner about to be led off by one of Tarchon's men on the right. Beside him would sit the mourning Megales or Arruns, if the two are the same. The female divinity

[59] Both the typical female demon and a queenly figure appear on the left and the right respectively of Florence 5741, an urn with the matricide of Alcmaeon (see n. 8 above). The demon is dressed like the attendant on the far left of no. 9, but differs from her in being winged. Eriphyle on Florence 5741 is fully and elaborately draped in a chiton, a robe, and a mantle.

Divinities did not always have to follow the standards of dress established for mortals. For example, Eris, like the nude woman on nos. 6-10, appears nude except for jewelry (tiara, earrings, necklace, and armlet), crossed-bands, mantle draped over her right arm and about her waist, and high-strapped sandals. (Once Grafen Gheradesia, now lost, *ES* 2:pl. 164 and 3:153-56.) Turan (Venus) may be fully draped (BrK 1:pl. 13 no. 28 Volterra 227) or nude (BrK 2:pl. 104 no. 2 Florence 5769). She, unlike Eris or the woman on nos. 6-10, generally appears winged on the urns.

[60] Her pose and position on the urns preclude her acting as a protecting divinity like Turan on the urns mentioned in n. 62 above, for she in no way prevents the prisoner from being taken away. For Turan's role as a divine protector, see Small, "Matricide," pp. 134-35 and "Lucretia," pp. 354-55.

[61] The tray of foodstuffs she carries and the lack of wings distinguish her from the usual demon, for which see n. 5 above.

[62] "Interim legati alia moliri . . . A quibus placide oratio accepta est, iis litteras ab Tarquiniis reddunt et de accipiendis clam nocte in urbem regibus conloquuntur." Livy 2.3.6-7.

on the left could be Cacu's sister (Caca), who, though unmentioned by Gellius, would certainly be concerned about her brother. Her extreme abjection, as well as that of Megales/Arruns, probably refers to the ultimate death of Cacus at the hands of Hercules rather than the immediate imprisonment by Tarchon from whom the seer escaped. The woman beside Caca would be one of her attendants.[63] The fallen woman on no. 9 and the kneeling woman on no. 8, as associates or servants of Caca, may have tried to come to Cacu's aid.[64]

No. 6 supports this hypothesis, because its scene forms a transition between nos. 1-5 and 7-9. The three figures on the right match their counterparts on no. 2, but the mourning woman on the left comes from nos. 7-9. Cacu playing the lyre in the presence of Caca would provide the link to nos. 7-9 where he appears without his customary lyre, but with a sword (nos. 8-9)—a plausible attribute in the light of Gellius's description of him as a leader of a military force. The absence of Caeles Vibenna should mean that the warrior on the right is not Aulus, but a representative of Tarchon, and the mourning man is Megales/Arruns. His physique and heroic nudity distinguish him from Artile in the first group who looks obviously younger (nos. 1-2) or at the least has the short hair of a youth (nos. 3-5), and is always partially or fully draped. If actually Arruns, he is of an appropriate age to accompany Cacus, as recorded in Gellius, or to lead men in his own right, as happened at the battle of Aricia.[65]

[63] Because Caca resembles Vesta in function (cf. Chapter I), like her, she may also have a servant (on nos. 7-9) to carry ". . . missos Vestae pura patella cibos . . ." (Ovid, *Fasti* 6.310; cf. Holland, *Janus*, p. 321). Since this passage, according to Bömer (*Komm*, p. 361), refers to the rites associated with worship of ancestors, it is possible that the presence of the temple attendant may allude to the subsequent death of Cacu. The oinochoe she carries on no. 9 could be used to pour a libation. On urns with the sacrifice of Iphigenia, different attendants similarly assist by bringing the tray with foodstuffs and the oinochoe, in addition to playing instruments (double-flutes and cithara) and mourning (e.g. Perugia 329, BrK 1:pl. 43 no. 17). The knife the attendant on no. 8 holds ready could be used either for the sacrifice of an animal or for keeping away unwanted shades. Compare Hom., *Od.* 11.23ff. and especially 48-50, and the fifth century Attic red-figure pelike by the Lykaeon Painter which illustrates this scene. Boston 34.79, *ARV²*, p. 1045 no. 2; *Para*, p. 444; and Touchefeu-Meynier, pp. 135-36 no. 227 and pl. XXI fig. 1.

[64] In this light no. 7 seems somewhat anomalous: the second servant, to the right of the middle, is the one about to bind Cacu and paradoxically is about to do so within a sanctuary. Possibly the fact that such a setting was appropriate for Caca, a goddess of fire, overrode the religious considerations of the sanctity of the altar as a refuge. No matter what the interpretation offered for this group of urns the taking of a prisoner within a temple area is inappropriate—hence Iphigenia (Eur. *IT* 468-69) ordered Orestes and Pylades to be freed.

[65] Hamburg (*Urnas*, pp. 38-39) offers a different explanation, especially for no. 8. The nude woman holds the prophecy, given to her by her husband, Artile. The pris-

RES GESTAE OF CACU

Finally, the only two urns of the group with inscriptions preserved corroborate the suggested interpretation. Like nos. 2 and 4 of the first group, the praenomens allude to the legendary ancestors of the owners of the urns. No. 8 is an Arnth and no. 9 a Larth, in turn the son of another Larth. Although the four inscribed urns come from three tombs—Purni, Sentinate, and Cumeresa—only two families are involved, since the inscription for no. 8—Arnth:Sentinate:Cumeresa— shows an intermarriage between the Sentinates and the Cumeresas. Moreover, nos. 8 and 9 establish a connection between the Cumeresa (no. 8) and Purni (no. 9) urns, because they were made in the same workshop.[66] If Pairault-Massa's theory for Volterran urns, that crowning and base mouldings function as signatures of different ateliers, can be applied to Chiusine urns, then nos. 2 and 4 should be from the same workshop as nos. 8 and 9, since the first two have mouldings of egg-and-dart comparable to that on no. 8.[67] Not only the small number of objects in the two groups, but the striking homogeneity in origin and ownership demonstrate the close relations that could exist between families and workshops over a period of time, and the control that a patron could exert over the choice of subject for his cask. The virtual appropriation of a subject by a limited number of related families makes it likely that the two groups do depict family legends in a manner analogous to the Etrusco-Roman scene in the François Tomb.

Conclusion

The mirror (no. 1) by its inscriptions establishes the alliance of Cacu with the Etruscans, his profession as a seer, and the otherwise un-

---

oner replaces Cacus. Thus Artile on nos. 1-4 not only escaped the ambush of the Vibennae, but later also took one of them prisoner. The whole group then represents the same story as in the François Tomb, but for the absence of Artile in the painting and Tarchon on the urns. The similarity in choice of figures between nos. 1-5 and 7-9, however, does not have to mean that two events within one adventure are depicted. When a limited number of types is used, slight variations become significant. Compare how the alteration of the pose of the left dueller on an urn in Verona from collapsing (as on Volterra 374) to kneeling changes the scene from the aftermath of the duel between Eteocles and Polyneices to that between Aeneas and Turnus. See Small, "Aeneas." Finally, the scene on nos. 7-9 is not one of liberation, but of imprisoning, on which see n. 58 above.

[66] Thimme II, p. 120 n. 20.

[67] Pairault, *Recherches*, pp. 37-76. Although no. 9 does not have the egg-and-dart moulding, it has been connected stylistically to the same workshop (n. 66 above). No. 2, by its simpler composition, rougher workmanship, and flatter relief, should be earlier than the others. No. 5 is the only urn that differs stylistically from the rest of the group.

known episode with the Vibennae. It, with the urns (nos. 2-5), demonstrates not only that the cycles of Etrusco-Roman legends must have been fuller than what has survived, but also that Etruria was actively producing its own version of events during the same period that the annalists in Rome were vigorously pursuing their history. The Etruscan and Roman sources, when studied together, are mutually enlightening. The mélange of the separate story of Gellius becomes intelligible. In both cases, the purposes and interests of the creators determine the point of view; for neither the Etruscans nor the Romans produced an "unbiased" account. On the mirror and the urns, but not in Gellius, the viewer's sympathy lies with Cacu and his companions. As Gellius focussed on people and events immediately affecting Rome, so the stories the Etruscans chose were localized. That is, only Chiusi of the three major centers of urn production depicts the adventures of Cacu, because they involve local figures whose descendents—the owners of the urns—wished to recall them and the glories of the past. Against this background of narrow regional interests Rome so extended its sway that the absorbed areas even in the late fourth century B.C. began to define their own history in terms of their relation to Rome, for all the figures under discussion are known today only in events involving Rome. After the rise of Augustus and the establishment of canonical accounts by Vergil and Livy, among others, only whispers remained of even these shared Etrusco-Roman legends. The past had become Roman.[68]

[68] For the imperial representations of Cacus, see Appendix I n. 1.

· III ·

GREEK MODELS AND ETRUSCAN LEGENDS

THE natural interest of "Greek" South Italians in mainland Greek culture, as well as the abundance of Greek material discovered on Italian, and especially Etruscan, soil, helps obscure the differences between the two areas.[1] Because so many Italian artists chose Greek subjects rendered in a Greek manner, the similarities to Greek works become so overwhelming that a scholar may falsely interpret the Italian offshoots solely from a Greek stance. That is, the success of a piece depends on how well it mirrors known or surmised Greek works rather than on whether it embodies its own tradition. Yet within the koine of the late fourth century B.C. and after, Italian artists constantly and consciously expressed their own native ideas. The study of iconographical sources for the adventures of Cacu will demonstrate some of the methods of Etruscan artists, and at the same time will establish their independent, local concerns.

The first Etruscan artists who decided to portray Cacu faced one major obstacle: no Greek representations existed, for Cacu was solely an Italian figure. Two solutions were possible: the creation of a new form or the use of established types, so combined as to produce a new scene. Because no art in the classical and Hellenistic periods appeared *ex nihilo*, only the second choice was practicable. In fact, the nature of iconography militates against a wholesale production of entirely new types. While the style or manner of rendering figures can vary without altering the content of a scene, iconography is effective only when artist and viewer agree on specific interpretations for attributes and actions. For example, a draped woman with an aegis, helmet, and spear must be Athena or the symbols become meaningless. Poses similarly depend on the story. A warrior taking leave of his wife cannot take an attacking attitude without untoward implications. Moreover, classical artists employed standard figural types for periods far longer than those possible for styles,[2] partly

---

[1] This chapter forms the basis for and is a fuller version of the paper, "Models," which I presented at the V^c Colloque International sur les Bronzes Antiques in Lausanne, 8–13 May 1978.

[2] On the longevity of types, consider Brendel's study, "Persian," of one particular example from its Hellenistic origin to the fifteenth century A.D.

because they delighted in, not so much the creation of new forms, as the use of existing ones in novel contexts. Thus the figure of Aristogeiton from the Tyrannicides appears later as Theseus fighting the Pallantids on the Hephaisteion and as Jason stealing the Golden Fleece on an Apulian vase.[3] Individual figures could be further reduced to their component parts of stance, gesture, and expression; or two or more figures could be combined to make a transferable unit. In other words, specific principles guided artists in the formation of new scenes.

Characters, event, moment, action, and setting together place limits on an artist's search for motifs. As the central actor and a precisely defined figure, Cacu was the logical starting point. The choice of event in his life—the ambush by the Vibennae—decided the other participants. The Vibennae presented no special problem since warriors were common. Artile's main distinction was youth. Auxiliary figures could then be added to the nucleus of indispensable actors according to the tastes of the individual artists (App. I, nos. 3-5). The moment selected—the prelude to (no. 1) and the actual ambush (nos. 2-5)—set the poses. To impart surprise (no. 1), Cacu should sit serenely strumming his lyre—a specific, identifying pose of a seer as recognizable an "attribute" as the aegis of Athena. For the attack itself (nos. 2-5), Cacu should be interrupted in his playing, and Artile deeply worried about the whole situation. In both moments, for a plausible ambush the two Vibennae should surround their quarry—an arrangement that also suited the compositional preference of Etruscan artists for strong end verticals. Finally, the event should obviously take place outside.

While Cacu's age and attribute narrowed the field to handsome young lyre-players, his profession of seer determined exactly which handsome young lyre-player. Since no models of similar native Etruscan candidates existed, the Etruscan artist had no option other than to turn to the multitude of works imported from South Italy and Greece. Of the possibilities, only Apollo fit the requirements. He too was a kind of seer who played a string instrument.

Once Apollo became the type for Cacu, it was natural, and certainly simplest, for the artist to choose some scene from that god's cycle to be a model for the adventure of Cacu. As an early Apulian pelike from Ruvo and now in Naples shows,[4] the Etruscan artist did

---

[3] For the Tyrannicides: Richter, *SSG*, figs. 608-15. For Theseus on the east frieze of the Hephaisteion: Morgan, "Heph II," pl. 82 a and b. For Jason, the lower register on the body of Munich 3268, Apulian volute-krater by the Sisyphus Painter: *RVA* I, p. 16 no. 51; *APS*, p. 9 no. 1 (15); and Trendall, *Early*, pl. 19.

[4] Naples H 3231 (81392), from Ruvo. According to Trendall the vase is "near in style to the Ariadne Painter," as quoted in Schauenburg, "Marsyas," p. 50 n. 55 (with

not have far to look (Fig. 14). Its version of the musical contest between Apollo and Marsyas offers precisely all the elements essential for a pictorial rendering of the ambush of Cacu.[5] Most important of all, a similar unit of two figures forms the center of focus. Apollo, seated in the middle, inclines his head slightly, as he strums his lyre with both hands. His feet gently cross; his drapery, though pulled over his head, leaves his upper torso bare. Below Apollo a shaggy Marsyas sits on a rock. He leans forward to rest his head on his right hand in sad acknowledgement of his loss and perhaps with full comprehension of the fate awaiting him. In his left hand he holds his flutes; their case, in the form of a skin, lies behind the rock. The surrounding figures represent the divine witnesses to the event and the Muses as judges. The two central figures of Apollo and Marsyas correspond directly to Cacu and Artile on no. 2 in pose, placement, and relative proportions.[6] The Etruscan artist altered only minor details: the two figures now assume the same groundline; Artile obviously holds no flutes; and Cacu's legs are uncrossed. The placement of the Vibennae corresponds compositionally to the two Muses flanking Apollo and Marsyas on the pelike. Furthermore, it cannot be claimed that the Etruscans in ignorance took over and misinterpreted the motifs associated with the musical contest, because they knew Apollo and Marsyas as Apollo and Marsyas. Several objects, contemporaneous with the Naples pelike and the mirror (no. 1), portray the contest. For example, the tondo of a Faliscan kylix in Berkeley shows the familiar seated Apollo approached by a somewhat gangly Marsyas, who delicately waves about his long arms (Fig. 15).[7]

---

bibliography). Froning (p. 42 no. 31) dates it to the end of the fifth/beginning of the fourth century B.C. For a good discussion (especially of the two women on the lower left): Hauser, pp. 68-69.

[5] Because three major studies have been made of the appearance of the musical contest on vases within the past twenty-five years, only those objects which directly affect the depiction of Cacu are considered here. Similarly the later pictorial evidence falls outside the present scope. The iconographical studies are: Clairmont; Schauenburg, "Marsyas," with an "addendum" "Bes. Marsyas"; and Froning. Compare also the treatment, limited to Attic examples, in Metzger, *Rep*, pp. 158-68.

[6] The mirror (no. 1) is roughly contemporaneous with the South Italian vases, but the urns (nos. 2-5), which are iconographically closer to the vases, are over a century later. Two factors explain the situation. It is extremely likely that there are gaps in survival for both groups. Secondly, iconography is conservative, and therefore long-lived (cf. n. 2 above).

[7] Faliscan kylix, Berkeley 8.935. *EVP*, p. 107 and pl. 25 fig. 1. Froning (p. 43 no. 40) dates the vase to the beginning of the fourth century B.C. Clairmont, p. 168 no. 32. The following list attempts to be complete for Etruscan objects with the contest between Apollo and Marsyas. Representations of Marsyas's encounter with Athena and his punishment are not included. (1) Berlin 2950, calyx-krater, Diespater Group; *EVP*, p. 73 no. 3; Clairmont, p. 165 no. 16; Froning, p. 40 no. 5. (2) Villa Giulia 6153, Faliscan stamnos; Clairmont, p. 168 no. 33 and pl. 6; Froning, p. 43 no. 44. (3)

GREEK MODELS

To express their individuality artists frequently made minor adjustments to their models. A remarkable number of the variations on the vases with Apollo and Marsyas also appears in the scenes with Cacu and Artile. For example, the Cacu of no. 4 who leans back with his right arm over his head and his lower legs crossed resembles Olympus, the pupil of Marsyas, on an Attic pelike in Leningrad (Fig. 16).[8] Although their bodies extend in opposite directions and the position of their left arms differ somewhat because Olympus lacks a lyre, the conception of the pose remains the same. Moreover, the intently listening Marsyas needed only a slight movement in the tilt of his head and his hand which supports it to produce the woeful Artile of no. 3. In fact, that precise adaptation occurs on another Attic representation of Marsyas in Sarajewo.[9] The flutes this Marsyas holds become Artile's diptych.

A Lucanian volute-krater in the Louvre[10] demonstrates that a composition, once established, can force variants in the story to adhere to its pictorial format (Fig. 17). While the arrangement and attitude of four of the five figures conform to the four figures in the center of the Naples vase,[11] the characters filling two of the positions have been changed. Marsyas is not the gloomy satyr, but now stands on a rise in the ground to the right. The flute-case, held behind his back in his left hand, and the knife in his right hand securely identify him as the contestant. The krater, then, portrays a moment, slightly previous to that on the Naples pelike. Apollo has just begun to play, as Marsyas leans forward to listen. The morose satyr either tries to block out the music of the cithara by holding his ears or else sadly realizes

---

Villa Giulia 6154, Faliscan stamnos, replica of Villa Giulia 6153; Clairmont, p. 168 no. 34; Froning, p. 43 no. 45. (4) Villa Giulia 6473, Faliscan calyx-krater; Clairmont, p. 168 no. 29; Froning, p. 43 no. 47. (5) Villa Giulia 13135, cista from Praeneste; Giglioli, *Arte*, p. 293 fig. 1; Schauenburg, "Marsyas," p. 55; Helbig⁴ III:815-17 no. 2946. (6) Villa Giulia, Castellani Collection 50668, oinochoe, Castellani Caeretan Painter; Del Chiaro, *EVP Caere*, pp. 39-40 no. 59 (340-300 B.C.) and pl. 40. (7) Tarquinia, Museo Nazionale Inv. No. RC 2263, stamnos, Tarquinia Marsyas Painter; Del Chiaro, "Gasp," pp. 261-64, pl. 127 fig. 2.

[8] Leningrad 1795, from Kerch, Marsyas Painter. *ARV²*, p. 1475 no. 3; Clairmont, p. 168 no. 24; *FR*, pl. 87; Metzger, *Rep*, p. 162 no. 18 and pl. 21 fig. 3 (detail); Froning, p. 42 no. 29 (ca. 335 B.C.).

[9] Sarajewo 39, fragment of calyx-krater, unattributed. Clairmont, p. 166 no. 20; Schauenburg, "Marsyas," pl. 36 fig. 2; Froning, p. 42 no. 24 (early fourth century B.C.).

[10] Louvre K 519, Brooklyn-Budapest Painter, Side A. *LCS*, p. 114 no. 594; Schauenburg, "Marsyas," p. 51 no. 5 and pl. 32; Froning, p. 43 no. 42 (380-360 B.C.); Small, "Models," pl. 83 fig. 4.

[11] Apollo and the satyr retain their general positions, as do the flanking figures. The two maenads (the right one holds a thyrsus) on the left recall the two Muses of the Naples vase in their stance.

that Apollo's skill is just too great for Marsyas to overcome. At the same time the vase indicates that a different version of the contest was current in Lucania, because Marsyas, not Apollo, is shown grasping the knife[12]—an action which implies that the punishment of flaying for the loser had been agreed upon in advance by both contestants and not decided at the end of the trial by Apollo. Finally, the vase specifically relates to the iconography of Cacu ambushed in the close parallel between Caeles Vibenna (waiting on the left on no. 1) and its Marsyas. Both raise their left thighs to support their right arms. Only the angles of the sword and knife are varied. Cacu and Apollo also closely correspond to each other. Both cross their draped legs, incline their heads at the same angle, and raise their right hands, though at different levels.

Once the types drawn from representations of Apollo and Marsyas came into the repertory of the Etruscan artist, he could and did apply them to other scenes. The second set of adaptations appears on the urns with Cacu? the prisoner (App. I, nos. 6-9). Except for his age and drapery, Megales/Arruns on no. 6 is just like Artile on no. 2 and in turn Marsyas on the Naples pelike. Megales/Arruns remains consistent throughout the series; the only variation occurs in the tilt of his head from slight on no. 8 to strong on nos. 6, 7, and 9. In addition the female demon on no. 8 assumes a pose related to his; she differs only in being portrayed in a frontal view and kneeling on the

---

[12] Only two other Lucanian examples of this type survive. (1) New York 12.235.4, skyphos fragment, Palermo Painter; *LCS*, p. 53 no. 273 and pl. 23 fig. 1; Schauenburg, "Marsyas," p. 50 no. 1; Froning, p. 42 no. 38 (end of fifth century B.C.) and pl. 12 figs. 1-2. (2) Taranto 20305, oinochoe, Schwerin Group; *LCS*, p. 69 no. 351 and pl. 32 fig. 9; Schauenburg, "Marsyas," p. 51 no. 4 and pl. 34 fig. 3; Froning, p. 43 no. 41 (380-370 B.C.). There may also be an Etruscan example, for which see no. 7 (Tarquinia, Museo Nazionale RC 2263) in n. 7 above.

The form of the knife may be significant, for its broad blade makes it a machaira, a knife associated with both Apollo and Marsyas. The Greeks called it the "Delphic machaira," because Machaireus killed Neoptolemus with it at Delphi. (Hesychius, s.v. Δελφικὴ μάχαιρα. *Homeric Hymn to Apollo* 535-56. Strabo 9.3.9. Roux, pp. 34-38.) According to Agatharchides (*apud* Pseudo-Plutarch, *De Fluviis* 10.5), a second century B.C. grammarian, the stone was also present in the River Marsyas: "Γεννᾶται δ' ἐν αὐτῷ λίθος καλούμενος μάχαιρα· ἔστι γὰρ σιδήρῳ παραπλήσιος· ὃν ἐὰν εὕρῃ τις τῶν μυστηρίων ἐπιτελουμένων τῆς θεᾶς, ἐμμανὴς γίνεται καθὼς ἱστορεῖ Ἀγαθαρχίδης ἐν τοῖς Φρυγιακοῖς." Interestingly the shape of the machaireus is the same as that of the Roman secespita which was used in sacrifices: "secespita autem est culter oblongus ferreus, manubrio eburneo, rotundo, solido, vincto ad capulum argento auroque, fixo clavis aeneis, quo flamines, flaminicae, virgines pontificesque ad sacrificia utuntur, . . ." Servius, *ad Aen.* 4.262. Virtually the same description is found in Festus L 472-73, s.v. "secespitam," where the passage is attributed to Antistius Labeo (L 472), a Roman jurist who died in A.D. 10-11. Schaewen, pp. 53-56 and pl. VII.1. In other words the choice of the machaira/secespita on these vases was extremely appropriate for the protagonists and its ultimate function.

left, not the right, knee. Caca, likewise, comes from the same source. On an Apulian oinochoe in Melbourne[13] Marsyas stands, on the left, with crossed legs and leans against a pillar, while Olympus sits on the right with his head cradled sadly on his hands, the one lying on top of the other (Figs. 18-19). When the stance of Marsyas is combined with the position of the head and hands of Olympus, the figure of Caca on nos. 6-9 results.[14]

The Cacu of this group has less of a lap than on nos. 1-5. That is, he balances himself between sitting and standing. The same effect would be achieved by placing a support under the lightly stepping Apollo on the Melbourne oinochoe (Fig. 19). Cacu on no. 8 comes closest to this Apollo, as he is about to be led away by his captor. A Paestan flask in Paestum,[15] conversely, portrays Marsyas in a similar halfway position. This Marsyas and the Cacu of nos. 7-9 share one other characteristic: they are both bound. The manner of their binding, however, differs. Marsyas's hands are tied behind his back, while Cacu holds his hands crossed in front of him. As is to be expected, the majority of ancient prisoners adhere to the type of Marsyas, for the more immobilized a prisoner the less likely his escape. The alternative used for Cacu is almost exclusively Etruscan, and even then limited in its occurrence.[16] Marsyas appears so bound on a mirror in

---

[13] National Gallery of Victoria 90/5, Felton Painter (370-350 B.C.). *RVA* I, p. 172 no. 49. Trendall, "Felton," pp. 45-52 and pl. 27. Schauenburg, "Bes. Marsyas," pp. 318ff. and pl. 130 figs. 1-2 and pl. 131 fig. 1.

[14] A figure related to "Caca" appears on another vase by the Brooklyn-Budapest Painter: nestoris, London F 179; *LCS*, p. 113 no. 582 and pl. 58, upper left and detail, bottom middle; Trendall, *Indigeni*, no. 5. A young satyr similarly places his arms, as he leans over Dionysos's shoulder rather than on a pillar; his legs also cross in a like manner. Note the close resemblance between the papposilenus on the right and Marsyas on the Louvre krater (cf. n. 10 above). In fact, Trendall (*LCS*, p. 111) considers this use of stock figures to be characteristic of the Brooklyn-Budapest Painter. In other words, both the Etruscan artists *and* the South Italian vase-painters employ the same modus operandi for constructing "new" scenes.

[15] No inventory number, in Case 33, from the area of Loc. IV. Trendall, "Postscript," pp. 163-64 (forerunner of developed Apulianizing). Schauenburg, "Marsyas," p. 51 no. 6 and pl. 35 figs. 1-2. Froning, p. 44 no. 51.

[16] To my knowledge, not one of the extant Greek or Graeco-Italian representations of Marsyas bound, or the related pictorial types (the captured Silenus led before Midas, Amycus punished, and the sacrifice of the Trojan Captives) portray the victim with his hands tied in front. Two Apulian column-kraters, however, do show a prisoner, perhaps Lykaon, kneeling or seated with his hands bound in front. (1) London F 173. Schauenburg, "Achilleus," pp. 225-26 and pl. 49 fig. 3. Trendall, *Indigeni*, no. 37 (370 B.C.). *RVA* I, p. 76 no. 73 and pl. 26 fig. 3. (2) Ruvo J 1709. Schauenburg, "Achilleus," p. 225 no. 1 (note that he identifies both vases as Lucanian). Sichtermann, *SlgJatta*, p. 46 no. 65 (as Apulian Ornate, related to the Iliupersis Painter, according to Trendall). Trendall, *Indigeni*, no. 38.

A related type may appear on Etruscan urns. Two figures, identified as prisoners in

ETRUSCAN LEGENDS

the Villa Giulia where he raises his hands toward Apollo, testing the sharpness of his knife on his left palm (Fig. 20).[17] The most notable example, however, comes from the François Tomb where significantly Mastarna is freeing, not imprisoning, Caeles Vibenna.[18] He extends his fettered hands toward Mastarna who pulls the two ends of the rope taut with his left hand, as he severs the section joining the wrists.

Because the figure of Cacu? the prisoner on nos. 7-9, like the unit of Cacu and Artile ambushed on nos. 1-5, is distinctive, its genesis could be determined. Unlike Cacu and Artile it is not a direct borrowing, but represents a second stage—the amalgamation of local and imported types. The derivation of the Vibennae on nos. 1-5 is not as clear and perhaps denotes a third phase. While it has been shown that the brothers work compositionally like the two Muses on the Naples pelike and in one case (no. 1) Caeles takes the stance of Marsyas on the Louvre krater, they also function as a pair on other Etruscan funerary urns. For example, Deiphobus and Hector in the same places and in the same attitudes as the Vibennae prepare to attack Paris seeking refuge at an altar on urns from Volterra.[19] Only the dress of Deiphobus, on the left, has been altered from full armor to heroic nudity. Similarly, these two warriors occur in scenes from Chiusi, but the omission of the victim separating them changes the depiction to a duel, as the left warrior advances with sword held ready toward the right warrior still drawing his.[20] Although the ultimate origin of the two figures may have been Greek, the Etruscan artist for nos. 1-5 would have selected them from previously Etruscanized types. The contest between Apollo and Marsyas would have

---

a sanctuary, sometimes sit with their hands crossed, but lack the rope (Volterra 208, BrK 2:pl. 76 no. 4); at other times one hand grasps the wrist of the other (Florence 5773 and 5772, BrK 2:pl. 75 nos. 1-2 respectively). The latter seems to be a modification of the seated Paris, patiently awaiting Helen before sailing, where his right hand rests gently on his left wrist (Volterra 430, BrK 1:pl. 18 no. 3).

[17] Villa Giulia 12983, ex Barberini Collection, from Praeneste. Gerhard, *ES* 4:pl. 296. Helbig⁴ III 831 No. 2962 (early Hellenistic).

[18] See Chapter I n. 38 for references. This detail also appears in Alföldi, *ERL*, pl. VIII. So odd did a prisoner with hands manacled in front seem that Hamburg (*Urnas*, pp. 38-39), on the basis of the scene from the François Tomb, misinterpreted the urns with Cacu? the prisoner (nos. 7-9) as a scene of liberation. See Chapter II n. 58.

[19] For example, Milan, Museo Archeologico Civico, and Volterra 240, BrK 1:pl. 3 nos. 6-7 respectively.

[20] For example, Chiusi 950 and Copenhagen 1215d; BrK 2:pl. 10 no. 5 and 2:261-62 (with photographs) respectively; Small, *Studies*, nos. 35 and 36, with photographs. The same type occurs on Volterran urns, such as Volterra 163 and 393. Volterra 163: No BrK; Ronzitti-Orsolini, pp. 80-81 no. 10; Small, *Studies*, no. 37, with photograph. Volterra 393: BrK 2:31 no. 5a; Ronzitti-Orsolini, pp. 78-79 (top) no. 9; *CUE* I, pp. 44-45 no. 49; Small, *Studies*, no. 38, with photograph.

particularly appealed to him, because it not only contained the models for Cacu and Artile but also included figures with which he was already familiar. Likewise the dead man on no. 9 with his right hand over his head may derive either from related wounded figures on the urns[21] or from Cacu on no. 4 and hence the Leningrad pelike. The insertion of a column on no. 7 presents the same situation. Does it indicate an Etruscan sanctuary, as on urns with the death of Myrtilos,[22] or does it reflect the vases with the musical contest which offer a tripod on a column as a reward to the winner?[23]

The use of stock types has another facet. While the group of the Vibennae, which represents other characters in Volterra and Chiusi, can be considered a universal Etruscan type, others enjoy a more limited circulation. The unit of Cacu and Artile occurs only on Chiusine urns.[24] Similarly, different forms of certain types were preferred by the artists of each area. In Chiusi horses, limited to the head and a portion of the chest, were frequently located among the figures as on nos. 2-6, 8, and 9, while in Volterra the tendency was to move the horse, with the forequarters completely portrayed, to the edge of

---

[21] For example, both dying warriors on Siena 731 collapse with their right arms over their heads. Like Appendix I, no. 8, from the Sentinate-Cumeresa Tomb, Sarteano; ex Palazzo Bargagli. BrK 2:pl. 16 no. 4. Thimme II, pp. 149-50 Urn no. 3. Small, *Studies*, no. 72.

[22] For example, on two urns from Volterra: Florence 93484, BrK 2:pl. 53 no. 2, and Laviosa, *Scultura*, pp. 98-99 no. 18; and Berlin E 57, not in BrK, *CUE* I, pp. 170-71 no. 247. Two such columns appear in another killing at an altar on an urn from Chiusi, now in Palermo: Inv. No. 8456, BrK 2:pl. 82 no. 2.

[23] For example: (1) Attic volute-krater by the Kadmos Painter, Ruvo J 1093; *ARV²*, p. 1184 no. 1 Side A; Clairmont, p. 165 no. 8; Sichtermann, *SlgJatta*, pp. 20-21 no. 10 and pl. 13; Froning, p. 40 no. 2 (and no. 8, end of fifth century B.C.); and (2) Apulian volute-krater by the Lycurgus Painter, Rome, Museo Barracco; Schauenburg, "Marsyas," pp. 51-52 no. 9 and pl. 33 fig. 2; Froning, p. 43 no. 46 (360-340 B.C.). On the relation between the tripod and column and the dithyramb, see Froning, pp. 29-40; compare also Raubitschek, *Hearst*, pp. 71-74 on Hearst 5490, Attic bell-krater by the Kadmos Painter, *ARV²*, p. 1185 no. 13, Side A (Froning, p. 40 no. 10), with *choreutai* (names inscribed) performing a dithyramb in the guise of Apollo and Marsyas.

[24] The motif of Cacu and Artile occurs in one other Chiusine scene in addition to the two groups with Cacu. On an urn from Cetona, now in Copenhagen, the two figures similarly form the focus of attention. The Cacu of nos. 7-9 has been converted into a woman who holds an axe upright in her left hand, while she drapes her right arm around her male companion to the left. Compositionally he works like Caca on nos. 6-9. The equivalent of Artile/Megales weeps at the base of the altar. To the right of the central group sits a demure, draped woman with crossed hands. From either side two archers approach in a manner reminiscent of the Vibennae on nos. 1-5 except for the change of weapons. The beard and pilos of the archer on the right has led to an identification of him as Ulysses and the scene as drawn from the Trojan cycle. Brunn (BrK 1:129-30, pl. 98 no. 8) interprets it as Ulysses and the Suitors, Vagn Poulsen (*EtrSam*, p. 58) as Achilles and Penthesilea. Only this urn survives with this representation. Copenhagen H 296 (H. I. N. 59). Poulsen, *BildEtr*, pl 134.

the frieze.[25] Caca on nos. 6-9 mourns by leaning against a pillar, but the Volterran artist generally opts for a tearful woman cushioning her face on her hand, with its elbow resting on the other hand held across her chest.[26] The four subsidiary figures on no. 3 with only minor adaptations often function together as a rescue squad on Chiusine urns and almost always as a frame to the main scene.[27]

The same principles apply to the mirror (no. 1). The head of the woodland creature, who peers over the rocks at the action below, takes a position regularly reserved for onlookers on mirrors, like the satyr watching Poseidon's abduction of Amymone.[28] This kind of setting, especially with its symmetrical balance, reflects Etruscan preferences, for the Greek and South Italian scenes with Apollo and Marsyas limit their landscape to the rocks on which the contestants sit, as on the Naples pelike, with a lone tree sometimes behind it, as on the Louvre krater. Because the frieze area on the Chiusine and Volterran urns is laid out horizontally, such vertical compostions as on no. 1 were generally impracticable.[29]

---

[25] For example, two urns with a banquet scene: Volterra 195, BrK 2:pl. 101 no. 3; and Florence 78523, from the Tomba Inghirami, Volterra BrK 3:pl. 102 no. 6, *CUE* I, pp. 114–15 no. 165.

[26] For example, the woman on the left end of Volterra 342 (a meeting between mother and son?), BrK 2:pl. 106 no. 1, *CUE* I, pp. 24–25 no. 1. Also compare Juturna, near the right edge, on an urn with Aeneas and Turnus in the Palazzo dei Principi Aldobrandini, Florence, BrK 2:pl. 17 no. 2 (as Eteocles and Polyneices); Ronzitti-Orsolini, pp. 86–87 no. 12; Small, "Aeneas," p. 52, with n. 19.

The Volterran type of weeping figure also appears on urns from Perugia. In one instance, the scene may actually represent Marsyas, seated on rocks, as a prisoner bound to a tree (Fig. 21). On the right a man approaches in a short tunic (garbed like a Roman sacrificer?). The fully draped mourning woman stands to the left of Marsyas, with a second woman seated to her right. The scruffiness of the urn makes a secure identification difficult, since it cannot be ascertained whether the figure of Marsyas has pointed ears; his pose precludes the inclusion of a tail. Perugia, Museo Archeologico, storeroom off the cloisters at the base of the staircase to the museum proper. Huls, "Urne," pp. 133–40.

[27] For example, Achilles just after beheading Troilus on Palermo 8461, BrK 1:pl. 54 no. 14; and then taking refuge at an altar on Chiusi 667bis, BrK 1:pl. 65 no. 36 and Thimme I, p. 113 fig. 51. Also the motif appears in general battle scenes, as on an urn in Turin, Matausni urn no. 2, Thimme I, p. 75 fig. 22.

[28] Vatican, Museo Gregoriano. *ES* 1:pl. 64 and 3:65–66. Compare also the Silenus viewing a woman's toilet. Private collection of E. Gerhard, now? *ES* 2:pl. 212 and 3:202–203.

[29] Perugia, however, used casks which were taller than they were wide. Nonetheless, vertical compositions even there were a rarity. An example is Perugia 235 red (321 green) with an attack on a city gate. BrK 3:240–41, with fig. 58.

Do note, though, that the landscape chosen for the mirror (no. 1) is repeated with slight modifications on urns from Volterra with Philoctetes on Lemnos. Both put the protagonist(s) between two trees, almost forming an arbor, against a rocky background, and have the ambushers flank this central unit. For example on Volterra 332: BrK 1:pl. 69 no. 2; Pairault, *Recherches*, pp. 200–202, pl. 79b–80a.

GREEK MODELS

Conclusion

The earliest representations of the musical contest between Apollo and Marsyas appear during the last quarter of the fifth century B.C. in Athens, from where the type spread shortly thereafter to Italy. In both areas the subject remained popular throughout the fourth century B.C., the end of which period marks the introduction of the Etruscan series with Cacu. Crucial for the establishment of the transfer of the iconography from the Greek musical contest to the Etruscan Cacu is the appearance in both model and adaptation of the identical pair: the Greek Apollo and Marsyas become the Etruscan Cacu and Artile. Although the two figures can be traced to two separate Greek originals, they work as an indivisible unit in both the Greek and Etruscan examples considered here.[30] Furthermore, except for the stock Etruscan figures, the variations the Etruscans used for Cacu ambushed and Cacu? the prisoner come from only the Greek variations of the musical contest between Apollo and Marsyas. The Etruscan borrowings of the Greek were culled from Attic and the entire range of South Italian wares; no one area can be singled out as the sole influence. In addition to the stock Etruscan figures, such as the Vibennae brothers, which occurred throughout Etruria, some types were limited to one Etruscan area. For example, only Chiusi of the major urn centers portrays the adventures of Cacu;[31] certain types, such as the horses and the mourning woman, varied from city to city. Thus iconography in Hellenistic Etruria is just as distinctive and local as style. In other words, the presence of a koine by no means obviates the existence of strong regional expressions, and vice versa.

[30] Except for the example in n. 25 above no other scenes—Greek, Etruscan, or Roman—utilize the two figures together. The type of the distraught Marsyas, however, enjoyed a wide and an independent circulation. A study of these occurrences lies outside the present discussion. Suffice it to note that when one type can represent a number of different characters, identifications can be difficult. For example, the Belvedere torso (Vatican 1192; Helbig[4] I:211-13 No. 265) has been interpreted as Marsyas (Carpenter, *MAAR*, pp. 84-91) and Amycus (Eckhart). The latter resembles Marsyas in personality and subsequent fate. His boastful challenge to Pollux led to punishment. As a result it is not surprising that Etruscan artists chose figures from the musical contest as a model for the encounter between Amycus and the Argonauts—another story not depicted on any extant Greek works. Compare: Marchese, "Mito," pp. 61-62; Weis, "Cista," p. 3.

[31] Compare Chapter II, p. 55. Each of the three cities (Chiusi, Volterra, and Perugia) frequently demonstrates its individuality and separateness by the choice of subject. For instance, in addition to the example of Cacu, only Volterra depicts the Recognition of Paris (see n. 19 above). If the same subject has been selected, then the moment or the rendering may differ. See my discussion the urns with the Seven against Thebes and their relation to the pediment from Talamone in *Studies*, chap. 4, "Conclusion—Choice of Subject on Late Etruscan Funerary Urns."

Disparate kinds of objects made of different materials can share the same figural types and scenes. In this case, an Etruscan bronze mirror of the late fourth to early third century documents the transmission of Greek motifs from Greek and South Italian vases to Etruscan funerary urns. The abundant survival of objects with the contest between Apollo and Marsyas attests that the Etruscans had no dearth of models, whatever their original form or ultimate provenience might have been.

Finally and most importantly for the present study, the Etruscan artists logically and knowingly chose the musical contest as a model for Cacu ambushed by the Vibennae, because the two protagonists in the contest and the ambush were alike in character and profession. Did the presence of Marsyas in the contest help foster his later connection with Cacus as attested in the Gellius passage from the second century B.C. *or* was the association already known in the late fourth century B.C. so that the contest became doubly entrancing as a model for Cacu? In either event, the Etruscan artists with discrimination selected each component, be it a single gesture or a many-figured group, from the contemporary repertory. In fact, it is this very amalgamation of *all* the elements—Attic, South Italian, and Etruscan—available to the Etruscan artist that makes the mirror and the urns truly Etruscan.

· IV ·

MARSYAS IN THE FORUM

ESSENTIAL for the establishment of the Etruscan adaptation of a Greek pictorial model was the conversion of the two-figure group of Apollo and Marsyas into Cacu and Artile. Of the two Greek figures, Apollo would appear to be the more important, for he and Cacu resemble each other in pose, physique, and function, while Marsyas is comparable to Artile only in pose. Yet Marsyas must have had some role in the pictorial transfer beyond a suitable stance, since he, not Apollo, has been associated by Gellius with Cacus. To understand their relationship it is necessary to distinguish the two disparate characterizations of Marsyas; for he was not just the foolish satyr who found Athena's discarded flutes, mastered the art of playing them, and then injudiciously challenged Apollo to a musical contest. He also enjoyed a considerable reputation for wisdom. Although Marsyas ranged all over the Mediterranean, only in Italy did he escape literally and figuratively from Apollo's knife, first to assume a role of significance in the practice and spread of augury, and then to become a symbol of Rome itself. This Marsyas alone is the subject of the present study.[1]

Even the uncomplimentary literary sources on the musical contest preserve traces of the other Marsyas. To begin, he had to be a worthy opponent of Apollo. He played the flutes so well that, when he either equalled Apollo's skill or surpassed it, Apollo cheated and changed the rules for the second round so that he could not possibly lose, since Marsyas was unable to play the flutes upside down and sing simultaneously, as Apollo could with the lyre.[2] Nor were skill (τέχνη)

---

[1] No references—literary or pictorial—to Marsyas, much less to the musical contest, have survived prior to the second half of the fifth century B.C. The earliest literary mention is Herodotus 7.26 (n. 47 below); the first representation seems to be Myron's group on the Acropolis in Athens (Pliny, HN 34.19 [57]). The disparagement of Marsyas appears to have been particularly Athenian, as the representations demonstrate; for only one South Italian vase, to my knowledge, includes Athena: New York, Metropolitan Museum of Art 12.235.4; skyphos fragments, the Palermo Painter; LCS, p. 53 no. 273, pl. 23.1; Froning, p. 38, pl. 12.1-2. The only facet of the musical contest of importance for my study is the iconographical model the vases provided for the ambush of Cacu, and that aspect has been treated in Chapter III with references there to the extensive scholarship devoted to the contest.

[2] Apollodorus, Bibl. 1.4.2; Diod. Sic. 3.59.2-6; and Lucian, Dial.D. 18 (16) 245. Lucian also claims foul judging on the part of the Nymphs. Similarly, according to

MARSYAS IN THE FORUM

and craft (σοφία) the only characteristics of ability that Marsyas possessed.[3] Diodorus Siculus records:

> Marsyas the Phrygian . . . was admired for his intelligence (συνέσει) and chastity (σωφροσύνη); and a proof of his intelligence they find in the fact that he imitated the sounds made by the pipe of many reeds and carried all its notes over into the flute, and as an indication of his chastity they cite his abstinence from sexual pleasures until the day of his death.[4]

Marsyas's chastity presents another facet of the reasonable Marsyas, but in itself is not as important for the present inquiry as his intelligence. To be an inventor, Marsyas obviously had to be clever;[5] Apollo merely became the best practitioner on an instrument, the lyre, invented by another god, Hermes.[6] Furthermore, Marsyas composed music and generously taught others to play the flute and his melodies.[7] There is good reason, then, to consider Marsyas intelligent. While the highest accolade may be Alcibiades' witty likening of Socrates to Marsyas in Plato's *Symposium*,[8] the example par excellence of the wise Marsyas is his statue as an old silenus in the Forum Romanum. The statue was so important that during the Empire copies of it were erected in provincial cities and used as devices on their coins.

---

some variants, Apollo gave Midas his donkey ears so that all would know the true quality of Midas's hearing after the king had judged Marsyas the better instrumentalist. See Fulgentius, *Myth.* 3.9 and Hyginus, *Fab.* 191.

[3] ". . . συντεθειμένων δ' αὐτῶν παρ' ἄλληλα τοῖς δικασταῖς ἐπιδείκνυσθαι τὴν τέχνην, . . ." Diod. Sic. 3.59.3. "ἐνταῦθα λέγεται 'Απόλλων ἐκδεῖραι Μαρσύαν νικήσας ἐρίζοντά οἱ περὶ σοφίας, καὶ τὸ δέρμα κρεμάσαι ἐν τῷ ἄντρῳ ὅθεν αἱ πηγαί." Xenophon, *An.* 1.2.8.

[4] Μαρσύαν τὸν Φρύγα, θαυμαζόμενον ἐπὶ συνέσει καὶ σωφροσύνῃ· καὶ τῆς μὲν συνέσεως τεκμήριον λαμβάνουσι τὸ μιμήσασθαι τοὺς φθόγγους τῆς πολυκαλάμου σύριγγος καὶ μετενεγκεῖν ἐπὶ τοὺς αὐλοὺς τὴν ὅλην ἁρμονίαν, τῆς δὲ σωφροσύνης σημεῖον εἶναί φασι τὸ μέχρι τῆς τελευτῆς ἀπείρατον γενέσθαι τῶν ἀφροδισίων.
[Diod. Sic. 3.58.3. Translation from *LCL* 2.271.]

[5] Marsyas was also credited with inventing the syrinx (e.g., Metrodoros of Chios and Euphorion *apud* Athenaeus 4.184 and 184a respectively) and a gadget, the *phorbeia*, to prevent the cheeks from becoming unbecomingly puffed out while playing the flutes (Simonides *apud* Plutarch, *Mor. Cohib. Ira* 6 and *apud* Tzetzes, *Chil.* 1.372-74).

[6] The locus classicus for the story is the *Homeric Hymn to Hermes* 24-61 and 418-523.

[7] Marsyas as a composer: Plato, *Laws* 3.677d; Pliny, *HN* 7.56 (204); and Pausanias 10.30.9. Marsyas as a teacher: Plato, *Symp.* 215C; Pausanias 10.30.9; Scholiast *ad* Aristophanes, *Eq.* 9; and Hyginus, *Fab.* 273.11. Another tradition makes Daphnis the teacher of Marsyas: Alexander the Aetolian *apud* Hypothesis *ad* Theocritus, *Id.* 8; and Alexander Polyhistor *apud* Plutarch, *Mor. De mus.* 5 (1132 F).

[8] Plato, *Symp.* 215 B-C and especially 216 D which says, ". . . καὶ αὖ ἀγνοεῖ πάντα καὶ οὐδὲν οἶδεν, ὡς τὸ σχῆμα αὐτοῦ. τοῦτο οὐ σιληνῶδες; σφόδρα γε."

MARSYAS IN THE FORUM

The Iconography of the Marsyas in the Forum

Only the existence of a statue of Marsyas in the Forum Romanum is incontrovertible.[9] Its exact location, time of erection, pose, and purpose remain open to reconstruction. Nor are these interrelated problems simplified by the fact that the type persisted from at least the end of the Republic throughout the Empire; for each period tended to interpret the Marsyas for its own age, and the altered Marsyas in turn formed the basis for the next stage in the development of the figure. By the time of the latest extant Marsyas, the earliest phase had been almost entirely forgotten.

Horace (App. III, A 1) provides the first surviving literary reference: ". . . tomorrow I must be up early in the morning, to meet at the Marsyas, who says that he cannot bear the face of the younger of the Novii." Outside of establishing the existence of the statue in the thirties B.C., Horace gives two other pieces of information: (1) the name Marsyas alone is sufficient to identify the statue, which appears to have been a landmark well-known enough to serve as a common meeting-place; and (2) the pose of the statue must be of such a nature as to allow Horace humorously to conclude that Marsyas "cannot bear the face . . ." In support of the first, Seneca (App. III, A 2) and Pliny (App. III, A 3) similarly refer to Marsyas when recounting the story about Julia's nocturnal revels, while Acron and Porphyrion, respectively second and early third century A.D. commentators on Horace,[10] elaborate on both points:

> "Marsya" is said to be the place (or statue) in the vicinity of the rostra where accusers were accustomed to gather, since formerly their cases used to be pleaded there. . . . for the place had received its name from the statue. (Acron *ad* 120; App. III, A 5)

> "Vultum ferre . . ." That is, of the youngest brother of the Novii, a certain money-lender . . . who had been accustomed to lend at interest and to feast at the place which is called "At the Marsyas." Moreover these Novii were very shrewd moneylenders, and Horace jokes about this matter. Thus he says: I think

---

[9] Only the major general scholarly studies on Marsyas in the Forum are cited in this note. Additional references will be found where they specifically apply in the notes below and in Appendix III, which includes all the primary sources pertaining to Marsyas. Jordan, *Marsyas*; Heisterbergk; A. Reinach, "Marsyas"; H. D. Johnson, *Tribunal*; Gioffredi; Paoli, "Statue."

[10] There is some question whether Acron's scholia are truly his or actually a compilation made in the fifth century A.D. See OCD², pp. 6 and 960.

Marsyas held one hand erect, since he cannot bear the impudence of those moneylenders; next because bail used to be fixed at the statue of Marsyas. (Acron *ad* 121; App. III, A 5)

The two Novii were brothers at that time, of whom the younger it is said had been a turbulent money-lender. Moreover satirically and elegantly [Horace pronounces] this dictum, just as if Marsyas raises his hand, because he cannot bear this Novius in the Forum. . . . (Porphyrion *ad* 120.121; App. III, A 7)

Porphyrion puts the statue in the Forum Romanum, and Acron, more specifically, says it was "in rostris." Where precisely this phrase means the statue stood will be considered later.

The Anaglypha Traiani (App. III, B 1; Figs. 22-23), found in the central area of the Forum Romanum between the Comitium and the Column of Phocas and dated to the reign of Hadrian (A.D. 117-138), confirm the general location of the Marsyas. The two relief panels show portions of the Forum Romanum, whatever the buildings may be in the background. A statue of a nude male figure on a high, squared base, placed under a fig tree, appears at the left end of one panel and is repeated in almost the same view on the right end of the other panel. The preservation, unfortunately, is similar in both cases. The heads, right arms, and most of the right legs are missing. Nonetheless, the stance, the treatment of the torso, the boots, and the wineskin, balanced on the left shoulder and gripped in the left hand, permit an identification as Marsyas when compared to the reverse type on silver denarii minted by Lucius Marcius Censorinus in 82 B.C. (App. III, B 2; Fig. 24). A number of these coins from different dies has survived. All show an old silenus with balding head, slight paunch, and tell-tale tail in the same pose and with the same attributes of wineskin and boots as the figure on the Anaglypha Traiani. The action of the missing sections of the latter silenus becomes clear. He throws his head back to look upward, as he raises his right arm almost straight up in the air with the hand flexed back at the wrist and the fingers splayed.[11]

The gesture of the arm and head of the Censorinus silenus is distinctive and not to be confused with the common pose of *adlocutio*. Two reverses of coins dated to ca. 81/80 B.C., and consequently

---

[11] While the right hand is invariably flexed and the fingers separated, on the coins the arm itself sometimes bends back at a sharpish angle over Marsyas's head. Since that positioning generally appears on the coins where little room has been left between the top of Marsyas's head and the upper edge of the coin, it is safe to conclude that exigencies of space made those die-cutters, guilty of less careful planning than the others, slightly alter the gesture of the statue as just described in the text.

virtually contemporaneous with the Censorinus denarii, demonstrate the difference. On a denarius serratus of A. Postumius Albinus[12] a togate figure looks straight at a legionary eagle and salutes it by raising his right upper arm to shoulder height and his hand with the fingers held together to the level of his forehead (Fig. 25c). The equestrian statue of Sulla, portrayed on an aureus struck by A. Manlius,[13] holds his hand and arm similarly, but with a slightly more extended and less contracted bend at the elbow than that of the Albinus figure (Fig. 25a). He too gazes straight ahead. Quintilian, writing in the first century A.D., explains why: ". . . instructors in the art of gesture will not permit the hand to be raised above the level of the eyes or lowered beneath that of the breast; since it is thought a grave blemish to lift it to the top of the head . . ."[14] In other words, Horace does indeed speak "satirically and elegantly" (App. III, A 7) when he says that "Marsyas cannot bear the face . . . ," for he has seized upon an ambiguity in the pose of Marsyas—not present in the standard *adlocutio*—which allows him to interpret the combined gesture of head and arms as one of aversion and rejection. That is, the angle of the head prevents Marsyas from looking at Novius, as the hand is lifted way up to denounce.[15] At the same time, the poet helps to establish that the Silenus on the Censorinus coins, which is the same figure as that on the Anaglypha Traiani, must be the Marsyas in the Forum.

Servius records other appearances of such statues of Marsyas:

(1) . . . But in the free (liberis) cities there was an image (simulacrum) of Marsyas, who is under the protection of father Liber. (App. III, A 8)

(2) FATHER LYAEUS who, as we said above [just quoted], is rightly the god of liberty; whence also Marsyas, his minister is a sign of liberty in cities.

---

[12] Crawford, *RRC*, p. 389 no. 372/2 (dated 81 B.C.), with pl. XLVIII.5.

[13] Crawford, *RRC*, p. 397 no. 381/la (80 B.C.), with pl. XLVIII.22. For an excellent color reproduction: Sutherland, fig. 77 (opposite p. 56). For the actual statue: *TDAR*, p. 500, s.v. "Statua Sullae."

[14] "Tolli autem manum artifices supra oculos, demitti infra pectus vetant, adeo a capite eum petere . . . vitiosum habetur." Quintilian, *Inst.* 11.3.112. Translation from *LCL* 4.301, 303.

[15] Quintilian (*Inst.* 11.3.120) specifically advises ". . . aut manu sublata denuntiant . . ." To a certain extent, the movement resembles the Mediterranean habit of tossing the head back to say no. It is not, however, the same as the gesture of "*aposkopein*," as maintained by Kapossy, p. 74. "*Aposkopein* is the characteristic gesture accompanying the expression of wonder at the radiant appearance of the deity. The adorant protects his eyes from the glory of his god by shadowing them with his right hand, raised to his brow." The last phrase clearly excludes the Marsyas in the Forum who extends his hand above his head. The quotation is from Brilliant, *Gesture*, p. 11.

MARSYAS IN THE FORUM

[and]

... Marsyas, his minister, placed by cities in the forum, is perhaps a sign of liberty (indicium libertatis), who by his raised hand (erecta manu) calls to witness that nothing is lacking in a city. (App. III, A 9)

Even if the location "in the forum" and the characteristic "raised hand" were not sufficient in themselves to attest to the replication of the Marsyas from the Forum Romanum, the reverses of the bronze coins struck by a number of provincial cities (App. III, C; Fig. 26), primarily during the second and third centuries A.D., would demonstrate the statue's popularity. Typical is the series of bronzes issued by Alexandria Troas (App. III, C 6; Fig. 26a). Like the Censorinus Marsyas an old, paunchy Silenus in boots carries a wineskin resting on his left shoulder and grasped in his left hand; the gesture of the right hand, however, has been altered slightly, but significantly. Although these Greek imperial coins may show Marsyas in different views,[16] with his head slightly tilted back[17] or held straight,[18] or even in varying settings,[19] never do they ever depict his right hand reaching above his head. Instead, his action resembles the *adlocutio* of the Postumius and Manlius reverses in height, extension, and hand with fingers held together. The die-cutters, and presumably the sculptors of the copies in the provincial forums, could not have seen the original in Rome.[20] All they must have known was a bare description of the pose, attributes, and dress, such as Servius records when he says

---

[16] For example, to right, Alexandria Troas (App. III, C 6; Fig. 26a); to left, Neapolis (App. III, C 20; Figs. 26b, c); or, more rarely, to front, Ninica Claudiopolis (App. III, C 11).

[17] For example, Neapolis (App. III, C 20; Fig. 26b, c). Note, however, that the position of the head can vary within the coinage of one city. An example from Alexandria Troas (App. III, C 6) at the American Numismatic Society shows Marsyas with his head held straight, but one in the Cabinet des Médailles (Fig. 26a) has him with his head tilted back.

[18] For example, Coela and Parion, App. III, C 2 and 5 respectively.

[19] For example, Marsyas stands alone (Alexandria Troas—App. III, C 6; (Fig. 26a); within the sanctuary of Astarte/Europa (Sidon—App. III, C 18; Figs. 26e, f); within a gateway (Berytus—App. III, C 15; Figs. 26i, j); facing a palm tree (Tyre—App. III, C 19); and with Astarte, a trophy and a Victory on a column (Tyre—App. III, C 19; Figs. 26g, h). Marsyas's associates on these coins do not affect or bear upon the arguments pursued here, but form a separate problem. All that does matter is his assured presence in the fora and not elsewhere.

[20] In addition to the coins, several inscriptions about the erection of statues of Marsyas have survived, for which see App. III, D. It is worthwhile noting that Acron and Porphyrion, the two ancient commentators on the Horace passage (App. III, A 5, 7, and 1 respectively) by their cogent explanations of the gesture prove that the actual statue in the Forum Romanum must have still been standing during their lifetimes and have been viewed by them. In other words, the Greek imperial die-cutters of the second and the third centuries A.D., if they had visited Rome, could have seen the statue.

the hand was raised ("erecta manu"), but does not specify how it was positioned. A "raised right hand," if not descriptively qualified, signified one thing alone to a citizen of the empire—the *adlocutio* of the emperor.[21] Hence the meaning of the rest of Servius's sentence becomes apparent: ". . . his raised hand calls to witness that nothing is lacking in a city," because it is the gesture of the emperor who ensures the well-being of the individual cities.[22]

Marsyas and Augury

Because the imperial use of the Marsyas depended on a reinterpretation of the gesture of the right hand of the Marsyas in the Forum, the original purpose of that Marsyas still remains to be considered. The two *Aeneid* passages that provoked Servius's glosses and the subject of the glosses themselves indicate the area in which an explanation should be sought. To Aeneas's statement in 3.19-20, "I was bearing sacrifices to the Dionaean mother and the divinities for auspices of the works begun, . . ."[23] Servius comments on the "divinities," unnamed by Vergil, whom Aeneas would have invoked; and in 4.54ff. tells of Dido's attempts to learn the will of the gods. Especially see line 65, "Alas, the ignorant minds of seers!"[24] That is, both cases concern augury and the gods involved.

The Censorinus coins provide the crucial evidence. No descriptive literary references to the Marsyas have survived in addition to those already quoted; and the sources on augury only say that an augur, when taking the auspices, may sit or stand,[25] but are silent on the

---

[21] Brilliant, *Gesture*, p. 69, with a general discussion of the gesture on pp. 65-69, its appearance and use under the Severans and in the third century A.D. on pp. 165-70, and *passim*.

[22] The Servian distinction that the Marsyas appeared in only "free cities" has led scholars (especially see Paoli, "Marsyas" and "Statue"), since Eckhel (4:493) in the late eighteenth century, to conclude that Marsyas was not merely an "indicium libertatis," but a symbol of the *ius Italicum*. The latter represents a legal status, conferred by the emperor on non-Italian provincial cities, equivalent to the rights and privileges of cities in Italy during the late Republic. (*OCD²*, p. 559; Berger, p. 530.) Although it once seemed that only cities known to have the *ius Italicum* also had statues of Marsyas, Paul Veyne ("Marsyas") has shown that enough exceptions exist of cities with a Marsyas, but without the *ius Italicum*, to make the scholarly connection between the two untenable. While other scholars have been skeptical of Marsyas's association with the *ius Italicum*, Veyne presents the strongest and most complete case against that identification. He also cites the previous scholarship both for and against the connection.

[23] "Sacra Dionaeae matri divisque ferebam/auspicibus coeptorum operum, . . ." Vergil, *Aen.* 3.19-20.

[24] "Heu, vatum ignarae mentes." *Aeneid* 4.65.

[25] Cicero, *Div.* 1.17 (31), says of Attus Navius, "itaque sue inventa ad meridiem spectans in vinea media dicitur constitisse, cumque in quattuor partis vineam divisisset . . ." See Pease, *Comm*, p. 145. Compare Servius, *ad Aen.* 6.197, "VESTIGIA PRESSIT quia ad captanda auguria post preces immobiles vel sedere vel stare consueverant."

precise position of the different parts of the body during an actual sighting. The pictorial material is scarcely more helpful. Representations of figures gazing skyward, and even pointing at flying objects, exist, but never with both the fingers separated and the wrist flexed back on the extended arm.[26] While depictions of seers and haruspices in action occur frequently enough—Cacu is a case in point—illustrations of augurs performing are extraordinarily rare.[27] The one feature necessary and common to all the augurs, however, appears to be the scanning of the sky and that is precisely the action of Marsyas on the Censorinus coins. It is quite obvious from the tilt of his head that he is looking up and from the position of his right arm and hand that he is calling attention to whatever he has seen in the sky.

The idea of Marsyas acting as an augur may seem strange at first, but nothing in his nature contradicts the possession of such a skill. On the one hand, he enjoyed a considerable reputation for wisdom; on the other, he could have the oracular abilities of a Proteus or a

---

[26] Even the number of objects with figures looking at the sky are few. The closest to the Marsyas are the following, all produced over a rather long span of time. (1) The boy, on the right, noting the first swallow of spring on an early fifth-century Attic red-figure pelike. Leningrad, Hermitage 615, from Vulci, Pioneer Group. *ARV²*, p. 1594 no. 48 and *Para*, p. 507. Neumann, *Gesten*, p. 20 fig. 7. (2) An onlooker, according to Mark I. Davies, or Daedalus, according to Hampe, on a third century A.D. terra sigillata vase from North Africa. Heidelberg 7115. Hampe, "Dädalus," pp. 25-30, and pl. 17. (3) A late fifteenth century illustration of *Aeneid* 1.390-93 with Venus, Aeneas, and Achates sighting the augury of the twelve swans. British Museum, King's Ms. 24 f. 59, written by Bartolomeo Sanvito and possibly illuminated by him. I thank Thomas S. Pattie of the British Library, Department of Manuscripts, for this information; for a good color illustration, Croft, p. 14 bottom.

Representations of dancing satyrs with right hands raised above their heads are generally not analogous, because the position of the legs and the left arm differ from that of the Marsyas in the Forum. For instance, a satyr on the far right of an Apulian skyphos by the Parasol Painter shows the closest resemblance with is right hand shooting straight up, but with a sharp bend at his knees. He also grips a winesack in front of him in his left hand. (Paris, Louvre CA 3291; *RVA* I, p. 23 no. 101.) Marsyas on another Apulian bell-krater similarly raises his right hand, but lets his left arm hang by his side and, more importantly, appears to jump off his feet in wonderment at Athena playing the flutes. (Boston 00.348; *APS*, p. 18 no. 1; Schauenburg, "Marsyas," p. 43 and pl. 30.)

[27] Only two comparable examples are known to me. (1) Vel Satie in the François Tomb stands stock-still (even his hands are covered by his toga *picta*) in profile and casts his eye upward for the sighting; note Arnza, the dwarf beside him, about to release a bird, which is the second according to the Rebuffats ("Tombe," p. 100). They also offer the excellent suggestion that Vel Satie is a sixth-century ancestor of the owner of the tomb and hence a contemporary of the Vibennae. For general scholarship on the tomb, Chapter I n. 38; for a good photograph of Vel Satie, Pallottino, *EtrP*, p. 121; and for the augural implications, Goidanich, pp. 107-18. (2) A fragment of a relief in Rome, Museo Nazionale Romano (Terme) shows a temple pediment with Romulus and Remus taking the auspices. From what I have been able to make out from the scrappy preservation, none of the figures seems overly similar to the Marsyas. The relief has been dated to the Flavian era and assigned to the Temple of Quirinus. Helbig⁴ I:727-29 No. 1013. E. Strong, *Scultura*, pp. 72-74, 74 fig. 48.

Nereus, for like them he was a river god.²⁸ More importantly, the Romans specifically associated Marsyas with augury. Silius Italicus rationalizes the appearance of Marsyas in Italy after the musical contest with Apollo: "But this people [the Marsi] got their name from Marsyas, the settler who fled in fright across the sea from Phrygian Crenai [Apamea-Celaenae], when the Mygdonian [Phrygian] pipe was defeated by Apollo's lyre."²⁹ Gnaeus Gellius adds the information that Marsyas founded his own city, Archippe, in Marsian territory on Lake Fucino.³⁰ The similarity between the names, Marsyas and Marsi, may help explain the connection of the two. Yet the fact that the Marsi enjoyed a reputation as enchanters and augurs may also reflect Marsyas's supernatural knowledge.³¹ Furthermore, Servius states that "Some, however, say that those sent from Phrygia by Marsyas the king, at the time when Faunus ruled, were the ones who taught the discipline of augury to the Italians."³² Likewise Gnaeus Gellius

---

²⁸ In his possession of intelligence Marsyas belonged to the group of refined, learned sileni, like the one captured by Midas (see Chapter I n. 30 for references). For Proteus: Chapter I n. 31 and accompanying text. For Herakles' struggle with Nereus to learn the location of the garden of the Hesperides: Apollod., *Bibl.* 2.5.11. On the oracular nature of rivers: Ninck, pp. 47-99. For sileni worshipped as river-gods: Preller-Robert, 1:729-30. Finally, of the four Near Eastern rivers that were called "Marsyas," the branch of the Meander in southern Asia Minor was the most famous. On its banks stood the Phrygian city of Apamea-Celaenae (*PECS*, p. 445) where Apollo hung Marsyas's skin according to Herodotus 7.26 (quoted in n. 47 below). See also *RE* XIV:cols. 1985-86 "Marsyas 1-4"; Waser, p. 2806.

²⁹   Sed populis nomen posuit metuentior hospes,
            cum fugeret Phrygias trans aequora Marsya Crenas,
            Mygdoniam Phoebi superatus pectine loton.
[Silius Italicus, *Pun.* 8.502-504. Translation from *LCL* 429.]
Silius Italicus refers to Apamea-Celaenae as Crenai, because the contest, according to some (e.g. Pliny, *HN* 5.106) took place at Aulocrene, a gorge near Apamea-Celaenae.

³⁰ Gnaeus Gellius *apud* Pliny, *HN* 3.12 (108), "Gellianus auctor est lacu Fucino haustum Marsorum oppidum Archippe, conditum a Marsya duce Lydorum; . . ." So also Solinus 2.6-7, "Archippen a Marsya rege Lydorum, quod hiatu terrae haustum dissolutum est in lacum Fucinum: . . ." Gellius is careless in these two fragments when he calls Marsyas "the leader of the Lydians," because elsewhere (*apud* Solinus 1.8-9; text in Chapter I n. 6) he implies that he is Phrygian. The confusion between the two peoples may have arisen, because the Phrygians were conquered by the Lydians. Nonetheless, compare the comments of Dionysius of Halicarnassus (*Ant. Rom.* 7.1.4) on Gellius's accuracy, for which see Chapter II n. 49 and accompanying text. In any case, as a native of Apamea-Celaenae (n. 28 above), Marsyas had to be Phrygian.

³¹ The Marsi as enchanters, e.g.: Horace, *Epod.* 17.9, "Marsa . . . nenia"; Aulus Gellius, *NA* 16.11.1, ". . . Marsis hominibus, . . . vi quadam genitali datum ut et serpentium virulentorum domitores sint et incentionibus herbarumque sucis faciant medellarum miracula." The Marsi as augurs, e.g.: Cicero, *Div.* 1.58 (132), "non habeo denique nauci Marsum augurem, . . ."; and *Div.* 2.33 (70), "Difficilis auguri locus ad contra dicendum. Marso fortasse, . . ." See also Pease, *Comm*, p. 289, s.v. "1. Soranum"; Letta, pp. 53, 95-99.

³² "Nonnulli autem dicunt a Marsya rege missos e Phrygia, regnante Fauno, qui disciplinam auguriorum Italis ostenderunt." Servius, *ad Aen.* 3.359.

MARSYAS IN THE FORUM

elsewhere tells that Cacus "with Megales the Phrygian . . . was sent as an envoy by Marsyas the king to Tarchon the Tyrrhenian. . . . [Later] the Sabines received Megales who taught them augury."[33] In other words, an Italian tradition that lasted at least six hundred years from the time of Gellius to that of Servius related Marsyas and augury.

Marsyas's Phrygian origin made him not just a logical possessor of augural ability but also indicates the form of augury he would inculcate.[34] The Roman sources concur that the Phrygians were among the first, if not the first, to practice augury from the observation of birds[35]—and that is precisely what the Marsyas in the Forum must be doing. He has recently arrived from Asia Minor, as implied by the winesack he carries for sustenance and the travelling boots he wears. The slight bend in his legs suggests that he has just ceased walking[36] and is confirming his choice of stopping-place by looking for a favorable omen in the sky.[37]

The "Indicium Libertatis" and the Site of the Statue

Servius provides a clue to the particular augural practice Marsyas and his followers brought to Italy when he calls the silenus an "indicium libertatis." Like the statue in the Forum, this phrase changes in meaning between the Republican and Imperial periods. As the *adlocutio* of Marsyas on the Greek Imperial coins and in Servius alludes to the emperor's guarantee of civic freedom (*libertas*) of which Marsyas is a sign (*indicium*), so in the Republican period the raised arm makes Marsyas an "augur" and the use of *libertas* denotes which sphere.

In discussing the erection of the Temple of Jupiter on the Capitoline, Livy says that the site must be prepared as follows:

> And that the site might be free (libera) from all other religious claims and belong wholly to Jupiter and his temple, which was

---

[33] Gnaeus Gellius *apud* Solinus 1.8-9. For text, see Chapter I n. 6.

[34] Remember that the idea of Marsyas as a teacher was also common to the stories devoted solely to his flute-playing, for which see n. 7 above.

[35] Cicero, *Div.* 1.41 (92): "Phryges autem et Pisidae et Cilices et Arabum natio avium significationibus plurimum obtemperant, quod idem factitatum in Umbria accepimus." Cicero, *Div.* 2.38 (80): "An Pisidarum aut Cilicum aut Phrygum ista inventa dicemus?" Isidorus, *Etym.* 8.9.32: "auguria autem avium Phryges primi invenerunt." For brief discussion and other ancient references: Pease, *Comm*, p. 260.

[36] I thank H. Anne Weis for the two observations about the travelling boots and the bend in the knees.

[37] Aeneas offers an excellent parallel to Marsyas. Like the silenus he was a refugee from Asia Minor who also waited for a divine sign—the sow and piglets—to tell him where to settle in Italy. See *Aeneid* 3.388-95 and 8.81-85.

MARSYAS IN THE FORUM

building there, he [Tarquinius Superbus] determined to annul the consecration of several fanes and shrines which had been first vowed by King Tatius at the crisis of the battle against Romulus, and had afterwards been consecrated and inaugurated. At the very time when he began this task the gods are said to have exerted their power to show the magnitude of this mighty empire. For whereas the birds permitted that the consecrations of all the other shrines should be rescinded, they refused their consent for the shrine of Terminus. This omen and augury was thus construed, . . .[38]

The premise of the rite of "exauguration" was to ensure that no divinity, known and particularly unknown, at a proposed site would be offended by the introduction of a new divinity.[39] Specifically the area was to "be free from all other religious claims." The crucial word is the adjective, "free" or "*libera*," the noun form of which can

---

[38] Et ut libera a ceteris religionibus area esset tota Iovis templique eius quod inaedificaretur, exaugurare fana sacellaque [Tarquinius Superbus] statuit, quae aliquot ibi, a Tatio rege primum in ipso discrimine adversus Romulum pugnae vota, consecrata inaugurataque postea fuerant. Inter principia condendi huius operis movisse numen ad indicandam tanti imperii molem traditur deos. Nam cum omnium sacellorum exaugurationes admitterent aves, in Termini fano non addixere; idque omen auguriumque ita acceptum est, . . .
[Livy 1.55.2-4. Translation from *LCL* 1.191.]
The other ancient passages, which mention this rite, in chronological order, are: (1) Cato, *Orig*. 1.23 *apud* Festus L 160, s.v. "Nequitum," ". . . et Cato Originum lib. I (23): 'Fana in eo loco conpluria fuere: ea exauguravit, praeterquam quod Termino fanum fuit; id nequitum exaugurari' "; (2) Cicero, *Leg*. 2.8 (21), ". . . urbemque et agros et templa liberata et effata habento"; (3) Livy 5.54.7, "hic cum augurato liberaretur Capitolium, Iuventas Terminusque maximo gaudio patrum vestrorum moveri se non passi; . . ."; (4) Festus L 108, s.v. "Liberata," "*Liberata* ponebant pro effata, hoc est locuta"; (5) Servius, *ad Aen*. 1.446, ". . . unde tamquam in luco sacro inducit Didonem Iunoni templa construere. morem autem Romanum veterem tangit; antiqui enim aedes sacras ita templa faciebant, ut prius per augures lucus liberaretur effareturque, tum demum a pontificibus consecraretur, ac post ibidem sacra edicerentur"; and (6) Servius, *ad Aen*. 9.446, "et cum in omnibus Tarpeius esset inventus, in quo erant multa diversorum numinum sacella, actum est, ut exinde ad alia templa numina evocarentur sacrificiis, quo posset libere et sine piaculo templum Iovis exaedificare. cumque omnes dii libenter migrassent, Terminus solus, hoc est limitum deus, discedere noluit, sed illic remansit."

On the rite of exauguration: Catalano, pp. 281-88, 333-34, and 341. Magdelain, "*Auguraculum*," pp. 266-69; Piccaluga, *Terminus*, pp. 192ff.; and Stambaugh, pp. 567-68.

[39] Exauguration is not the same as, nor should it be confused with, "evocatio" (Catalano, pp. 283-88). On a grand scale it may be related to the ritual destruction of cities through the reversal of the foundation rites, as in Carthage in 146 B.C., for Servius, *ad Aen*. 4.212, says, "nam ideo ad exaugurandas vel diruendas civitates aratrum adhibitum, ut eodem ritu quo conditae subvertantur; . . ." See also Rykwert, pp. 70-71.

be "*libertas.*"[40] Thus Marsyas the "indicium libertatis" in its original usage meant Marsyas the symbol of the one responsible for ritually freeing the land.[41] The action of Marsyas in the statue confirms this reading of "*libertas.*" The augur performing the exauguration in Livy observes the flight of birds, as Marsyas does on the Censorinus coins.[42] Thus the general association between Marsyas and augury preserved in the literary sources is based on an actual and specific contribution of Marsyas to Roman augural lore.

The "freeing" or "liberatio" applied not just to religious buildings, but also to the augural *templum* in the sky, the city (*urbs*) itself, and the *ager romanus antiquus*.[43] Hence Marsyas at one time was of such importance to the Romans that he earned a place as prominent as the Forum Romanum for his statue (Plan 4; Figs. 29-30). Acron (App. III, A 5) says the statue stood "in rostris." Despite the common practice of placing statues on the rostra, Marsyas was not a likely choice, because the subjects were human, not semi-divine figures of mixed human-animal origin.[44] "In rostris" must refer, then, to the general

---

[40] Lewis and Short, p. 1056, s.v. "liber" and p. 1058, s.v. "libertas." Compare *MythVat* 3.12.1, which indulges in a lengthy discussion of possible meanings of and derivations for the god Liber, among which "liberari" is used in the same sense as here of "freeing" and even "cleansing": "Dicitur Liber, . . . sive, ut dicunt, quia hic deus mares, missis seminibus, liberet. Nam per Junonen feminae, per Liberum mares liberari dicuntur et purgari. Liber etiam vocari meruit, quod a curis homines *liberet*; sive Liber, quia sacra ejus ad purgationem animae pertinent." The passage ends, "Liber ergo ab eo quod *liberet*, nuncupatus est." In the middle of the section Marsyas is mentioned, for which see Appendix III, A 11. Note that not here or in any of the other passages referring to the Marsyas in the Forum was the silenus ever related to the goddess Libertas; the two were never associated in antiquity. Similarly a reading of *libertas* as licentiousness, a common trait of sileni, makes no sense in the contexts of the two Servian passages (App. III, A 8-9).

One other scholar has connected Marsyas with augury, although not as presented here. Zmigryder-Konopka considers the *libertas* to refer broadly to the freedom or right to take one's auspices. I have not seen this article, but Catalano (pp. 131-35 n. 64), who disagrees with the conclusions, provides a lengthy summary.

[41] Edwin Flinck (pp. 20-21), in fact, has already connected the god Liber, in a way similar to that argued here for Marsyas, with the rite of exauguration, which he calls a "Beschwörung" ("exorcism"). Recall that Servius (App. III, A 8) specifically refers to Marsyas as "in tutela Liberi Patris." In any case, because of Marsyas's (and Liber's) Eastern origins there may be a connection with a similar Mesopotamian foundation rite which calls for the removal or exorcism of a particular divinity as part of the dedication of a house. See Ellis, pp. 185-86 no. 45 (text, translation, and bibliography).

[42] Livy, 1.18.7, describes the accoutrement of the augur, "Augur ad laevam eius capite velato sedem cepit, dextra manu baculum sine nodo aduncum tenens, quem lituum appellarunt." The Marsyas in the Forum does not accord with this description of an augur, because he is not in *esse* a Roman augur, but the semi-divine bringer and teacher of a specific augural rite to the Romans.

[43] So Magdelain, "*Auguraculum*," p. 266 and "Inauguration." Hermon, p. 24.

[44] For example, Cicero, *Phil.* 9.7.16, "senatui placere Ser. Sulpicio statuam pedestrem aeneam in rostris ex huius ordinis sententia statui, . . ." For other literary sources

vicinity of the rostra rather than to the rostra itself. The Anaglypha Traiani, the only other extant source with information about the location, puts Marsyas under a fig tree, which stands in the same plane as the figures instead of in the background with the buildings. This separation of the statue indicates that it did not belong among the monuments lining the sides of the central area of the Forum Romanum, but that it must have stood in the central area itself where the people gathered to hear the emperor. Accordingly the statue appears on both panels as a visual reference of orientation for the viewer. The fig tree pinpoints the exact spot. A small, squared area, midway between the north and south sides of the Forum, but close to the east end and directly opposite the center of both the Republican and the Augustan rostra—hence the "in rostris"[45]—remained unpaved throughout the Republic and the Empire to allow the flourishing of the three trees most sacred to Rome, the olive, the vine, and the fig, which shaded Marsyas.[46]

---

and a general discussion: *TDAR*, pp. 450-51, s.v. "Rostra." For an idea of what the rostra with its honorary statues would have looked like, compare the frieze with the *adlocutio* of Constantine on his arch in Rome. *PDAR*, 1:104-105.

[45] I follow Welin (p. 91) in my analysis of the Anaglypha Traiani, and like him (pp. 89-90) I believe that the literary sources (App. III, A) refer to the new, not the old, rostra, because none dates to the period of the old rostra, and, unless an author indicates otherwise, he should be alluding to the contemporary arrangement. Although it is interesting to note that Zanker's plan (no. 1, opposite p. 40 in *Forum*) of the Forum Romanum for ca. 42 B.C., showing both rostra, rightly puts the Marsyas in the center of the Forum with the result that the statue stands virtually equidistant from both rostra. In other words, the statue, placed in the central, cleared area, is "in rostris" with respect to both the old *and* the new rostra. When Julius Caesar reorganized the western end of the Forum, he demolished the old rostra. The new or Augustan rostra, dedicated after 42 B.C. and inaugurated in 29 B.C., was then moved from between the old Comitium and the Forum proper to the west end of the Forum. *TDAR*, pp. 450-55. *PDAR*, 2:272-83. Zanker, *Forum*, p. 40.

[46] eadem [ficus] fortuito satu vivit in medio foro, qua sidentia imperii fundamenta ostento fatali Curtius maximis bonis, hoc est virtute ac pietate ac morte praeclara, expleverat. aeque fortuita eodem loco est vitis, atque olea umbrae gratia sedulitate plebeia sata.
[Pliny, *HN* 15.20 (78).]
TDAR, pp. 207-208. *PDAR*, 1:397. There were two other major fig trees in Rome (Pliny, *HN* 15.20 [77-78]): (1) the ficus Ruminalis, under which Romulus and Remus were suckled by the wolf; and (2) the ficus Navia, near the statue of the seer, Attus Navius, in the Comitium ("colitur ficus arbor in foro ipso ac comitio Romae . . .")— it may have once been the original ficus Ruminalis miraculously moved there by Attus Navius. The ficus Ruminalis, which grew outside the Forum, does not apply to this discussion. The other tree, however, has sometimes been cited as the one sheltering Marsyas. Since there were two fig trees in the Forum and only one was really "in rostris," Marsyas (in addition to the reasons given in the text) belongs in the middle of the Forum. In fact, no text puts him in the Comitium; it is his association with the fig tree on the Anaglypha Traiani that muddles the situation. In any case, while the Marsyas seems more appropriate in the central area of the Forum, a location on its edge, as other scholars argue, would not vitiate Marsyas's basic augural nature. The

MARSYAS IN THE FORUM

The location particularly suited Marsyas. He naturally belonged in an area which not only was kept free of permanent encumbrances,[47] but could remain so only through his agency. Even during the Empire, when space was limited, that section of the Forum stayed predominantly open and unbuilt. Moreover, there is the possibility that the tree represents part of the ritual of exauguration, because the augur used trees to mark the physical boundaries of his *templum*, the area in which the auspices applied.[48] Although this fig tree had no apparent connection with the ficus Ruminalis, the symbolic association, particularly with its special veneration, may have been sufficient to recall the birth of Romulus and Remus and the origins of Rome. Romulus would have had need of Marsyas's rite before he could build his settlement. Thus Marsyas under a fig tree could commemorate the founding of Rome.

Set in the pavement in front of Marsyas's enclosure was an inscription, "Lucius Naevius Surdinus, son of Lucius, Praetor between citizens and foreigners."[49] Together the location of the inscription and

---

idea that Marsyas stood in the Comitium goes back to Jordan (*Marsyas*, pp. 11-13), and was first refuted by Loeschke, *AA*, col. 14-15.

Jean Gagé ("Megales") maintains that the two statues of Attus Navius and Marsyas were actually one and the same and originally portrayed Megales of the Gellius passage (See Chapter I n. 6). His conflation of statues is entirely untenable. Livy (1.36.5) says, "Statua Atti capite velato, quo in loco res acta est, in comitio in gradibus ipsis ad laevam curiae fuit; . . ." If the head were veiled, then the statue cannot be the bareheaded (save for the fillet) Marsyas, not to speak of the obvious problem of the necessary metamorphosis of Attus Navius from human to silenus, nowhere recorded. While the exact placement of the statue of Attus Navius remains outside of the present discussion, nonetheless its location in the Comitium again separates it from the Marsyas. Finally, no mention exists of a statue of Megales in the Forum Romanum.

[47] Dudley, pp. 76-77. Parenthetically, it may not be accidental that the site for the Marsyas is near the Lacus Curtius (*PDAR*, 1:542-44), once a source of water and thereby suggestive of Marsyas the river god. Similarly the hanging of Marsyas's skin in the agora at Apamea-Celaenae (". . . ἐξ αὐτῆς τῆς Κελαινέων . . . ἐν τῇ καὶ ὁ τοῦ Σιληνοῦ Μαρσύεω ἀσκὸς ἀνακρέμαται . . ." Herodotus 7.26) may indicate that Marsyas himself carried the association with marketplaces from the East to the West rather than the location being a purely Roman concept.

[48]
    Olla vera(a) arbos quirquir est, quam me sentio
    dixisse, templum tescumque me esto in sinistrum.
    Olla ver(a) arbos quirquir est, quam me sentio
    dixisse, te(m)plum tescumque me esto (in) dextrum.
     Inter ea conregione conspicione cortumione, utique
    ea ⟨rit⟩e dixisse me sensi.

     In hoc templo faciundo arbores constitui fines apparet
    et intra eas regiones qua oculi conspiciant, . . .

[Varro, *Ling.* 7.8-9.]

Varro is quoting an old formula, reflecting an old ceremony. Magdelain, "Auguraculum," p. 259.

[49] "L. NAEVIUS L. F. SURDINUS PR. INTER CIVIS ET PEREGRINOS." *CIL* VI:37068. *PDAR*, 1:397. Zanker (*Forum*, p. 24) dates the inscription to 10 B.C.; while

the office Surdinus held indicate that the tribunal for the foreign praetor stood during the Augustan period beside the three trees[50] and, more importantly, the statue of Marsyas. While the original juxtaposition of the tribunal and the statue may have been fortuitous—for example, the space available was there—the proximity of the two fostered a causal relation about a century later. That is, aided by the logical misunderstanding of the raised right hand of the statue and in a like manner, the augural sense of Marsyas as the "indicium libertatis" receded. Instead during the middle-to-late Empire, if Marsyas were to be a symbol of *libertas*, it must be the political kind, and obviously related to foreigners, or else why would the foreign tribunal stand beside his statue? Thus colonial cities desiring "to be miniatures, as it were, and in a way copies" of Rome,[51] would naturally adopt as an ideal symbol the statue of Marsyas with his right hand raised in an *"adlocutio,"* and place copies of it in a similar position in their own fora and on coins.[52] In other words, both the original iconography and the purpose of the statue were simultaneously and similarly misinterpreted in such a mutually reinforcing way that the Marsyas in the Forum underwent a complete transformation from an augural figure to a political being.

The first extant use of the civic Marsyas occurs on the coinage of Cremna under Hadrian (App. III, C 8), but the majority of examples not unnaturally dates to the period of the Severans when the focus of the emperor switched more and more from Rome to the provinces.[53] Septimius Severus greatly increased the number of cities which enjoyed the *ius Italicum*; Caracalla by the Constitutio Antoniniana

---

Dudley (pp. 96-97) puts Surdinus's praetorship ca. 15 B.C. For a detailed discussion of the inscription and its implications: Welin, pp. 77-82. There as an exact replica of this inscription (*CIL* VI:1468, with addendum in 31662) on the back of the relief with Mettius Curtius plunging into the abyss. The relief was found on the site of the Lacus Curtius, and is now in the Museo Capitolino Nuovo. Helbig⁴ II:404-406 No. 1602. *PDAR*, 1:544, fig. 673.

[50] *TDAR*, pp. 540-41; Welin, pp. 93-96; Zanker, *Forum*, p. 25. The tribunal was a temporary wooden structure which could be collapsed and removed when space was needed.

[51] ". . . cuius istae coloniae quasi effigies parvae simulacraque esse quaedam videntur, . . ." A. Gellius, *NA* 16.13.9. Translation from *LCL* 3.181.

[52] The Lupa Romana with Romulus and Remus suckling is another example of the same kind of symbol. See particularly Veyne, "Marsyas," pp. 95-97. Moreover, Marsyas's long-standing connection with Liber, already a god associated with the freedom of cities (cf. n. 40 above and App. III, A 8-9), only strengthens and enhances the new political role of Marsyas.

[53] Appendix III, C lists all the cities known to me that issued coins with Marsyas in the Forum as a device. Appendix III, D gives the imperial inscriptions that generally imply the existence of statues, now lost, because they come primarily from bases. In any case, the inscription on a base from Furni (App. III, D 1) clearly states that Gentius Proculus Rogatianus presented the statue to his city, Furnos Minus.

vastly added to the ranks of Roman citizens.[54] In fact, it is notable that the Marsyas in the Forum appears primarily in those areas, North Africa and especially Asia Minor, which were most favored by the Severans' provincial policy. No examples of the Marsyas have survived from Spain, Gaul, or any of the northern provinces. Perhaps because Marsyas had ultimately come from Asia Minor to Rome, he may have had a special appeal to the eastern cities when several centuries later he reversed his path to return home as a Roman.

The Date of the "Original"

The only surviving statue of the Marsyas in the Forum found outside of Rome was excavated at Paestum (App. III, B 3; Fig. 27). The bronze shows a stocky, bearded silenus (note the pointed ears and tail) with a rather elongated torso compared to the almost stubby legs, whose feet are shod in the usual boots. The figure lacks both arms and the top of his head. Nonetheless, the position of the right shoulder where the stump of the arm remains proves that the arm was extended straight up.[55] For an *adlocutio* the angle at the base of the arm is much less sharp and nearly horizontal, as the classic example of the Augustus of Prima Porta demonstrates.[56] The statue, then, represents the Censorinus, rather than the Imperial, Marsyas. The only major difference apparent between the Censorinus and Paestum statues is the slighter tilt to the Paestum head, whose lips are slightly parted, as if in speech. The place where the statue was erected also accords with the Rome Marsyas; for the Paestum bronze was discovered on the edge of the open, central area of the forum.[57] Even its height (1.035 m.) follows the Republican custom in Rome described by Pliny: "It would seem not to be proper to omit the fact noted by the annals that the statues of . . . persons, erected in the forum, were three feet in height, showing that this was the scale of these marks of honour in those days.[58] Thus iconography, location,

[54] Sherwin-White², pp. 275-87 (Chapter XII, "The Union of East and West under the Severi"). See also *CAH* XII:24 (Septimius Severus) and 45-48 (Caracalla).

[55] A marble statuette, found in Rome, also appears to be of the same type (App. III, B 4; Fig. 28). It too lacks its right arm, but like the Paestum bronze the arm was probably raised high—at least as far as I can tell from the drawing in Jordan, *Marsyas*, pl. III C.

[56] Rome, Vatican 2290. Helbig⁴ I:314-19 No. 411. For a good photograph: Bianchi-Bandinelli, *Center*, p. 183, fig. 197.

[57] Brendel, "Funde," p. 640.

[58] "Non omittendum videtur, quod annales adnotavere, tripedaneas iis statuas in foro statutas; haec videlicet mensura honorata tunc erat." Pliny, *HN* 34.11 (24). Translation from *LCL* 9.145, 147. According to Vitruvius (*De Arch*. 3.7) a foot measured, ". . . pes altitudinis extam habet partem . . ."

and size confirm a date, based on stylistic evidence, in the third-to-second centuries B.C.

While the creation of the original type of the Marsyas in the Forum must then be either contemporary to or earlier than the Paestum bronze, it can only be extraordinarily speculative in the absence of any additional data to attempt to date the "original" more precisely. The Censorinus coins and the Anaglypha Traiani, over and above the problems of scale and preservation, as later representations, necessarily reflect more of the style of their own periods than that of the actual statue in the Forum Romanum. Furthermore the situation is complicated by the fact that the Marsyas in the Forum Romanum need not have been the first of the series. Although sileni were frequently depicted in Italy from the archaic period on,[59] the earliest incontrovertible Marsyas does not occur until the late fifth century on Lucanian ware, and even then it is the Marsyas of the musical contest.[60] The literary sources offer little help. That Gnaeus Gellius in the second century B.C., the earliest of those extant, knows of Marsyas's augural connection merely supports the date of the Paestum statue. Similarly, even if the time of the introduction of exauguration could be established, it does not inevitably follow that Marsyas's statue appeared at the same time.

Although the date of neither the "original" in the Forum nor the creation of the type itself—if the two are distinct entities—can be ascertained, the place of origin at least is quite clear. The type is so thoroughly Roman in conception and purpose that it must have been invented in Italy—albeit after a Greek model like the thoroughly Etruscan rendering of the ambush of Cacu. It could never have been looted from Pergamon or any other Greek site and have been carried to Rome.[61] No comparable Hellenistic or earlier examples, as would

[59] A small Etruscan bronze, ca. 500-480 B.C., in the British Museum (474; Walters, *CatBr*, p. 66) may even be a bootless forebear of the Censorinus Marsyas. Bearded, with pointed ears and tail, this silenus takes virtually the same pose. He balances a winesack on his left shoulder, and raises his right hand in a "proto-*adlocutio*" to a little above shoulder height.

[60] The earliest of the Lucanian group are the skyphos fragments by the Palermo Painter in New York (12.235.4). See Chapter III n. 12 for that and the other Lucanian examples.

[61] The idea that the statue was of Greek workmanship goes back at least to Jordan *Marsyas*, pp. 9-10) who also suggested (pp. 14-16) that the statues were fountain figures because of their discovery in marketplaces. As explained in the text, the location was originally based on the "exaugural" functions of Marsyas. Adolphe Reinach ("Marsyas") created the most involved genesis for the statue. Because of certain legendary connections to the Romans, the people of Apamea-Celaenae gave the statue, which actually depicted a local Apamean hero, to Cn. Manlius Vulso in 188 B.C. Other Greek sites of origin, such as Pergamon (Carcopino, *Passion*, pp. 129-30) have also been proposed.

be necessary, have ever been found in Greek areas. In fact, the surviving sources written by Greeks in Greek areas for Greeks appear to have been unaware of Marsyas's augural functions despite the possibility that the musical contest with Apollo might be a euhemerization of a conflict between an augural Marsyas and a prophetic Apollo over the right to practice divination.[62] Finally, even the ancients, and in particular a Greek, considered the Marsyas in the Forum Roman. Charax of Pergamon wrote in the second century A.D.:

> They took care to honor also the cities which the Italians inhabit by erecting there the statue of a supernatural being, a sort of old man similar to a Silenus, in order that the community of worship was one more bond. As for the shackles one put on him, they symbolize the state of subjection, the cities which have statues of this type being enchained to them. (App. III, A 6)

The custom described and the witty reversal of the use of Marsyas as the "indicium libertatis" in the last sentence prove that the passage is about the Marsyas in the Forum. Not only does Charax associate the statue solely with the Italians, i.e. the Romans, but he has humorously seized upon one of its most Italian features, the boots—only in Italy does Marsyas appear so shod—and has converted them to shackles which cover the same area of the ankles.[63]

The Censorinus Coins

While the time of Marsyas's introduction into Italy may be hazy, his prominence during the late Republic is unmistakable. The devices on the Censorinus denarii, minted in 82 B.C. in the middle of the conflict between Sulla and the old Marian faction, have been interpreted as propagandistic symbols of the Populares. (fig. 24) On the obverse facing right is the laureate head of Apollo, the tutelary god of the Marians. On the reverse, the Marsyas in the Forum provides the cornerstone of the theory. His name forms a punning reference to

---

[62] The imagery for the musical contest and divination is nearly identical. As the oracle-giver sings or chants his prophecy (cf. the seer from Veii who "*cecinerit*" Livy 5.15.10—Chapter II n. 6), so Apollo could accompany his lyre. The relation was apparent to ancient authors. In the same section Pliny slips from a discussion of the discovery of augury directly to the invention of musical instruments: The paragraph (*HN* 7.56 [203-204]) begins, "Auguria ex avibus" and proceeds to "geminas tibias Marsyas in eadem gente." Compare Strabo 10.3.10 (C 468): "αἱ δὲ Μοῦσαι καὶ ὁ Ἀπόλλων, αἱ μὲν τῶν χορῶν προεστᾶσιν, ὁ δὲ καὶ τούτων καὶ τῶν κατὰ μαντικήν."

[63] I thank H. Anne Weis for the observation about the boots. Veyne ("Marsyas," pp. 88-92) gives an excellent analysis of the Charax passage and was the one to suggest the interpretation of the shackles as boots.

the Marcii, one of whose members, Lucius Marcius Censorinus, struck the coins. Marsyas wears a pileus or freedman's cap, which, in conjunction with the fact that Marsyas is a symbol of civic *libertas*, shows Marian support for increasing the Roman enfranchisement of the Italians. Finally, the statue on the column to the right of Marsyas, as a Victory, represents the obvious Victory the Marians hope to achieve.[64]

Although the coins do allude to contemporary affairs, it is not in the same way as just outlined because of a misreading and misinterpretation of the devices. As has been seen, the type of Marsyas in the Forum in the late Republic signifies augural, not civic, *libertas*. The Paestum bronze, whose head is detailed and well worked, proves that the raised band, visible on Marsyas's head on some of the coins, must be a fillet (or possibly a wreath) and not a pileus, which Marsyas has never worn and has no reason to wear here. A fillet makes sense, because Roman statues of divinities were commonly adorned with them.[65]

That Marsyas does play on the name of the gens, Marcius, is not to be denied,[66] but the reason for his selection depends more on his augural nature, because all the devices on the coin refer to augury. If Censorinus wished to suggest his ancestry, he could better have chosen his purported forebear, the Sabine Ancus Marcius, as did his older brother, Caius Marcius Censorinus, in 88 B.C.[67] The warring Ancus, however, had no overt connections with augury, while Marsyas epitomized both the family and augury. Remember that according to Gnaeus Gellius Megales, an "envoy" of Marsyas, escaped to the Sabines to whom he taught augury. If Marsyas were responsible for the Sabine skill in augury, then he probably helped the Marcii

---

[64] Kapossy (pp. 74-79) is idiosyncratically representative of the position. That is, he does not believe that Marsyas is wearing a pileus, as among others *TDAR*, p. 499, but, along with Gagé (*Apollon*, pp. 391-93), does maintain that the use of Marsyas refers to the Marsi who were of importance during the 80s B.C. Against that interpretation: Luce, p. 32 n. 40. Finally, Kapossy alone interprets the head on the obverse as Concordia, against which see Luce, p. 39 n. 71.

[65] "Et iam tunc coronae deorum honos erant et larum publicorum privatorumque ac sepulchrorum et manium, . . ." Pliny, *HN* 21.8 (11). The "tunc" refers to the period of Scipio Serapio, mentioned in 21.7 (10), who was consul in 138 B.C. (*OCD²*, p. 963). Pliny (App. III, A 3) records two instances involving Marsyas which date to the time of the triumvirs and of Augustus. The practice of putting chaplets on the Marsyas may have led Vergil to adopt it playfully for the capture of Silenus in *Eclogue* 6.19, ". . . iniciunt ipsis ex vincula sertis," which Ovid echoes in *Metamorphoses* 11.91, ". . . ruricolae cepere Phryges vinctumque coronis . . ." Compare also Charax, quoted in the text and in App. III, A 6.

[66] So also the generally skeptical Crawford in *RRC*, p. 378.

[67] The obverses of one group of denarii and two groups of asses: Crawford, *RRC*, p. 357 no. 346/1 (denarii) and p. 360 no. 346/3-4 (asses), with plate XLV.15 and 17 respectively. On the Sabine elements of Ancus Marcius: Poucet, *Sabine*, pp. 148-54.

acquire this knowledge; for a renowned seer was one of their ancestors:

> Then [212 B.C.] fresh religious scruples were aroused by the verses of Marcius. A noted seer had been this Marcius, and when in the preceding year search was being made by decree of the senate for such [prophetic] books, they had come into the hands of Marcus Aemilius, the praetor urbanus, who was in charge of the matter. He had immediately turned them over to the new praetor, Sulla. Of the two prophecies of this Marcius the authority of one, made known after the event, was confirmed by the outcome and lent credibility to the other also, whose time had not yet come. In the earlier prophecy the disaster at Cannae had been predicted. . . . Then the second prophecy was read, being not only more obscure because the future is more uncertain than the past, but more difficult also in the way it was written. "If you wish, Romans, to drive out enemies, the sore which has come from afar, I propose that a festival be vowed to Apollo, to be observed with good cheer in honour of Apollo every year." . . . In charge of the conduct of that festival shall be the praetor who is then chief judge for the people and the commons. The decemvirs shall offer the victims according to Greek rite. . . . The fathers voted that a festival should be vowed and held in honour of Apollo . . .[68]

---

[68] Religio deinde nova obiecta est ex carminibus Marcianis. Vates hic Marcius inlustris fuerat, et cum conquisitio priore anno ex senatus consulto talium librorum fieret, in M. Aemili praetoris urbani, qui eam rem agebat, manus venerant. Is protinus novo praetori Sullae tradiderat. Ex huius Marcii duobus carminibus alterius post rem actam editi comprobata auctoritas eventu alteri quoque, cuius nondum tempus venerat, adferebat fidem. Priore carmine Cannensis praedicta clades . . . erat. . . . Tum alterum carmen recitatum, non eo tantum obscurius quia incertiora futura praeteritis sunt, sed perplexius etiam scripturae genere. "Hostis, Romani, si expellere vultis, vomicam quae gentium venit longe, Apollini vovendos censeo ludos, qui quotannis comiter Apollini fiant." . . . Iis ludis faciendis praeerit praetor is qui ius populo plebeique dabit summum; decemviri Graeco ritu hostiis sacra faciant. . . . censuerunt pratres Apollini ludos vovendos faciendosque . . .
[Livy 25.12. Translation from *LCL* 6.383, 385, and 387.]
The "Marcius *vates*" and the Marsyas in the Forum even share the same divinatory sphere; for, according to Palmer (*ACR*, pp. 146-50), two of the three surviving Marcian fragments are about augural ritual, and one of these two specifically concerns the observation of birds. According to Cicero, *Div.* 1.40 (89), there was more than one Marcius involved. His or their floruit appears to have been "legendary"; that is, it is a compilation of his songs that is being consulted and not the actual person. Pease, *Comm*, p. 253 (with other ancient references). Münzer, "Marcius," pp. 1538, 1541 no. 2. Gagé, *Apollon*, pp. 224-27. Fowler, *Festivals*, pp. 179-82. Alföldi, "Apollo," pp. 170-72.

Thus Censorinus on his coins not only recalls the "Marcius vates" by the augural Marsyas on the reverse of his coins, but by the head of Apollo on the obverse commemorates the role the carmina Marciana played in the establishment of the ludi Apollinares during the Punic Wars (212 B.C.).[69]

The statue of the Victory on the reverse could, then, reflect the Roman success in the Punic Wars in addition to the contemporary desire for victory over Sulla, if it were not for the fact that the statue cannot represent a Victory.[70] Because the lower part of the statue has the triangular shape of long, skirted drapery, the figure is a woman; but if the two ridged, angular "projections" on the right are wings, then she lacks arms; and if they are arms, she has no wings. A readily identifiable Victory on the reverse of another denarius struck a little earlier by Lucius's brother, Caius, illustrates the difference.[71] She too has the diminutive form for a figure squeezed into a small space. Nonetheless, her wings manage to curve fully and gently behind her back; and her arms, with a wreath in one of the hands, are distinctly visible in front of her. Similarly, the Victory on a column on the imperial coins with Marsyas from Sidon (App. III, C 18; Fig. 26e) and Tyre (App. III, C 19; Fig. 26g) portray her with wings and her right hand holding a wreath. The woman on the later Lucius Censorinus coin has to be someone else.

Unlike the usual composition for double devices in profile, the statue neither faces Marsyas nor in his direction, but stands to the right with her back to him.[72] In this odd arrangement the coin may preserve the actual, physical relationship between the two statues. Pliny mentions a possible candidate:

> The custom of erecting . . . statues on pillars (columnarum) is of earlier date [than that of erecting memorial chariots]. . . . Also, it does not at all surprise me that statues of the Sibyl stand near the Beaked Platform (iuxta rostra) though there are three of them—one restored by Sextus Pacuvius Taurus, aedile of the

---

[69] Crawford (*RRC*, p. 361) similarly interprets the issues (no. 346) of Caius Censorinus, just discussed in the text and in n. 67 above. On the use of Apollo as a "factional symbol": Luce, pp. 28-39; Alföldi, "Apollo," pp. 165-74.

[70] For example, Crawford (*RRC*, pp. 377-78 no. 363) identifies the statue as Victory.

[71] Crawford, *RRC*, p. 357 no. 346/2a, with pl. XLV.16.

[72] Again compare the coins just mentioned from Sidon and Tyre (App. III, C 18 and 19 respectively). There the Victory is also placed on the right on a column, but she takes part in the scene by facing left, to the center, as she offers her wreath. Moreover, the trophy on the left on the coins from Tyre give a reason for her presence; the Sidon example may be an excerpt from a fuller figured scene.

plebs, and two by Marcus Messalla. I should think these statues and that of Attus Navius, all erected in the period of Tarquinius Priscus . . .[73]

Procopius helps to pinpoint the site of "near the rostra": "And he [Janus] has his temple in that part of the forum in front of the Senate-house which lies a little above the 'Tria Fata.' "[74] (Plan 4). Since the "Tria Fata" refer to the three Sibyls,[75] the place where Procopius saw their statues was probably nearly or right on axis with the statue of Marsyas.[76] The location and the type of statue, on a column, are crucial, for the first puts the statue in the same area as the Marsyas and the second describes the device on the coin. Note that the pictorial difficulties of depicting two additional statues of the Sibyl, as well as the fact that one suffices as a symbol, obviate the necessity of rendering all three, as they were in the Forum. The Sibyl should, as a figure on a column, be standing, not sitting. As much as can be made out from the coins, she extends one arm (probably the left) downward and bends the other at the elbow with perhaps an object held vertically in that hand. Lactantius, quoting Varro, may explain the gesture: ". . . the tenth [Sibyl] of Tibur, by name Albunea, who is worshipped at Tibur as a goddess, near the banks of the river Anio, in the depths of which her statue is said to have been found, holding in her hand a book."[77] Obviously the two statues were not the same, but a book is a likely attribute for a Sibyl, and held upright fits the Censorinus representation.[78]

---

[73] . . . celebratio . . . antiquior columnarum . . . equidem et Sibyllae iuxta rostra esse non miror, tres sint licet: una quam Sextus Pacuius Taurus aed. pl. restituit; duae quas M. Messalla. primas putarem has et Atti Navi, positas aetate Tarquinii Prisci . . .
[Pliny, *HN* 34.11 (20, 22). Translation from *LCL* 9.143, 145.]
Pliny adds a little later, ". . . Atto enim ac Sibyllae Tarquinium, ac reges sibi ipsos posuisse verisimile est." *HN* 34.11 (29).

[74] ". . . ἔχει ['Ἰανος] δὲ τὸν νεὼν ἐν τῇ ἀγορᾷ πρὸ τοῦ βουλευτηρίου ὀλίγον ὑπερβάντι τὰ Τρία Φᾶτα." Procopius, *Goth.* 1.25.19. Translation from *LCL* 3.245, where the passage is cited as 5.25.19 in the combined *History of the Wars*.

[75] From at least as early as the third century A.D. the three statues of the Sibyl were thought to be the Three Fates. Cyprian, *Epistles* 21.3.2, is the first extant citation as such according to *TDAR*, p. 539, with additional literary sources.

[76] As Procopius's placement of these statues clarifies Pliny's "iuxta rostra," it provides further corroboration that the similar phrase, "in rostris," used for the Marsyas (Acron, App. III, A 5) also meant in the rostra's section of the Forum, i.e. merely at the west end.

[77] ". . . decimam Tiburtem nomine Albuneam, quae Tiburi colatur ut dea iuxta ripas amnis Anienis, cuius in gurgite simulacrum eius inventum esse dicitur tenens in manu librum." Lactantius, *Div. Inst.* 1.6.12. Translation from *ANF* 7.16.

[78] To my knowledge, the only other uncontested extant representations of the Sibyl are on coins which show only her head. It is interesting to note that they were all

MARSYAS IN THE FORUM

The selection of the Sibyl strengthens the augural references. Her books were not just a primary source for consultation and advice during difficult times,[79] but were directly associated with the Marcii. In the same passage about the carmina Marciana quoted above, Livy also says: ". . . the senate made a decree that in regard to the festival to be held and the sacrifices in honor of Apollo the decemvirs should consult the books."[80] Since the *decemviri sacris faciundis* were the guardians and interpreters of the Sibylline Books, the ludi Apollinares were sanctioned only with the Sibyl's approval,[81] and her appearance on the coins would acknowledge that fact.

Most important of all the Sibyl makes an especially pointed and unmistakable allusion to contemporary events. Dionysius of Halicarnassus records:

> These oracles [of the Sibyl] till the time of the Marsian War, as it was called, were kept underground in the temple of Jupiter Capitolinus in a stone chest under the guard of ten men [the *decemviri*]. But when the temple was burned after the close of the one hundred and seventy-third Olympiad [83 B.C.], either purposely, as some think, or by accident, these oracles together with all the offerings consecrated to the god were destroyed by the fire. Those which are now extant have been scraped together from many places, . . .[82]

---

minted in Rome between 65 and 43 B.C. See: Crawford, *RRC*, p. 439 no. 411, p. 475 no. 464/1, p. 484 no. 474/3, and p. 500 no. 491/2 (?); and Alföldi, "Apollo," with many coins illustrated in the plates. Salomon Reinach does suggest two possible standing, draped female statues as candidates. The one in Naples (*RépStat* 1:460 top) broadly fits the coin and the description of Lactantius in that she holds a scroll (i.e. a book) in her lowered left hand and gestures with her right hand. The arms of the other statue (*RépStat* 1:455 bottom) are differently disposed.

[79] So Dionysius of Halicarnassus, *Ant. Rom.* 4.62.5:

χρῶνται δ' αὐτοῖς, ὅταν ἡ βουλὴ ψηφίσηται, στάσεως καταλαβούσης τὴν πόλιν ἢ δυστυχίας τινὸς μεγάλης συμπεσούσης κατὰ πόλεμον ἢ τεράτων τινῶν καὶ φαντασμάτων μεγάλων καὶ δυσευρέτων αὐτοῖς φανέντων, οἷα πολλάκις συνέβη.

[80] ". . . senatus consultum factum est ut decemviri de ludis Apollini reque divina facienda inspicerent." Livy 25.12.11. Translation from *LCL* 6.387.

[81] On the *decemviri* and the Sibylline Books: Latte, *RRG*, pp. 160-61, 397-98. On the Sibyl, the *decemviri*, and the Ludi Apollinares: Gagé, *Apollon*, pp. 224-25; Radke, "XVviri," pp. 1114-48.

[82] οὗτοι διέμειναν οἱ χρησμοὶ μέχρι τοῦ Μαρσικοῦ κληθέντος πολέμου κείμενοι κατὰ γῆς ἐν τῷ ναῷ τοῦ Καπιτωλίνου Διὸς ἐν λιθίνῃ λάρνακι, ὑπ' ἀνδρῶν δέκα φυλαττόμενοι. μετὰ δὲ τὴν τρίτην ἐπὶ ταῖς ἑβδομήκοντα καὶ ἑκατὸν ὀλυμπιάσιν ἐμπρησθέντος τοῦ ναοῦ, εἴτ' ἐξ ἐπιβουλῆς, ὡς οἴονταί τινες, εἴτ' ἀπὸ ταὐτομάτου, σὺν τοῖς ἄλλοις ἀναθήμασι τοῦ θεοῦ καὶ οὗτοι διεφθάρησαν ὑπὸ τοῦ πυρός. οἱ δὲ νῦν ὄντες ἐκ πολλῶν εἰσι συμφορητοὶ τόπων, . . .

[Dionysius of Halicarnassus, *Ant. Rom.* 4.62.5-6. Translation from *LCL* 2.467, 469.]

MARSYAS IN THE FORUM

The synchronization of events is crucial: the Capitoline and the Sibylline Books were destroyed in 83 B.C.; the Censorinus coins were issued the following year in 82 B.C. Thus all the devices on them are mutually reinforcing and interlocking allusions to augury and prophecy and the pivotal role of the Marcii in Rome's affairs. As their divinatory skill once saved Rome during the Punic War, so should it enable them to prevail against Sulla now; as their carmina led to institution of the ludi Apollinares, so would the current members of their gens now ensure that the Sibylline Books were properly reconstituted. Their actual help was probably considerably less than their aspirations, since Sulla succeeded in his. Interestingly the two families must have once cooperated, for, according to Livy, an ancestor of Sulla was the praetor *urbanus* at the very time the carmina Marciana were consulted, and hence, of necessity, was also involved in the establishment of the ludi Apollinares.[83] As a result the anti-Sullan content of the coins may have been somewhat tempered.[84]

As a footnote to this discussion, the close ties between the Marcii and Marsyas, as substantiated by the coins, do not in themselves prove that some member of that family erected the statue of Marsyas in the Forum. That individuals did put up statues in the Forum is implied by Pliny and actually recorded for some of the imperial examples of the Marsyas in the Forum.[85] Nonetheless, the first point

---

The same event is briefly mentioned in Pliny, *HN* 13.27 (88), ". . . tertius [liber Sibyllae crematus] cum Capitolio Sullanis temporibus"; and at greater length in Plutarch, *Vit. Sull.* 27.6:

ἐν δὲ Σιλβίῳ φησὶν οἰκέτην Ποντίου θεοφόρητον ἐντυχεῖν αὐτῷ λέγοντα παρὰ τῆς Ἐνυοῦς κράτος πολέμου καὶ νίκην ἀπαγγέλλειν· εἰ δὲ μὴ σπεύσειεν, ἐμπεπρήσεσθαι τὸ Καπιτώλιον· ὃ καὶ συμβῆναι τῆς ἡμέρας ἐκείνης ἧς ὁ ἄνθρωπος προηγόρευσεν· ἦν δὲ αὕτη πρὸ μιᾶς νωνῶν Κυντιλίων, ἃς νῦν Ἰουλίας καλοῦμεν.

[83] Livy 25.12.4, "Is protinus novo praetori Sullae tradiderat." (For the rest of the passage: n. 68 above and accompanying text.) Did Sulla himself intend a parallel to the Ludi Apollinares when he established his own annual games after the fall of Praeneste in 82 B.C.? Compare Velleius Paterculus 2.27.6:

Oppugnationi autem Praenestis ac Marii praefuerat Ofella Lucretius, qui cum ante Marianarum fuisset partim praetor, ad Sullam transfugerat. Felicitatem diei, quo Samnitium Telesinique pulsus est exercitus, Sulla perpetua ludorum circensium honoravit memoria, qui sub eius nomine Sullanae Victoriae celebrantur.

In any event, Sulla seems to have used the opportunity to make his own changes regarding the Sibylline Books, for he is the one generally credited with increasing the *decemviri* to fifteen (n. 81 above).

[84] Luce (p. 38) suggests that Marsyas on the reverse and Apollo on the obverse refer to the rivalry in the musical contest between the two and hence to that between Marius and Sulla. It should be remembered that the Marsyas used on the coins is not the brash satyr, but the wise silenus of the Forum. Because the two Marsyae were generally considered discrete figures in antiquity and all the devices taken together have such strong augural overtones, I think an allusion to the contest unlikely.

[85] For example, Pliny implies private erection of statues when he refers to public

only establishes the possibility and the second its practice in a different period and area. Since evidence is lacking, the questions of the time of erection and the doer of the deed must still remain open.

Conclusion

A mythological figure popular throughout the ancient world tends to be judged from whatever view dominates in the surviving sources. As a result Marsyas is best known today as the foolish challenger of Apollo to a musical contest. Yet an equally strong tradition in Italy alone revered him for his teaching of augury, although even there the changes Marsyas underwent in the Empire almost buried knowledge of that aspect.[86] In other words, the ability to adapt to contemporary needs may foster survival, but may also entail an almost total transformation. The three most significant qualities of the Marsyas in the Forum—the action of the figure, the location in the Forum Romanum, and the connection with *libertas*—were originally united in the Marsyas to embody the bringer of the rite of exauguration to the Romans, but were also perfectly suited to the imperial symbol of Rome and guarantor of civic freedom. The reinterpretation of the individual elements came about for entirely logical reasons. The raised right hand merely descended slightly from an overhead position to an *adlocutio*; the erection of the statue in the cleared, central area of the Forum Romanum with the later juxtaposition to the foreign tribunal resulted in a fortuitous association between the two monuments; and so the meaning of *libertas* easily slipped from augural freeing to civic freedom. Before and even after his transformation the Marsyas in the Forum was a thoroughly Roman creature who always served totally Roman purposes from the time of his obscure origins through the late Republic with his appearance on the Censorinus coins to the end of the Empire.

---

dedications, as in *HN* 34.13 (28-29), "hanc primam [statuam Cloeliae] cum Coclitis publice dicatam crediderim . . ." For an imperial example: Furni, App. III, D 1.

[86] The consistent separation of the two Marsyae in antiquity implies that the foolish Marsyas did not evolve through suffering into the wise Marsyas; like Socrates (cf. n. 8 above) the latter was always smart.

· V ·

AUGURY AND THE STATE

CACU and Marsyas have been studied separately to establish that both were associated with divination in Italy. Because the two played their major parts during the same periods, they were subject to the same events. Nonetheless, they adapted themselves differently. Why they changed as they did, and why both were ultimately relieved of their prophetic responsibilities is partly explained by their individual natures, but can only be truly understood against the background of the historical developments of Rome of the first century B.C.; for no other period witnessed so marked a transformation in these two figures.

According to Cicero, "the highest and most important authority in the State is that of the *augurs*, to whom is accorded great influence."[1] Although the need for and use of augury permeated Roman life from the time of the foundation of Rome under Romulus through the Empire, control over augury was hotly contested and dramatically challenged only twice—in the sixth and the first centuries B.C. It is not that other periods were free of augural disputes, but that these two ages were marked by skeptical attitudes on the part of the rulers and major alterations of the system. Since the changes introduced in the sixth century lasted more or less intact until the first century B.C., they must be considered before the "reforms" of Augustus can be treated.

The Tarquins were responsible for the introduction or fostering of the three dominant types of public divination espoused by the Romans.[2] The first of them, Tarchon, the legendary founder of Tarquinia, recorded and helped disseminate the art of hepatoscopy taught him by Tages.[3] As a result, divination from entrails first appears in

---

[1] "Maximum autem et praestantissimum in re publica ius est *augurum* cum auctoritate coniunctum." Cicero, *Leg.* 2.12.31. Translation from *LCL* 409.

[2] The distinction between public and private divination was made by the Roman themselves, as Livy 1.56.5 shows: "Itaque cum ad publica prodigia Etrusci tantum vates adhiberentur, hoc velut domestico exterritus visu Delphos ad maxime inclitum in terris oraculum mittere statuit."

[3] Tarchon as founder of Tarquinia: Strabo 5.2.219. Tarchon was also credited with founding Pisa (Cato, *Orig.* 2.45 *apud* Servius, *ad Aen.* 10.179) and Mantua (Servius, *ad Aen.* 10.198).

AUGURY AND THE STATE

Rome under the Tarquins.[4] An Etruscan king, ruling in an alien city (Rome), would in a crisis naturally revert to his native religious practices. Although hepatoscopy was not formally incorporated into the Roman state religion until the first century A.D. under Claudius, Etruscan haruspices were consulted on an individual basis in the earlier periods, and in the later Republic were organized into a regular college, composed only of Etruscans.[5]

Tarquinius Priscus's encounter with Attus Navius involves the same type of augury as that which the Marsyas in the Forum brought to Italy. When the king wanted to increase the number of tribes in Rome, according to Livy:

> Since this was a matter in which Romulus had obtained the sanction of augury before acting, it was asserted by Attius [sic] Navius, a famous augur of those days, that no change or innovation could be introduced unless the birds had signified their approval. The king's ire was aroused by this, and he is reported to have said, in derision of the science, "Come now, divine seer! Inquire of your augury if that of which I am now thinking can come to pass." When Attius, having taken the auspices, replied that it would surely come to pass, the king said, "Nay, but this is what I was thinking of, that you should cleave a whetstone with a razor. Take them, and accomplish what your birds declare is possible!" Whereupon, they say, the augur, without a sign of hesitation, cut the whetstone in two.... Auguries and the augural priesthood so increased in honour that nothing was afterwards done, in the field or at home, unless the auspices had first been taken: popular assemblies, musterings of the army, acts of

---

[4] For Tarchon as the one who plows up the divine seer Tages: Lydus, *De ostentis*, prooemium 2-3. Compare Cicero, *Div*. 2.23 (50-51) for an unknown rustic as the "discoverer" of Tages; see Pease, *Comm*, pp. 435-37 for a discussion of the other ancient sources for this tale. A third century B.C. Etruscan mirror from Tuscania and now in the Museo Archeologico, Florence (Inv. no. 77759) portrays Tarchon, second from the left, pensively watching a liver being interpreted by the second figure from the right. Pallottino, "Specchio," pp. 49-87 with illustrations on pp. 51-52 and a plate opposite p. 86.

Pease (*Comm*, pp. 49-50) cites Livy 1.54.4-5 (see n 2 above), along with Servius, *ad Aen*. 8.345, as the first recorded use of haurspices, which occurred during the reign of Tarquinius Superbus.

[5] Pease, *Comm*, pp. 49-50. Latte, *RRG*, p. 158. Rawson, "Caesar." Cicero, *Div* 1.2 (3), speaks of a gradual introduction of hepatoscopy and in the same passage explains why the early Romans were so receptive to foreign practices:
> Deinde auguribus et reliqui reges usi, et exactis regibus, nihil publice sine auspiciis nec domi nec militiae gerebatur. Cumque magna vis videretur esse et impetriendis consulendisque rebus et monstris interpretandis ac procurandis in haruspicum disciplina, omnem hanc ex Etruria scientiam adhibebant, ne genus esset ullum divinationis, quod neglectum ab eis videretur.

supreme importance—all were put off when the birds refused their consent. Neither did Tarquinius at that time make any change in the organization of the centuries of knights.[6]

At first Tarquinius Priscus evinces great skepticism. Even though he governs Rome, he is an Etruscan and presumably better versed in and more reliant on Etruscan methods of soothsaying, such as the hepatoscopy of Tarchon. Nonetheless, as a ruler of a foreign people he does allow the local Attus Navius to demonstrate the accuracy of his prophecy. Taking the auspices from the flight of birds goes back, of course, to Romulus and Remus. Tarquinius Priscus's acceptance of the system, then, becomes a reaffirmation of Roman religion by the first Etruscan king.[7] His endorsement ensures that this native Roman form of divination retains its control over state acts.

According to tradition, by the time of Tarquinius Superbus at the end of the sixth century B.C., not only was prophecy from celestial signs and livers well established, but the third and last major form of divination—the consultation of the Sibylline Books—was incorporated into the official Roman religion. Dionysius of Halicarnassus preserves the fullest account:

> A certain woman who was not a native of the country came to the tyrant [Tarquinius Superbus] wishing to sell him nine books filled with Sibylline oracles; but when Tarquinius refused to purchase the books at the price she asked, she went away and burned three of them. And not long afterwards, bringing the remaining six books, she offered to sell them for the same price. But when they [sic] thought her a fool and mocked at her for asking the same price for the smaller number of books that she had been unable to get for even the larger number, she again went away

---

[6] Id quia inaugurato Romulus fecerat, negare Attus Navius, inclitus ea tempestate augur, neque mutari neque novum constitui, nisi aves addixissent, posse. Ex eo ira regi mota, eludensque artem, ut ferunt, "Age dum," inquit, "divine tu, inaugura fierine possit, quod nunc ego mento concipio." Cum ille augurio rem expertus profecto futuram dixisset, "Atqui hoc animo agitavi," inquit, "te novacula cotem discissurum; cape haec et perage quod aves tuae fieri posse portendunt." Tum illum haud cunctanter discidisse cotem ferunt. . . . Auguriis certe sacerdotioque augurum tantus honos accessit ut nihil belli domique postea nisi auspicato geretur, concilia populi, exercitus vocati, summa rerum, ubi aves non admisissent, dirimerentur. Neque tum Tarquinius de equitum centuriis quicquam mutavit.

[Livy 1.36.3-7. Translation from *LCL* 1.131, 133.]
The last section echoes Cicero, *Leg.* 2.12.31 and *Div.* 1.16 (28).

[7] Since the Sabines under Titus Tatius entered into a joint rulership with Romulus, the first Roman, they cannot be considered in the same category of foreigners as the Etruscans. For the auspices of Romulus and Remus, see Chapter I n. 92 and accompanying text.

and burned half of those that were left; then, bringing the remaining three books, she asked the same amount of money for these. Tarquinius, wondering at the woman's purpose, sent for the augurs and acquainting them with the matter, asked them what he should do. These, knowing by certain signs that he had rejected a god-sent blessing, and declaring it to be a great misfortune that he had not purchased all the books, directed him to pay the woman all the money she asked and to get the oracles that were left. The woman, after delivering the books and bidding him take great care of them, disappeared from among men. Tarquinius chose two men of distinction from among the citizens and appointing two public slaves to assist them, entrusted to them the guarding of the books. . . . In short, there is no possession of the Romans, sacred or profane, which they guard so carefully as they do the Sibylline oracles.[8]

The order of incidents resembles that in the story of Tarquinius Priscus and Attus Navius. A prophetess presents herself *sua sponte* and initially meets rejection, followed by testing (in this case the questioning of the appropriate authorities), which similarly results in the acceptance of the new system. The major difference between the two lies in the reversal of the place of origin for the king and the prophetess. Tarquinius Superbus represents Rome; the Sibyl is clearly "not a native of the country."[9] The "moral" of the tale for the Roman indicates that a healthy skepticism will be exhibited before a foreign

---

[8] γυνή τις ἀφίκετο πρὸς τὸν τύραννον οὐκ ἐπιχωρία βύβλους ἐννέα μεστὰς Σιβυλλείων χρησμῶν ἀπεμπολῆσαι θέλουσα. οὐκ ἀξιοῦντος δὲ τοῦ Ταρκυνίου τῆς αἰτηθείσης τιμῆς πρίασθαι τὰς βύβλους ἀπελθοῦσα τρεῖς ἐξ αὐτῶν κατέκαυσε· καὶ μετ' οὐ πολὺν χρόνον τὰς λοιπὰς ἐξ ἐνέγκασα τῆς αὐτῆς ἐπώλει τιμῆς. δόξασα δ' ἄφρων τις εἶναι καὶ γελασθεῖσα ἐπὶ τῷ τὴν αὐτὴν τιμὴν αἰτεῖν περὶ τῶν ἐλαττόνων ἣν οὐδὲ περὶ τῶν πλειόνων ἐδυνήθη λαβεῖν, ἀπελθοῦσα πάλιν τὰς ἡμισείας τῶν ἀπολειπομένων κατέκαυσε καὶ τὰς λοιπὰς τρεῖς ἐνέγκασα τὸ ἴσον ᾔτει χρυσίον. θαυμάσας δὴ τὸ βούλημα τῆς γυναικὸς ὁ Ταρκύνιος τοὺς οἰωνοσκόπους μετεπέμψατο καὶ διηγησάμενος αὐτοῖς τὸ πρᾶγμα, τί χρὴ πράττειν ἤρετο. κἀκεῖνοι διὰ σημείων τινῶν μαθόντες ὅτι θεόπεμπτον ἀγαθὸν ἀπεστράφη, καὶ μεγάλην συμφορὰν ἀποφαίνοντες τὸ μὴ πάσας αὐτὸν τὰς βύβλους πρίασθαι, ἐκέλευσαν ἀπαριθμῆσαι τῇ γυναικὶ τὸ χρυσίον, ὅσον ᾔτει, καὶ τοὺς περιόντας τῶν χρησμῶν λαβεῖν. ἡ μὲν οὖν γυνὴ τὰς βύβλους δοῦσα καὶ φράσασα τηρεῖν ἐπιμελῶς ἐξ ἀνθρώπων ἠφανίσθη, Ταρκύνιος δὲ τῶν ἀστῶν ἄνδρας ἐπιφανεῖς δύο προχειρισάμενος καὶ δημοσίους αὐτοῖς θεράποντας δύο παραζεύξας ἐκείνοις ἀπέδωκε τὴν τῶν βιβλίων φυλακήν, . . . συνελόντι δ' εἰπεῖν οὐδὲν οὕτω Ῥωμαῖοι φυλάττουσιν οὔθ' ὅσιον κτῆμα οὔθ' ἱερὸν ὡς τὰ Σιβύλλεια θέσφατα.
[Dion. Hal., *Ant. Rom.* 4.62.1-5. Translation from *LCL* 2.465, 467.]

[9] On the Sibyls and their origins: Pease, *Comm*, pp. 50-51. See also Chapter IV nn. 73-82 and accompanying text. Recently compare Gagé, *Chute*, pp. 15-51.

religious practice will be accepted, but once adopted, it will be accorded the position and respect it deserves.

Although the figures credited with the introduction of the different kinds of divination may be legendary and even entirely fictitious, the implied relative chronology is accurate. That is, there seems to be no reason to doubt that the basic augural apparatus was established by the end of the sixth century B.C. It lasted more or less intact throughout most of the Republic with minor alterations as necessary. Not until the second century B.C. do the political uses of augury become truly apparent and so abused that the entire fabric falls apart in the next century. This is not the place to present a detailed discussion of the use of augury to obstruct government; the subject has been well and extensively treated by others.[10] Suffice it to note that the inception of the decline may be marked by the passage of the leges Aelia et Fufia around the middle of the second century B.C.[11] The two laws regulated the use of *obnuntiatio*, the announcement of unfavorable auspices, by magistrates and tribunes to cancel assemblies. As a result, about a century later a Bibulus would sit up all night awaiting an appropriate omen, naturally see one, and yet be ignored in his pronouncement thereof by a Julius Caesar.[12] At the same time, increasing exposure to other peoples, especially in the East, and a series of dire events, particularly the Social and Civil Wars of the first century, further weakened belief in the validity of a system which, on the one hand, others did not espouse, and, on the other, did not save the Romans from, worst of all, internal strife. While the skepticism of a Tarquin permitted a strengthening of religion, the disbelief of a first century Roman destroyed the old ways. Augustus, then, was faced not with the choice of a return to former practices, but with the necessity of a substitution, under the guise of a restoration, of a new augural structure. He initiated a two-part

---

[10] Taylor, *Politics*, chap. IV "Manipulating the State Religion," pp. 76-97. Rawson, "Religion," pp. 193-212.

[11] *OCD*², p. 601, with bibliography. See also n. 10 above.

[12] Lege autem agraria promulgata obnuntiantem collegam armis foro expulit ac postero die in senatu conquestum nec quoquam reperto, qui super tali consternatione referre aut censere aliquid auderet, qualia multa saepe in levioribus turbis decreta erant, in eam coegit desperationem, ut, quoad potestate abiret, domo abditus nihil aliud quam per edicta obnuntiaret. Unus ex eo tempore omnia in re publica et ad arbitrium administravit, ut nonnulli urbanorum, cum quid per iocum testandi gratia signarent, non Caesare et Bibulo, sed Iulio et Caesare consulibus actum scriberent, bis eundem praeponentes nomine atque cognomine, . . . [Suetonius, *Iul.* 20.]

On Bibulus, see Taylor, *Politics*, p. 82. Compare Cicero, *Dom.* 41, "Si et sacrorum iure pontifices et auspiciorum religione augures totum evertunt tribunatum tuum, quid quaeris amplius?"

program: the elimination of "superfluous" augural figures and rites, and the elevation of Apollo to supreme oracular deity.

The choice of Apollo was extremely astute. To the Romans in the Republic he was basically augurally neutral. While they were well aware of his worship as an oracular divinity in Greece, they did not directly honor him as such in their homeland.[13] During the first century B.C. Apollo's importance and popularity in Italy so increased that he was easily able by the time of Augustus to usurp the powers and the prerogatives of the "older" Roman divinities under whose ineffective sway the previous oracular system had collapsed.[14] Finally Apollo had particular personal appeal to Augustus, as his notorious dinner, the "cena δωδεκάθεος,"[15] and his vow of a temple to Apollo in 36 B.C. demonstrate.[16] To honor Apollo appropriately in his new Roman guise, a new temple within the *pomerium* was essential, for his main temple stood in the Campus Martius.[17] Augustus had the perfect site: "[Augustus] reared the temple of Apollo in that part of his house on the Palatine for which the soothsayers declared that the

---

[13] It has been generally held (e.g. Gagé, *Apollon*, pp. 685-93; Ogilvie, *Comm*, p. 474) that Apollo did not appear in Rome until the second half of the fifth century B.C. when he came as a god of healing (Apollo Medicus) and was rewarded with a temple dedicated in 431 B.C. (Livy 29.7). Simon ("Apollo," pp. 202-227) has recently presented a convincing case that he comes via the Latins during the time of the Tarquins in the sixth century B.C. She sees Apollo as closely associated with Jupiter during that period and hence with the Sibyl and divination. Even if Apollo did exercise his oracular abilities in Rome during the Republic, his position and powers remained very much inferior to Jupiter's.

[14] For example Luce, and Alföldi, "Apollo."

[15] Cena quoque eius secretior in fabulis fuit, quae vulgo δωδεκάθεος vocabatur; in qua deorum dearumque habitu discubuisse convivas et ipsum pro Apolline ornatum . . . Auxit cenae rumorem summa tunc in civitate penuria ac fames, adclamatumque est postridie omne frumentum deos comedisse et Caesarem esse plane Apollinem, sed Tortorem, quo cognomine is deus quadam in parte urbis colebatur.

[Suetonius, *Aug.* 70.]

See also Gagé (*Apollon*, pp. 485-88) who dates the dinner to 38/37 B.C., but Taylor (*Divinity*, p. 119) puts it as early as 40 B.C. On the possible temple to Apollo Tortor, whose location is unknown, see *TDAR*, pp. 19-20. Hill (p. 136) identifies the head of Apollo on the obverse of the Censorinus denarii (App. III, B 2) as that of Apollo Tortor, but there is no distinguishing or intrinsic reason for such an interpretation; also compare my comment on Luce in Chapter IV n. 84. The parallel between Augustus's "cena . . . δωδεκάθεος" and the celebration of the Lectisternium honoring the Twelve Gods (e.g. in 217 B.C., Livy 22.10.9) would not have been missed and surely heightened the impudence of Augustus.

[16] The temple, which became that of Apollo Palatinus, was actually vowed by Augustus in 36 B.C. during his conflict with Sextus Pompey and not at the Battle of Actium in 31 B.C. Eden, p. 190.

[17] *TDAR*, pp. 15-16. *PDAR*, 1:28-30. Simon, "Apollo," pp. 208-215, especially on the connection of Apollo with the triumph.

god had shown his desire by striking it with lightning."[18] The location resulted in several benefits for Augustus and Apollo. Built on a prominent crest of the Palatine, the temple overlooked and watched over a large part of Rome, and in turn could be seen as a significant landmark from afar (Plans 1-2). Because the area was and would remain primarily residential, new divinities would be unlikely to detract from Apollo's glory. In addition the site was among the most hallowed in Rome, as the place where Romulus, the founder, settled—a fact not lost upon Augustus, soon to be officially hailed as "pater patriae."[19] By erecting the temple within the area of his own home, Augustus demonstrated his customary beneficence in seeming to yield his private interests to the public welfare, but in actuality he succeeded in ensuring that his chosen god would remain under his personal control. How closely he allied himself to Apollo may be seen in his erection of a statue of himself "in the appearance and attitude" as well as "with all the attributes of Apollo" in the library he attached to the temple complex, again on his own land.[20]

Although the temple of Apollo was dedicated in 28 B.C., Augustus had to wait until 13 B.C. and his assumption of the office of Pontifex Maximus before he could make his next major move:

> [Augustus] collected whatever prophetic writings of Greek or Latin origin were in circulation anonymously or under the names of authors of little repute, and burned more than two thousand of them, retaining only the Sibylline books and making a choice even among those; and he deposited them in two gilded cases under the pedestal of the Palatine Apollo.[21]

---

[18] "Templum Apollinis in ea parte Palatinae domus excitavit, quam fulmine ictam desiderari a deo haruspices pronuntiarant." Suetonius, *Aug.* 29.3. Translation from *LCL* 1.167. Compare Cassius Dio 49.15.5. On the temple: Chapter I nn. 104-105 and accompanying text; *TDAR*, pp. 16-19; and Gagé, *Apollon*, pp. 523-81.

[19] Suetonius, *Aug.* 58. He received the title in 2 B.C. (*OCD*² p. 150.) Alföldi, *Vater*, pp. 92-98 (115-21).

[20] The two quotes, in full, are respectively: "Caesar in bibliotheca statuam sibi posuerat habitu ac statu Apollinis," Pseudo-Acron ad Horace, *Epist.* 1.3.17; and "Et tangit Augustum, cui simulacrum factum est cum Apollinis cunctis insignibus," Servius, *ad Ecl.* 4.10. After the passage of Suetonius, *Aug.* 29.3, quoted in n. 18 above, immediately comes the information about the library, "addidit porticus cum bibliotheca Latina Graecaque, . . ." So also Cassius Dio 53.1.3.

[21] Quidquid fatidicorum librorum Graeci Latinique generis nullis vel parum idoneis auctoribus vulgo ferebatur, supra duo milia contracta undique cremavit ac solos retinuit Sibyllinos, hos quoque dilectu habito; condiditque duobus forulis auratis sub Palatini Apollinis basi.
[Suetonius, *Aug.* 31.1. Translation from *LCL* 1.171.]

AUGURY AND THE STATE

As usual Augustus resolved several problems with one stroke. He did not merely declare the true oracles from the false, but destroyed all the prophecies which he did not find suitable. In other words, no political rival would be able to claim that Augustus was acting against some oracular response, as happened with Bibulus in the Late Republic. In fact, the lay, but politically important, person could no longer even obtain access to the new edition, for Augustus had "the Sibylline verses . . . copied off by the priests with their own hands, in order that no one else might read them."[22] A less obvious and more subtle advantage gained by Augustus was control over foreign cults, because each new deity worshipped in Rome could be admitted only after a consultation of the Sibylline Books.[23] Now Augustus with impunity could cite the Sibylline Books in support of the expulsion of foreign cults he disliked and, conversely, for the restoration of "old" rites and deities he favored.

Finally, and perhaps most importantly, the placing of the Sibylline Books in the Temple of Apollo Palatinus formed part of Augustus's efforts to strip Jupiter of his supreme authority.[24] When the Sibyl had come to Rome independently of Apollo, her books were logically stored in the then recently built temple to Jupiter Capitolinus, highest of all Roman gods and responsible in general for augury and personally for the auspices from thunderbolts.[25] The removal of the Sibylline Books from his temple effectively ended his control of augury, and marked the consummation of Apollo's augural authority, which the Augustan poets celebrated in their allusions to "augur Apollo."[26] Augustus had made Apollo not just the augural

---

[22] "καὶ τὰ ἔπη τὰ Σιβύλλεια . . . τοὺς ἱερέας αὐτοχειρίᾳ ἐκγράψασθαι ἐκέλευσεν, ἵνα μηδεὶς ἕτερος αὐτὰ ἀναλέξηται." Cassius Dio 54.17.12. Translation from *LCL* 6.325, 327. Compare Cicero, *Div.* 2.54 (112), "Quam ob rem Sibyllam quidem sepositam et conditam habeamus, ut, id quod proditum est a maioribus, iniussu senatus ne legantur quidem libri valeantque ad deponendas potius quam ad suscipiendas religiones; . . ."

[23] Latte, *RRG*, pp. 160-61. Similarly the authority of the Sibylline Books lay behind the temple to Apollo Medicus (see n. 13 above) and the institution of the ludi Apollinares in 212 B.C. (see discussion in Chapter IV).

[24] Altheim, *Religion*, pp. 358-59 (especially on the assumption by Mars Ultor of certain prerogatives once enjoyed by Jupiter).

[25] Compare n. 13 above and Chapter IV n. 82 on the Sibylline Books and the Temple of Jupiter Capitolinus. On Jupiter's authority over augury, see Catalano, pp. 155 and 315 n. 275.

[26] For example: Horace, *Carm.* 1.2.30-32, ". . .Tandem venias precamur,/Nube candentis umeros amictus,/Augur Apollo; . . ."; Horace, *Carm. Saec.* 61-65:
　　　Augur et fulgente decorus arcu
　　　Phoebus acceptusque novem Camenis,

deity, but the god of Roman religion, which now operated only under the emperor's auspices rather than vice versa. In fact, his very name, Augustus, symbolizes that authority. Suetonius's passage is instructive:

> Later he took the name of Gaius Caesar and then the surname Augustus, the former by the will of his great-uncle, the latter on the motion of Munatius Plancus. For when some expressed the opinion that he ought to be called Romulus as a second founder of the city, Plancus carried the proposal that he should rather be named Augustus, on the ground that this was not merely a new title but a more honourable one, inasmuch as sacred places too, and those in which anything is consecrated by augural rites are called "august" [augusta], from the increase [auctus] in dignity, or from the movements or feeding of the birds [avium gestus gustusve], as Ennius also shows when he writes: "After by augury august illustrious Rome had been founded."[27]

While the historian attributes the appellation to a rivalry between two senators, surely if the name displeased Octavian he would not have used it. Instead, as has been seen, it admirably suited his purposes.

To complete the transference of influence from the old religious centers, Augustus abandoned the Regia as the residence for the Pontifex Maximus for his own home on the Palatine with the concomitant allocation of the remaining third of his house to the divinity most closely connected with the Pontifex Maximus—Vesta, goddess of the hearth.[28] Ovid extols the new physical arrangement:

> Qui salutari levat arte fessos
> Corporis artus,
>
> Si Palatinas videt aequus aras, . . .

and Vergil, *Aen.* 4.376, "nunc augur Apollo, . . ."

[27] Postea Gai Caesaris et deinde Augusti cognomen assumpsit, alterum testamento maioris avunculi, alterum Munati Planci sententia, cum quibusdam censentibus Romulum appellari oportere quasi et ipsum conditorem urbis, praevaluisset, ut Augustus potius vocaretur, non tantum novo sed etiam ampliore cognomine, quod loca quoque religiosa et in quibus augurato quid consecratur augusta dicantur, ab auctu vel ab avium gestu gustuve, sicut etiam Ennius docet scribens: "Augusto augurio postquam incluta condita Roma est."
[Suetonius, *Aug.* 7. Translation from *LCL* 1.131.]

[28] *CAH* X 479. In other words, the religious center of Rome no longer was in the Forum Romanum, but on the Palatine in the emperor's own home. On Vesta: Chapter I nn. 104, 106-107, and accompanying text; Altheim, *Religion*, pp. 356-57 (note his comments there and on p. 351 on the Sorrento Base which "summarizes" Augustus's building program on the Palatine); and Guarducci, "Enea" (also on the Sorrento Base).

AUGURY AND THE STATE

> Vesta has been received in the home of her kinsman [Augustus]: so have the Fathers righteously decreed. Phoebus owns part of the house; another part has been given up to Vesta; what remains is occupied by Caesar himself. Long live the laurels of the Palatine! Long live the house wreathed with the oaken boughs! A single house holds three eternal gods.[29]

With the union under one roof and in one person of hearth, ruler, and augur Augustus had become a latter-day priest-king.

Thus far Augustus's augural actions have been considered broadly in the realm of the state religion. The editing of all written responses, along with the Sibylline Books, however, showed that he also acted against semi-official and private oracles. These types by their number and independence were harder to eliminate than the state forms where patience would frequently enable Augustus to accomplish the task with a minimum of trouble, as with the Sibylline Books. Only two of those removed, Marsyas and Cacus, concern this inquiry.

Marsyas presented no real problem to Augustus, because his augural importance had already begun to wane. His kind of auspices, the observation of birds, according to Cicero, had yielded earlier in the century to hepatoscopy.[30] Marsyas's association with *libertas* facilitated the transition as its connotations of civic freedom overrode its original meaning of the augural freeing of the *templum*. The reinterpretation of the pose and the placement of the statue in the Forum Romanum completed the transformation of the augural silenus into an ordinary follower of Bacchus, such as he had always been in the Greek world. In other words, while Augustus must have been concerned about Marsyas's practice of exauguration since Vegoia's prophecy on *limitatio* (a related rite) was placed along with the Sibylline Books in the Temple of Apollo Palatinus,[31] he was able to let

[29]
> . . . cognati Vesta recepta est
> limine: sic iusti constituere patres.
> Phoebus habet partem, Vestae pars altera cessit;
> quod superest illis, tertius ipse tenet.
> state Palatinae laurus, praetextaque quercu
> stet domus: aeternos tres habet una deos.

[Ovid, *Fasti* 4.949-54. Translation from *LCL* 259.]
Compare Chapter I n. 108. Another indication of the demotion of Jupiter Capitolinus may be that the "oaken boughs," traditionally associated with him, now decorate the house where Apollo has taken up residence. Compare Fowler, *Festivals*, p. 229 and Ogilvie, *Comm*, pp. 439-40.

[30] "Nam ut nunc extis (quamquam id ipsum aliquanto minus quam olim), sic tum avibus magnae res impetriri solebant." Cicero, *Div.* 1.16 (28). Pease, *Comm*, pp. 134-35.

[31] Servius, *ad Aen.* 6.72, quoted in Chapter II n. 30, with references also to discussions of Vegoia's writings on *limitatio* (Thulin, *Script*, pp. 17-18).

AUGURY AND THE STATE

natural events for the most part take their course. The process no doubt was aided by an emphasis on Marsyas's alter ego, the upstart satyr who challenged Apollo. Although the substance of the story about the contest was retained, Apollo's reaction to the flaying changed in the late first century B.C. from righteous anger to compassionate repentance—even if only after the fact—thereby reducing the emotional appeal of Marsyas's plight.[32] Marsyas, the bringer of exauguration to Italy, faded with little trouble and few machinations into almost complete oblivion.

Cacus, on the other hand, posed the greatest threat to Augustus's plans for reorganization. Because he lived at the top of the Scalae Caci virtually on Augustus's doorstep, he had to be removed. If Augustus were attempting to bring all types of augury under his control, he could hardly allow a private, independent seer to practice almost within Apollo's new sanctuary.[33] It is one thing to relieve religious figures and divinities of their powers and to leave them in charge of empty rites and sanctuaries (a process which results in an inevitable waning of influence through disuse), but it is another problem altogether to uproot a figure so well-established that a landmark will always be known by his name. Cacus required drastic measures. Augustus, as ever, used the mythological situation to his advantage, for Cacus's image was already somewhat tarnished. In the second century B.C. Cacus no longer appears just as the handsome, Apolline seer of the Etruscan mirror and urns, but has already become the unsuccessful, rather scurrilous opponent of Hercules. Because the earlier stories of the conflict speak of Cacus as a thief, it is possible that the rise in violence in Rome made this characterization particularly apt for that period.[34] In any case, it gave Augustus the basis he needed for thoroughly blackening Cacus's character and completing his downfall. The task was not easy. Vergil needed one-sixth of Book Eight of the *Aeneid* to dispose of Cacus so that Apollo could reign

---

[32] For example, Diodorus Siculus 5.75.3:

τὸν Ἀπόλλωνα νικήσαντα καὶ τιμωρίαν ὑπὲρ τὴν ἀξίαν λαβόντα παρὰ τοῦ λειφθέντος μεταμεληθῆναι, καὶ τὰς ἐκ τῆς κιθάρας χορδὰς ἐκρήξαντα μέχρι τινὸς χρόνου τῆς ἐν αὐτῇ μουσικῆς ἀποστῆναι.

Ingomar Weiler (p. 54) similarly believes that Apollo's remorse does not belong to the older saga.

[33] Compare Cassius Dio 56.25.5, "τότε δ' οὖν ταῦτά τε οὕτως ἐπράχθη, καὶ τοῖς μάντεσιν ἀπηγορεύθη μήτε κατὰ μόνας τινὶ μήτε περὶ θανάτου, μηδ' ἂν ἄλλοι συμπαρῶσίν οἱ, χρᾶν."

[34] See Chapter I, under the subheading, "Cattle Stealing." On violence in Rome and especially its increase from the second half of the second century B.C. on: Lintott, pp. 1-2 and Appendix A, pp. 24-34 (on theft).

supreme and unchallenged in his new home on the Palatine and throughout all Rome.

In conclusion the Tarquins and Augustus chose opposite courses to gain control of augury. The Etruscan kings ruled in an age of religious expansion in which new figures and rites, after discriminative testing, were invited to join and be incorporated into the Roman ranks. Augustus, inheriting a plethora of conflicting practices and practitioners, effectively trimmed the state religion to a core, controlled by and answerable only to him.

· VI ·
CONCLUSION

CACUS and Marsyas have so far been considered separately to establish their characters and their development. How they relate to each other remains to be explored.

The first contact between Cacu and Greek figures occurs in the late fourth century B.C. on the Etruscan mirror (App. I, no. 1) and the South Italian vases. Since Cacu was known and represented as a seer in that period, other diviners offered an appropriate model. The actual choice—Apollo of the musical contest—worked very well. The curious thing, however, was that Marsyas, not Apollo, was the one named in alliance with Cacus by Gnaeus Gellius. Because the annalist somewhat surprisingly ended the encounter between Cacus and Hercules with a reference to the teaching of augury to the Sabines by Megales, the companion of Cacus, the problem arose of ascertaining Marsyas's relation to augury. As king, did he merely have augurs as his subjects or did some more direct connection exist? The interpretation of the Marsyas in the Forum Romanum in Chapter IV confirmed the latter hypothesis. If Marsyas was the bringer of exauguration to Italy, then he would have come in contact with a number of the native practitioners of divination, such as Cacus.

Only one aspect of the association of Marsyas and Cacus can be ascertained without doubt. By the time of Gellius, Cacus as a "legatus" was evidently subordinate, but nonetheless cordial, to Marsyas. This relationship, in turn, has important implications when the "ius hostium," the converse so-to-speak of the *ius hospitium* (Chapter I), is applied to them. As descendants of friendly ancestors enjoy friendship with each other, so offspring of enemies continue the rivalry. In this case, in the Augustan period Cacus on the Palatine becomes a threat to Apollo, the archenemy of Marsyas. Parenthetically, Gellius also obeys this principle when he pits Cacus against Tarchon, who, as a direct descendant of Hercules, would naturally not favor Cacus.[1] If the *ius hostium* works backwards in time, as it

---

[1] Tarchon's imprisonment of Cacus in the Gellius passage may depend on an inheritance of his opposition from either his father or grandfather, Hercules, since Hercules begets Tarchon and Tyrrhenus directly or indirectly through his son, Telephus. (Lycophron, *Alex.* 1248-50, and Dion. Hal., *Ant. Rom.* 1.28, respectively.) Therefore Vergil (*Aen.* 8.506) allies a Tarchon with Aeneas and Evander, because both Tarchon

CONCLUSION

should, then the original encounter between Cacu and Marsyas, of which no traces survive, should also have been amicable. The Etruscan artists probably not only knew the story, but were consequently doubly enticed to use the contest as a model for the ambush. It worked visually and fittingly reversed the outcome of the Greek scene, for Cacus, the "legatus" of Marsyas, assumes the winner's position which Apollo had held "unfairly." The mirror even alludes to the connection between Cacu and Marsyas. The head of the silenus or satyr, who peeks over the rocks to watch the ambush, not only joins the two, but may be an actual emissary of Marsyas sent to ensure that all does turn out well for Cacu. Likewise, the grapevine that surrounds the entire scene may refer to Marsyas, who notably carries a winesack in the Forum Romanum.[2]

The lack of rivalry between Cacu and Marsyas may be another example of the kind of peaceful accommodation that marked the succession of founder-seers on the Palatine (Chapter I). Both practiced divination, but of different sorts. Cacu was the mortal seer who prophesied by singing; Marsyas was a semi-divine and sometime immortal, who taught humans how to perform a rite crucial for gaining protection from gods that might otherwise have been inadvertently slighted. As the legends of the sixth century B.C. show (Chapter V), several forms of prophecy did make room for each other and coexist. Cacu on the Palatine becomes, then, as in Diodorus Siculus (4.21), a local who welcomes the outsider, Marsyas. He may have either himself needed to use exauguration or wanted to make it available to others. In neither case would there be cause for conflict. If Cacu did become a disseminator of Marsyas's rite, his position in Gellius as envoy ("legatus") makes sense on the "mythological" level (Chapter II). That Cacu is not the one to teach augury to the Sabines may be due to Gellius's lack of knowledge about Cacu's own prophetic nature, as well as to the fact that Cacu's good image had already begun to suffer by the second century B.C. Gellius has probably gone too far when he ascribes the entire acquisition of augury rather than just the rite of exauguration by the Sabines to Megales' instruction.

As Cacu and Marsyas began their careers independently, so they also appear to have gone their separate ways sometime after the second century B.C., the time of Gellius's account. The later congru-

and Evander are enemies of Cacus. For the evolution of the lineage: Bayet, "Arcadisme," pp. 75-76; Martin, "Héraclès," p. 272 and n. 130 with the literary references. Similarly, Faunus in the Derkyllos account (Chapter I n. 66) receives Hercules ungraciously, as does his wife Bona Dea (Chapter I n. 95).

[2] In the handle of the mirror stands a boy. Except for the *pedum*—a possible Marsyan reference—he holds, he appears to have no connection to the main scene.

CONCLUSION

ences in imagery, livelihood (shepherds), and domicile (caves)[3] are probably fortuitous, due more to their being or becoming characters of ill-repute than to their former direct association with each other. Similarly it must be stressed that the two were never equated as one figure in antiquity; instead they remained distinct characters who interacted briefly. At last the strange prominence of the two—Cacus on the Palatine and in the *Aeneid*; Marsyas in one of the most important and conspicuous places in the Forum Romanum—finds an explanation. At first individually and then together both played essential roles in the legends about the foundation of early Rome and in the fostering of its augural practices. Although the two eventually outlived their original divinatory purposes, nonetheless they were so inextricably tied to Rome, its history and its religion, that they remained forever rooted to the city.

This study began with an image which likened Cacus and Marsyas to two balls of wool woven into the complex fabric of the legends of Rome. With their strands unravelled, it becomes necessary to reverse the process—to reconstitute the tapestry by considering how these two minor, but essential, figures work within and yet affect the design of the whole. That is, although the analysis of Cacus and Marsyas was divided into parts, nonetheless, each was treated primarily within his chronological development no matter what the source of the evidence, be it literature, art, history, topography, or religion. Here, instead, the focus will be on these individual areas and the light that Cacus and Marsyas shed on them.

Literature is evidence of the first recourse. It supplies not just de-

---

[3] For example, Apuleius (*Flor.* 3.1) calls Marsyas ". . . barbarus, vultu ferino, trux, hispidus, inlutibarbus, spinis et pilis obsitus fertur—pro nefas—cum Apolline certavisse, taeter cum decoro, agrestis cum erudito, belua cum deo. . . . monstri illius barbariam . . ." etc. While certain details may be more fitting for a satyr, the image of Marsyas is not much different from that of Cacus in *Aeneid* 8 ("semihominis" with "facies dira"—194; "monstro"—198; etc.). Similarly Livy (1.7.5) makes Cacus a "pastor," as Claudian (*Against Eutropius* 2.257) does Marsyas. Parenthetically, Cicero, *Div.* 1.42 (94), sees a connection between shepherds and augury, which may help explain the later professions of both Cacus and Marsyas: "Arabes autem et Phryges et Cilices, quod pastu pecudum maxime utuntur campos et montes, hieme et aestate peragrantes, propterea facilius cantus avium et volatus notaverunt; . . ." Finally, Cacus resides in a cave ("spelunca"—*Aen.* 8.193), as Marsyas's skin was hung in the one from which his river arose according to Xenophon, *Anabasis* 1.2.8 ("ἐνταῦθα λέγεται Ἀπόλλων ἐκδεῖραι Μαρσύαν νικήσας ἐρίζοντα οἱ περὶ σοφίας, καὶ τὸ δέρμα κρεμάσαι ἐν τῷ ἄντρῳ ὅθεν αἱ πηγαί."). The capture of Silenus by Midas (see Chapter I n. 30 for references) cannot be used as a comparison to the imprisonment of Cacus by Tarchon in Gellius, because the two appear to be separate characters since, to my knowledge, no ancient reference states that *the* Silenus and Marsyas are one and the same.

CONCLUSION

tails of, but reasons for actions. While the literary uses of Cacus and Marsyas have for the most part been left untouched, the way literature uses legendary history has not. In other words, whether or not Cacus symbolizes Turnus in the *Aeneid*[4] has not been a concern, but the manner in which Vergil incorporated Cacus into his poem has been. That a sizable portion of Book 8 is devoted to him at first seems disproportionate to his role in the legends of Rome. Yet he must be reckoned with as one of the "native" inhabitants of the earliest settlement on the Palatine. More important, however, was his role as seer—a position he could not be allowed to maintain once Augustus established Apollo in the same place. Vergil, aware of contemporary political needs, yet still desirous of preserving the past, skillfully worked within these constraints to fashion an account which served Augustus but did not violate tradition. This aspect of Vergil's craft has been little remarked, although it helped to determine which incidents in Rome's rich legendary past were included in the *Aeneid*. In contrast to the consummate artistry of Vergil, Gnaeus Gellius appears both ill-phrased and ill-informed. He recalls Flannery O'Connor's "food-chopper brains that nothing comes out of the way it went in."[5] But even in his case it has been possible to discern a kernel of historicity in the tangle by a careful dissection of each part.

The Etruscan artists worked in a manner similar to Vergil's. As Vergil freely borrowed from Greek sources, which he combined with local Roman forms for an epic on a thoroughly Roman subject, so the Etruscans creatively adapted Greek artistic models to produce representations of local tales. As Vergil was able to use not just Homer but other Greek authors, so the Etruscan artists depended not just on Tarentum but on all of Greek South Italy as well as Greece itself. The synthesis in both cases results in products clearly and distinctly identifiable as Roman and Etruscan. This relationship between pictorial model and offshoot has frequently been demonstrated for other periods, such as between late Roman and early Christian, but never before for the Etruscans using Greek art for representations of their own local legends. As a result it is apparent that slight changes in the model do not have to mean a misunderstanding on the part of the Etruscan adapter but may indicate a different, and even local story. Similarly a minor variation in a well-established type, such as the lowering of the right arm of the Censorinus Marsyas on Greek im-

---

[4] Buchheit, pp. 116-33.

[5] S. Fitzgerald, ed., *Flannery O'Connor—The Habit of Being* (New York, 1979), p. 68.

CONCLUSION

perial coins, tangibly demonstrates that the conception of Marsyas had changed between the late Republican and the Imperial periods.

As the minter carefully chose the devices on the Censorinus coins for his own political ends, so the Etruscan buyer would order a particular scene for his funerary urn. For the first time such a relationship between patron and artist has been documented in Etruscan art. All the urns discussed here either have inscriptions indicating that their owners were reputed descendants of one of the participants in the figured scene or were made in the same workshop. In other words, these urns portray not so much the "national" history of Etruria as the glorification of local heroes and events.

While coins and imperial reliefs have often been used as historical evidence, Etruscan representations, except for the François Tomb, have generally been ignored. Yet the mirror in the British Museum not only portrays an otherwise unknown event of the sixth century B.C., it also indirectly provides the first Etruscan corroboration of Roman hints that Lars Porsenna did indeed capture Rome. At the same time it furnishes the key to an explanation of the Gellius passage, which in turn suggests a possible interpretation of the second group of urns as Cacu? the prisoner. Just as significantly the mirror demonstrates that the Etruscan artists composed their scenes with the same care as the designer of coin devices. An understanding of all the parts is essential for an interpretation of the whole. Artile had previously been considered a minor figure merely accompanying Cacu rather than being the center of the action. Similarly the devices on the Censorinus coins work together to make a pointed political statement about the control of divination in Rome during the Social Wars. Particularly important is the correct reading of the individual devices, be it the statue of the Sibyl or the raised right hand of Marsyas himself.

In fact, throughout the study a strictly literal interpretation of the various bits of evidence has proved the most productive approach. The Etruscans and Romans were quite straightforward in their portrayals and preservation of events. This attitude is also obvious in their use of topography. Cacus inhabited a house, reached by a grand staircase, hence the part which survived never lost its original name, Scalae Caci. Marsyas, on the other hand, was a symbol of *libertas*, and as such occupied a cleared place in the Forum Romanum where he could practice and inculcate his speciality, exauguration. His case, however, differs from Cacus in that when his original purpose was no longer served his distinctive characteristics lent themselves to a second, but still, straightforward political interpretation. Thus both

CONCLUSION

he and Cacus in their own ways display the tenacity with which figures held on to their monuments in Rome. They could not be destroyed. Even conflation of several figures into one or a reduction of hallowed sites—common enough elsewhere—does not apply here. Either the purpose of troublesome features (Marsyas) had to be subverted or a new location (Cacus) had to be found.

The initial spur to the major transformations—as opposed to the slower, but inevitable process of evolution—was the need of Augustus to control divination. Whether it is the Vibennae ambushing Cacu, the Sabines learning augury from Megales, or Censorinus asserting his family's role in prophecy, divination in Rome was never separated from politics. In order to rule, the ruler or ruling party had to control prophecy lest he or they be predicted out of power. Cacus and Marsyas exemplify the problem in addition to substantiating two minor features of divination. The mirror with Artile portrayed as the pupil of Cacus provides one of the few proofs that the Etruscan nobility, like the Roman Republicans, did educate their children in the prophetic arts, whereas the Marsyas in the Forum is one of the extremely rare representations of an augural sighting of birds.

Together the sometime disparate areas of literature, art, history, topography, and religion over time formed the legends of Rome. While the very flexibility of the legends ensured their survival, the variety of the stories frequently resulted in conflicting versions. What really happened? Did Lars Porsenna, for example, capture Rome? Do the urns depict an actual ancestor of the Purnis, Sentinates, and Cumeresas or merely their claim to such an ancestor? Does the truth become impossibly muddled when real people, such as the Vibennae and Arruns Porsenna, are mixed with mythological figures, like Cacu, Marsyas, and Hercules? Or is it not that very interweaving of the divine and the real that makes the Roman tales legends and not history?

The Etruscan and Romans use legends not to tell what actually happened but what they wanted to have happened. The Romans went beyond simply presenting "history" from their point of view to an attempt at complete control over the past. Livy (2.15) eloquently describes Lars Porsenna's dignified departure from Rome, but Tacitus's one-line throwaway statement indicates the reverse outcome. A similar experience, the capture of Rome by the Gauls in 390 B.C., was openly discussed. Its occurrence so close to the writing of the first Roman histories at the end of the century militated against blatant manipulation. People not only might remember, but they were also becoming aware of current events as something to be remem-

CONCLUSION

bered, something fit for history. The earlier capture of Rome, however, was sufficiently removed in time to permit the greatest embellishment, which Livy's incredible specificity of characters and events shows.

As a result the main purpose here has been not so much to determine what occurred historically, but to analyze the legends for what they reveal about the period in which they were conceived. It is no coincidence that the Augustan period marks the final metamorphosis of Cacu and the fading of the "augural" Marsyas. Not only were codifications of Roman history encouraged, but the emperor, his adventures and his religious impulses, replaced the extraordinary variety of tales fostered by the numerous rival Republican families and cities. Instead of a constant influx of the new, as exemplified by a Cacu and a Marsyas during the Republic, the need for a continual reworking of Roman legends had diminished. It is not so much that the legends became fixed and unvarying during the Empire, but that the changes were of a different and a less dramatic nature than those wrought between the Republic and Augustus. The golden age of the legends of Rome had passed.

APPENDIX I
REPRESENTATIONS
OF CACU

Notes on Use

1. Numbers are continuous between the two groups, Cacu Ambushed and Cacu? the Prisoner.
2. Objects are arranged according to composition within each group.
3. The catalogue is as complete as possible for the pre-imperial representations of Cacu.[1]
4. Misattributions are listed and briefly discussed in Appendix II.
5. "Left" and "right" always refer to the viewer's position, except where specifically modified to denote the represented figure's limbs, etc.
6. Because this is an iconographical, not a stylistic, study, measurements for the objects are not given. Publications cited in the bibliography, at the end of each entry, contain this information.
7. A standard and basically self-explanatory format is used for the urns. No mention of covers or ends indicates that the first have not survived and that the second were undecorated. The mouldings on the cask, as decorative and not true architectural elements, are described from top to bottom. Emendations of the BrK drawings are generally cited in parentheses.

---

[1] In addition to the urns in this Appendix only two other extant representations can be securely assigned to Cacus. Both are imperial Roman medallions, one of Antoninus Pius in the Bibliothèque Nationale, Paris and the other of Marcus Aurelius in Vienna. They show Hercules victorious just after he has killed Cacus, who lies dead on the right. On the medallion of Antoninus Pius four men, much smaller in stature than the hero, thank him in a scene reminiscent of Theseus's reception by the Athenian children after he had slaughtered the Minotaur. The Marcus Aurelius example does not portray the four men. Vergil's and Propertius's characterizations of Cacus did not affect the pictorial tradition, for both representations depict Cacus in the form of a human, not a monster. For the medallions: *ML*, 1:2288-89; Münzer, *Cacus*, pp. 118-21; Brommer, "Caco," pp. 247-48 with fig. 375 (Paris medallion). Compare Brommer, *Denk*, 1:36. For the paintings with Theseus: Schefold, *DWP*, p. 170—VII, 2, 16 House of "Gaius Rufus" (1), exedra, east wall, Naples Inv. 9043; Bianchi-Bandinelli, *Center*, p. 110, fig. 115 and p. 111, fig. 116—Herculaneum, Basilica (Naples Inv. 9049) and Naples Inv. 9043 respectively.

REPRESENTATIONS OF CACU

Cacu Ambushed

1. London 633, from Bolsena.   Figs. 1-2
   Bronze mirror.
   Condition: For the most part extremely good, except for the head of the left warrior which has not survived.

   The basic description of the scene appears in Chapter I on page 4. Only additional details about the Vibennae and the decoration in the handle area are included here.
   Each of the Vibennae carries a shield (Caeles's device: a star within two concentric circles). Caeles was presumably bearded like his brother (cf. nos. 2-4 below). While Aulus grips the rim of his shield with his right hand, Caeles holds a sword vertically in his right hand which rests on his raised right thigh. Both turn their heads slightly to the center, but stand frontally with their weight on their inside legs. Caeles's outside leg is bent more than that of Aulus, because his right foot rests on a rock not, like Aulus's, behind the other foot on the same level. The ground is stippled. A small, chubby boy with a *pedum* held in his right hand behind his head occupies the handle and has nothing to do with the main scene which forms a distinct unit enclosed by a border decorated with an undulating grapevine.

   Date: Late fourth-third century B.C.

   Bibliography: Helbig, *BdI*, p. 216. Gardthausen, p. 33. Körte in *ES* 5:166-72 and pl. 127. Münzer, "Vibenna," pp. 598ff. Walters, *CatBr*, pp. 99-100 no. 633, with bibliography. Robert, "Cacus," p. 76 fig. 1. Messerschmidt, "Probleme," p. 77 fig. 12. Colini, p. 23 fig. 11 top. Heurgon, *Vie*, pp. 283-84. Bloch, *Prodiges*, p. 105 fig. 1. E. Richardson, *Etruscans*, pp. 221-27. Ruch, "Devin," p. 342. Hackens and Van den Driessche, pl. 259. Brendel, *EtrArt*, pp. 415-16 (third century B.C.), p. 415 fig. 315. Small, "Models," pl. 82 figs. 1a-1b. Small, "Cacu Imprisoned," fig. 1. Jannot, p. 477 no. 23.

2. Chiusi, Tomba della Pellegrina, Urn no. 3, still in situ.   Fig. 3
   Alabaster urn.
   Condition: Worn; some cracks through the figured scene; right mouldings chipped.
   Cover: Man, half-draped, also wears a lei, a wreath, and a ring on the fourth finger of his left hand. The phiale in his right hand, as well as most of his right arm, no longer survives. Inscription: cae sentinate larϑal cutna(1).

Crowning Moulding: Egg-and-dart; narrow fascia.
Base Moulding: Wide fascia.

Similar to no. 1 except for the following variations. Cacu now plays a cithara, not a lyre, held high. He wears a necklace with large bullae and drapery only to his knees. His legs are uncrossed. To the left of his head appears a tree, and to the right, instead of the second tree of no. 1, a bridled horse raises its left front leg. With his feet resting on a low rock, Artile sits on another rock with his back to Cacu. The youth, completely in profile, leans forward to rest his elbows on his drawn-up knees and his head in his hands. His drapery leaves his left shoulder, side, and legs uncovered from the mid-thigh down. Each Vibenna takes the same stance of extended right leg, with left, weight-leg bent, instead of standing in a nearly perfect mirror-image as on no. 1. Caeles looks slightly down to the right like Cacu, while Aulus faces the viewer. Aulus now draws his sword, as Caeles levels his for action. They are dressed as before except that fillets have been substituted for the helmets and the boots have been discarded. Between Aulus's feet lies a big, round pot with a large, loop handle fallen onto the body. The craggy setting and the satyr of no. 1 are not included.

Date: ca. 160 B.C. (Thimme I, p. 132.)

Bibliography: No BrK. Levi, "Chiusi," pl. 13a. Levi, "Pellegrina," p. 29 no. 1 and p. 28 fig. 24. Thimme I, pp. 104-108, 132, 104 fig. 47 (cover), and 105 fig. 48 (cask).

3. Siena 734, from Sarteano. Fig. 4
Alabaster urn.
Condition: Surface rather worn, especially the faces of the two figures on the right; chips in both mouldings.
Cover: Woman, holding drapery in her left hand and an object in her right hand; very worn; head missing.
Crowning and Base Mouldings: Each, a wide fascia.

To the scene on no. 2 have been added four figures in symmetrical balance. On each side a nude warrior, gripping a shield and wearing a helmet, a baldric, and a scabbard, falls onto his outside knee with his inside leg extended. The left warrior holds a sword almost vertically in his right hand which rests on rocky ground; the right warrior grasps the hilt of a sword whose blade is now missing (or never was?). Above and behind each of them another man moves to the outside, as he looks toward the center. The left man, who wears a mantle and a tunic with a large fold at the waist, raises his right hand, palm outward, to his shoulder and extends his left arm behind Caeles on the right. The man on the far right is similarly garbed (the BrK drawing does not include his mantle's fastening); he carries a shield (device: star? in relief) and possibly held a sword over his head—the frieze is not well preserved in this section.

The central group differs from no. 2 primarily in details which heighten the action. The Vibennae are dressed as on no. 1 except that Aulus lacks the baldric and has a plumed crest on his helmet; because their feet are not visible, they may (cf. no. 1) or may not (cf. no. 2) have worn boots. While the Vibennae assume mirror-image stances of bent, inside legs and the actions of their counterparts on no. 2, their bodies have been pivoted and their glances turned toward Cacu who no longer plays the cithara, now balanced on his right thigh (cf. no. 1). Instead Cacu lifts his right hand (his middle fingers were not raised as in the BrK drawing), still holding the plectrum (the lump-like mass on the BrK drawing), and looks up, almost beyond the viewer. His body is older than on nos. 1-2 with drapery covering only his thighs and right leg. The horse of no. 2 now stands at rest. Artile, as on no. 1, sits to the right with his legs crossed, but in a pose more closed like on no. 2, as he gazes to the left. His left hand supports his head (traces of red above the fingers), and his right hand clasps an object, rectangular in section, which is probably the diptych of no. 1 folded. He wears a tunic girt at the waist. Between him and Cacu is a round pot with a loop handle.

Date: Second century B.C.

Bibliography: BrK, 2:254 and pl. 119 no. 1. Körte in *ES* 5:167 no. 1. Robert, "Cacus," p. 76 fig. 2. Hamburg, *Urnas*, pp. 13, 38. Messerschmidt, "Probleme," p. 79 fig. 14. Colini, p. 23 fig. 11 below. Heurgon, *Vie*, p. 63 fig. 11. Small, "Models," pl. 83 fig. 2.

4. Florence 74233, from Città della Pieve, Purni Tomb.   Fig. 5
Alabaster urn.

Condition: For the most part extremely good, except for chips in the corners and the missing heads of the two warriors on the ends. Additional comments, including color notations, appear in the description below.

Cover: Man, holding a patera (chipped) in his right hand and a lei (right section missing) in his left hand (broken thumb; ring on fourth finger), lacks his head and right arm. Cracked in places. The alabaster of the cover is whiter than the somewhat yellow-hued cask.

Crowning Moulding: Wide fascia (inscribed: arnϑ:purni:curcesa [*CIE* 1345]); narrow, cut-back fascia; dentils.

Base Moulding: Inverted egg-and-dart; wide fascia.

The subsidiary figures of no. 3 are altered in pose and more elaborate in dress. The two warriors who were collapsing on the edges of the frieze are less moribund, more upright here, and kneel on their right knees on a stone (left) or on the ground (right). Both have on belted tunics (red on the left's waistband), and the right warrior possibly a mantle, the end of which hangs between his legs. The latter also wears a fillet, while the crown of the head of the left warrior is smooth. Instead of holding shields as on no. 3, the left figure clasps his empty scabbard at his waist and his counterpart rests his left hand on his, as he raises his sword to the right and looks back left over his shoulder. The warrior behind him, on the far right, wears buskins and a muscle cuirass over a tunic. His cohort on the left is dressed (green on the chest) as on no. 3, except that his mantle flutters to the left. His right foot, shod in a buskin, can be seen on the lower left just behind the leftmost warrior's right thigh; he attempts to draw his sword, but is restrained by the right hand of Caeles whom he is trying to push away. Aulus reaches up with his right hand to control the excited horse (yellow diamond on forehead; lower portion of muzzle missing). Because the weight of each brother falls on their bent, outside legs, their bodies incline symmetrically away from the center. To their dress on no. 3 are added baldrics, from which sheathed swords hang (Caeles's sword hilt no longer preserved); Caeles now also has a helmet with two crests (both broken) and a plume, and he still wears a mantle. Traces of brown remain in their beards, hair, and eyes. Cacu appears unconcerned about the surrounding melee, for he stares directly ahead with lightly creased forehead, and leans back, with his right hand still holding the plectrum over his head and his left hand resting on the top of his cithara (traces of yellow; right portion missing). Not just his position, but the smoothness of his nude body, in contrast to the detailed surfaces of the other draped figures, draw the viewer's attention. Cacu's mantle (traces of red) covers only his right leg; the elaborate necklace (traces of gold) of no. 2 reappears; and his right foot sports an open-toed, laced boot. Artile (traces of brown in hair and facial features), in a belted chiton (traces of red) to his knees and a mantle, reclines to the left on a rock with his left leg tucked under him and his right leg (buskin on foot) bent. Only on this urn does he not cradle his head; instead he extends his right hand, palm up, toward Caeles. At his side lie two vases (or sacks) connected to a carrying yoke. The tree of nos. 2-3 has been omitted.

Ends: Within arches are figures who hold torches diagonally in both hands with the flame end elevated toward the front of the cask.

Left: Female demon, winged at the head and shoulders and seated on rocks to the right, wears a belted chiton and a mantle about her lower torso. A snake coils up toward her.

Right: A triton, with his bipartite tail coiling to either side, faces front.

Date: Second century B.C.

Bibliography: BrK, 2:254-55 no. 1a and 255, with photograph. Körte in *ES* 5:167 no. 1a. Petersen, "Vibenna," p. 44 fig. 1. Robert, "Cacus," p. 77 fig. 3. Messerschmidt, "Probleme," p. 79 fig. 15. Giglioli, *Arte*, p. 398 fig. 1. Thimme II, pp. 122-23 no. 3 (Style III) and pl. IV figs. 1, 3.

5. Florence 5801 (72).[2] Fig. 6
    Alabaster urn.

Condition: Much of the surface gone, particularly on the left, with small chunks missing from the edges of the cask; traces of stucco, which may once have filled some of the more conspicuous gaps; in general, less well-preserved than on the BrK drawing.

Crowning Moulding: Fascia; cavetto.
Base Moulding: Wide fascia between animal paws.

A more open composition than on nos. 3 and 4 affects to varying extents the action of the figures. The leftmost figure is based on the

---

[2] According to the label in the Museo Archeologico this urn is from Chiusi, and Körte (BrK 2:256) identifies the stone as "alabastro chiusino." Thimme (II, p. 122 n. 22), however, believes it must be from Volterra because of its similarity to Volterra 205 (BrK 2:pl. 118 no. 1). Although it is true that both casks have animal feet, that resemblance in itself is insufficient to cast doubt on the provenience much less to assign both urns to the same workshop as Thimme does. The relation between the feet and the cask is not comparable on the two urns. On Volterra 205 the figured scene is placed between two "fluted" columns whose bases are formed by the feet, each with four toes; on Florence 5801, the feet, each with three toes, appear directly below the figured scene which is unframed. While such casks may be rare at Chiusi, the subject of Cacu, outside of this possible example, does not occur in Volterra. In other words, since Florence 5801 may present a problem for either place of manufacture, the fact that it does not fit Thimme's "workshop" makes it more likely that the urn is indeed Chiusine. Compare also the discussion on the origin of the urns in Chapter II. For good photographs of Volterra 205: Laviosa, *Scultura*, pp. 54-57 no. 8, pls. XXII-XXIV.

man standing on the left on no. 3: instead of raising his right hand he holds his sword vertically; in his left hand he clasps its scabbard at an angle to his body (the action of the similarly extended left arm of the man on no. 3 is unclear); and he is nude except for a mantle buttoned at the neck. A rescuer, almost like Caeles on no. 3, strides to the right with his sword drawn and its scabbard firmly gripped in his left hand. He wears a belted tunic (or two garments?) and a mantle hanging over his left arm. At his feet sits Artile in the general position and dress of no. 4, except that he holds his head in his right hand and rests his left hand on a stone. His drapery now covers his lower legs. The Vibennae, in the stance of no. 4, for the first time are in heroic nudity, but for their mantles billowing slightly behind their backs and around the left arm and thigh of Aulus. They also have on plumed helmets. Each is unsheathing his sword and carries a shield with a beaded rim (red strap-handle on Caeles's). Only Aulus (much of his face is damaged) is bearded. At the feet of Cacu a male figure takes the leg and body position of the lower left nude man on no. 3 in order to grab Caeles with both hands by his right calf. This rescuer is dressed like the second rescuer with the addition of a *pilos*. At his knees lies a yoke, finished with a bird's head on each end and carrying two pairs of "saddle-bags." Cacu takes the pose of no. 3, except that his head tilts to the right and his right hand holds the plectrum at waist level. His left fingers grip the strings of the lyre, held in place by a strap running over his left shoulder and wrapping around his left forearm. His drapery completely covers his crossed legs, but not his left foot. The last man on the right wears a belted tunic and a mantle over his left shoulder. He grasps a sheathed sword in his lowered left hand; and like his counterpart on no. 4 he reaches behind Aulus, but here to control the whinnying horse (with reins and halter). All the figures wear high boots, although not so indicated on the BrK drawing. Trees and foliage appear in the spaces between the figures, especially by their heads and feet; a palm stands on the far right.

Ends: Within a frame of a fascia and a cavetto sits a winged demon to the left on rocks (the left is covered with an animal skin, the right with a mantle). Their heads face front, and they lean on their left hands for support.

Left: The male demon rests his right hand on the head of a hammer. He wears a belted chiton and boots. The surface on his left wing and his face no longer survives.

Right: The female demon, with almost leonine hair, rests her right hand similarly on a torch, flame-end down. She wears a belted chiton and open-toed boots. Her face is damaged; traces of red remain on the outer edges of her wings.

Date: Second century B.C.

Bibliography: BrK, 2:256 and pl. 119 no. 2. Overbeck, *Gallerie*, p. 613 n. 91 and pl. 25 no. 21. Körte in *ES* 5:167-68 no. 2. Robert, "Cacus," p. 77 fig. 4. Messerschmidt, "Probleme," p. 79 fig. 16. De Ruyt, *Charun*, pp. 97-98 no. 106. Thimme II, p. 122 n. 22. Jannot, pp. 492-93 no. 73, pl. 6.5.

Cacu? the Prisoner

6. Berlin SK 1281 (E 51), from Chiusi. Fig. 7
    Alabaster urn.

Condition: The surface is worn; the triangular chunk missing from the lower left corner has been restored.

Crowning and Base Mouldings: Each, wide fascia (crowning, more regular than on BrK drawing).

The composition and three of the figures correspond to no. 2 except for minor variations. On the left, Caeles is replaced by a woman, leaning against a pillar (with an Aeolic capital) to rest her head on her left arm. Her hands are clasped, and her left leg crosses her right leg. She wears only a necklace, crossed bands (not on the BrK drawing), and a mantle draped over her head, behind her body on either side (right folds omitted on BrK drawing), and around her right lower leg. "Artile," instead of wearing, sits on a folded mantle placed on top of a rock; otherwise he differs from no. 2 primarily in his more open pose—his legs are separated and his right hand hangs limply on his right thigh. Cacu is nude except where his mantle falls over his left thigh. He looks to the left (but not down as on the BrK drawing). "Aulus" has now drawn his sword and no longer wears a mantle. Between his legs a krater is "suspended" diagonally. The tree has been deleted, and the horse has been moved from the right to the left of Cacu.

Date: Second century B.C.

Bibliography: BrK, 1:109 and pl. 85 no. 3. Schlie, p. 174 no. 3. Hamburg, *Urnas*, pp. 37ff. Rumpf, *Kat*, p. 31 and pl. 38 top (mislabelled E 50). Messerschmidt, "Probleme," p. 80 fig. 17. Clifford, p. 308 fig. 8. Brommer, *Denk*, 3:327 no. 5 (as Berlin 520).

7. Florence 5777 (98).[3]   Fig. 8
    Alabaster urn.
    Condition: Somewhat worn with chips along base moulding; cracked and repaired; lower legs of left figure damaged.
    Crowning and Base Mouldings: Each, a wide fascia.

Two female figures, similarly attired, have been added to the scene of no. 6, and the setting has been altered. On the left stands one of the new women with legs almost crossed. She wears a braided fillet(?), the ends of which hang on either side of her head, a folded-over chiton, crossed-bands, and buskins. She balances a tray, with foodstuffs and a patera, on her left hand and she brings her right hand to her chin. Beside her the nude woman of no. 6 (without the crossed-bands, but with an earring and a necklace) leans against the pillar, no longer visible because "Artile" has been raised to sit on an altar (crowning moulding—fascia, dentils, cavetto, fascia; base moulding—wide fascia) with his feet held together and resting on a stand (composed of opposed Aeolic capitals between plinths, with dentils below the upper member). His mantle falls down his back and under him. Between the stand and the altar a covered amphora with twisted (not plain as on the BrK drawing) handles rests against the altar, behind which rises an Aeolic pillar topped by a round, covered pyxis (damaged, loop handle on the right omitted on the BrK drawing). "Cacu" also sits on the altar on his mantle, its fastening at his neck precludes the necklace of no. 6; he wears a leafy wreath. Instead of the lyre, he holds an object, rectangular in section, in his left hand. He looks away to the left, as the second, added woman, on the right, binds his crossed wrists. Part of the cord already loops around his right wrist; the rest (not drapery as on the BrK drawing) is still held in her left hand. She raises the sword in her right hand behind her head. "Aulus" is now in heroic nudity with a mantle fluttering behind his back and about his right thigh. He also has on a fillet and a baldric for his scabbard. A Phrygian helmet, instead of a vase, lies between his legs. The horse and tree have been omitted.

Each End: An archway, with a closed, two-leaved, panelled door, is set within a simple frame of a wide fascia. The bottom portion of both ends no longer survives.

[3] Although the museum displays this urn without a cover, according to Thimme (II, p. 120 n. 20 and p. 120 fig. 12) one did survive of a man, wearing a wreath, a lei, and rings on his fourth and fifth fingers of his left hand.

REPRESENTATIONS OF CACU

Date: Second century B.C.

Bibliography: BrK, 1:106-107 and pl. 84 no. 1. Schlie, pp. 173-74 no. 1. Bianchi-Bandinelli, "Caratteri," pp. 24 and 27. Messerschmidt, "Probleme," p. 81 fig. 20. Clifford, p. 307 fig. 6. Thimme II, p. 120 n. 20 (early III style) and p. 121 fig. 12 (cover) and pl. III fig. 1 (detail). Brommer, *Denk*, 3:327 no. 6. Small, "Cacu Imprisoned," fig. 2.

8. Siena 730, from Sarteano. Figs. 9-10
   Alabaster urn.

Condition: For the most part very good, except for four missing heads (first figure on the left and three figures on the right); some traces of paint as noted in the description; base moulding scruffy, especially on the right.

Cover: Semi-draped man holds a lei in his slightly raised left hand (ring on fourth finger) and a patera (scar only remains) in his right hand (now missing along with his right arm from just below the elbow). The bottom of the two tasseled cushions against which he reclines has an elaborate fringe. The coverlet of the couch is inscribed with red paint in the letters: arnθ:sentinate.cumeresa; below runs an egg-and-dart moulding (not part of the cask as on the BrK drawing).

No crowning moulding.
Base Moulding: Wide fascia.

Similar to no. 7 except for the following variations and elaborations. The woman on the far left now also wears detached sleeves (traces of green on the left cuff) and a necklace, yellow like her crossed-bands and the beads of her waistband; her chiton top is no longer folded down, and its skirt is blue. She clasps a sword in her lowered right hand. The nude woman (left ankle and part of foot missing), to the right, holds in her left hand (ring on fourth finger) the object formerly held by "Cacu" on no. 7. In addition to her mantle, yellow necklace and crossed-bands, she wears a tiara (chipped on top). "Artile" is entirely similar to his counterpart on no. 7 except that he brings his left hand to his forehead rather than to the top of his head. On the ground the second added woman, dressed as on no. 7 but also with a necklace and detached sleeves, kneels on her left knee. She rests her head on her left hand and holds a sword in her right hand. Her eyes, like those of the two previous figures, are black. The altar has been replaced by rocks and the pillar by a bridled horse, to the left, between "Artile" and "Cacu," whose mantle falls over his left thigh and around his left arm. His wrists (left hand slightly damaged and missing most of thumb) are raised high and already bound with rope, the ends of which are blue and are firmly grasped by a completely nude man standing on the right, facing slightly to the left. This man also holds a sheathed sword with a baldric (the piece just below the rope) in his lowered right hand. A fourth man, now drawing his sword, corresponds to "Aulus" on nos. 6 and 7, but wears a belted (yellow bosses) tunic (traces of blue on the bottom of the overfold and on the skirt) which has slipped off his right shoulder. Drapery (his mantle?) falls between his legs. Excellent workmanship.

Each End: Within a frame of a simple fascia is the head of a demon, winged at the temples and wearing a torque.

Date: Second century B.C.

Bibliography: BrK, 1:107-108 and pl. 84 no. 2. Schlie, p. 174 no. 2. Hamburg, *Urnas*, pp. 37-38. Bianchi-Bandinelli, "Caratteri," p. 24. Messerschmidt, "Probleme," pp. 78, 80 fig. 18. Clifford, p. 307 fig. 7. Thimme II, p. 120 n. 20, p. 149 no. 2 and pl. III fig. 2 (detail). Brommer, *Denk*, 3:327 no. 8. Small, "Models," pl. 84 fig. 5. Small, "Cacu Imprisoned," fig. 3.

9.   Copenhagen H 298, from Città della Pieve,   Fig. 11
Purni Tomb

Alabaster urn.

Condition: Extremely good for the most part; some chips on the mouldings (chunk missing below the right foot of "Cacu"); traces of paint, as noted in description below.

Cover: Elaborately wreathed, semi-draped (left shoulder and lower torso) man holds a lei (portion above hand broken) in his left hand (ring on fourth finger) and a patera (lower edges badly chipped) in his right hand. He reclines against two tasseled cushions, placed on a coverlet, below the fringe of which runs an inscription: larϑ:purni:larϑal raufesa (*CIE* 1346). The arrangement and choice of elements closely recalls the cover of no. 8; Thimme (II, p. 120 n. 20) puts the two urns in the same workshop.

Crowning and Base Mouldings: Each, a wide fascia.

This urn is most analogous to no. 8, but with several adaptations related to no. 4, also from the same tomb. The four left-hand figures correspond to the four main figures on no. 8; the subsidiary, kneeling woman has been transferred back to the right of Cacu as on no. 7. The first woman, on the left, wears her hair long and tied with a fillet; her tunic top has been folded over. Instead of a sword she carries a small oinochoe in her lowered right hand. The nude woman (brown eyes) is entirely similar to no. 8 except that she no longer holds the rectangular object. A low, boxlike stool supports "Artile's" feet. The covered amphora of no. 7 leans at a sharp angle against the rocks. The horse now looks to the front and not to the left. "Cacu" rests his bound hands (left hand and part of right forearm broken away) on the hilt of his sheathed sword. Under each of his feet is a small pile of stones. He turns his head (with fillet) away from the scene on the right, which differs most from no. 8. A second horse (head to the right) is prevented from rearing by a nude man who holds its bridle (traces of red, as also on the left horse's bridle) firmly in his left hand and reaches around to the back of its head with his right hand. The man reflects the action of Aulus on no. 4 and recalls in pose the nude man on no. 8 who holds the rope binding "Cacu." His sword is still sheathed. Between him and "Cacu" the second, added woman, in a folded-over tunic, collapses with her right arm over her head—a position reminiscent of Cacu on no. 4. She wears a double bracelet on each wrist. The last figure on the right resembles no. 9 except in dress. He wears a fillet, a banded cuirass over a tunic, and a mantle fluttering behind his head.

Each End: Within a frame of a wide fascia (widest at the bottom) a winged, bare-breasted Scylla, to front, holds an oar diagonally in both hands with the blade to the front.

Date: Second century B.C.

Bibliography: BrK, 1:108 no. 2a. *BdI* 36 (1864):185. Poulsen, *Kat*, pp. 145-46 (Thimme notes that the inscription given here does not belong to this urn) and pl. 136. Messerschmidt, "Probleme," p. 81 fig. 19. Thimme II, p. 120 no. 1 and p. 134 (Early III Style). Brommer, *Denk*, 3:327 no. 7. Small, "Models," pl. 84 fig. 6.

APPENDIX II
MISATTRIBUTIONS TO CACUS

SCHOLARS now generally agree that no representations of Cacus (for depictions of Cacu, see Appendix I) occur before the Empire.[1] Most of the pre-imperial scenes assigned to Cacus purportedly showed him as the thief of Hercules' cattle; yet these objects, dated previous to the second century B.C. or more loosely prior to the Hellenistic period, by the arguments presented in Chapter I cannot ipso facto depict Cacus, for he only became a thief in the later period. Moreover, if Cacus did "live" during the sixth century B.C., then it would be extremely unusual for him to appear on contemporary objects—it took the Vibennae two centuries before they were depicted in the François Tomb[2]—much less on those of Greek manufacture;[3] for Cacus is an Etrusco-Roman figure. A brief comment accompanies each entry below to explain further why it should not portray Cacus. The objects are listed in general chronological order.

1. Louvre E 633, from Caere.
   Early Corinthian column-krater.
   Late seventh century B.C.

   A nude, bearded man forces a bearded prisoner, in a tunic and a petasos, to follow cows moving off to the right. Most recently the scene has been interpreted as Apollo and Hermes.

   Bibliography: Yalouris, pp. 171-73 no. 1 and 170-72 with illustrations. Krauskopf, pp. 21 and 71 n. 132.

2. London 560, from Capua.
   Etruscan bronze lebes.
   Sixth century B.C.

   In one of the engraved bands a figure is attached to a tree by his bound hands and feet. Hercules (with lionskin, club, and bow) moves off to the right behind his cattle. The scene may well represent the

---

[1] Yalouris, pp. 162-84. Brommer, "Caco," pp. 247-48. Krauskopf, pp. 21 and 71.
[2] For the floruit of both Cacu and the Vibennae, see Chapter I, pp. 13-16.
[3] The earliest extant Greek reference is the passage by Diodorus Siculus (4.21; Chapter I n. 56 for text) who wrote between 60 and 30 B.C.

MISATTRIBUTIONS TO CACUS

punishment of one of the thieves of Hercules' cattle—the problem is which one.[4]

Bibliography: *MonInst* 5:pl. 25 (the drawing most frequently reproduced). Walters, *CatBr*, pp. 80-81. Wolters in Münzer, *Cacus*, pp. 121-24. Haynes, *Utensils*, p. 16 fig. 1 and 17. Brommer, *Denk*, 1:36 (as questionable). Thuillier (as Cacus).

3. Oxford, Ashmolean Museum 211, from Gela.
   Attic black-figure lekythos.
   The Dot-Band Class.
   Sixth century B.C.

Gardner's interpretation is no longer held. On Side A Herakles is seen mounting a platform to play the cithara he holds. Completely distinct is Side B where a satyr reclines and plays the flutes, while Hermes approaches Paris with his cattle in a scene from the Judgement of Paris.

Bibliography: *ABV*, p. 484 no. 9. Gardner, "Cacus," pp. 70-76. Winter, pp. 272-73.

4. Nenfro relief in Tarquinia.
   Sixth century B.C.

One of the panels shows a bound prisoner preceding his guard who is in heroic nudity. The scene resembles the two human figures of no. 1 above. In this case the absence of cattle makes a connection with Cacus even more dubious than the other examples listed here. Moreover, nothing even identifies the guard as Hercules.

Bibliography: *NSc* (1942):36 fig. 11. Krauskopf, p. 71 n. 129. Pallottino, *Etruscans*, p. 285 and pl. 58.

5. Three Etruscan mirrors in:
   Collezione Borgia, now Naples?
   Paris, Louvre Br 1724
   Siena, Museo Archeologico (Room 3), from Chiusi.
   Fourth-third century B.C.

Messerschmidt (and after him Alföldi) interpreted the Louvre example as Cacu, on the right, writing down the wise sayings of the head, below on the left. Apparently he did not know the Siena and

---

[4] For references to examples, see Chapter I n. 87 and accompanying text.

Borgia examples which have inscriptions in the rim labelling the figures. Neither the name of Cacu nor of anyone associated with him appears—not to speak of the fact that Artile, and not Cacu, should be the scribe, who is called ALIUNEA on the Siena mirror. The head, URPHE on the Siena mirror, indicates that the scene is related to several Greek vases with the prophesying head of Orpheus as their subject. On the mirrors all the other figures are shadowy or unknown Etruscan characters, on whom see Bianchi-Bandinelli.

Bibliography: *ES*, 2:pl. 196 (Borgia—as suitors of Helen) and pl. 257a (Louvre—as the Kabirea). Bianchi-Bandinelli, "Clusium," pp. 543-52 and 545-46 fig. 10 (Siena). Messerschmidt, "Probleme," pp. 76 and 77 fig. 13. Cook, *Zeus*, 3:pt. 1, pp. 99-102 and pl. XVII (all three mirrors). Bisi, p. 744 fig. 906 (Siena). Alföldi, *ERL*, p. 229 n. 2. Schoeller, pp. 69-71.

6. London, BMCRR Romano-Campanian 113.
   Roman Republican coin (217-215 B.C.).
   Obverse: Female Head.
   Reverse: Hercules fighting a centaur.

For some unexplained reason Alföldi says "the centaur . . . may be Cacus." If a name must be given, Nessus is the more likely candidate, for Cacus did not become a centaur until the Renaissance (see Chapter I n. 10).

Bibliography: Alföldi, "Aspects," p. 70. For an illustration: Crawford, *RRC* 2:pl. VII fig. 5 no. 39/1.

7. Two Roman reliefs in Mainz and Darmstadt.
   Imperial.

These two reliefs of scrappy preservation from the provinces portray, among other scenes, Hercules seizing an opponent by the hair in preparation for a final blow from his club. The illustration of a very Roman story in the provinces, as well as the lack of any specific identifying characteristics for the victim, such as on the two imperial medallions (App. I n. 1), precludes a certain attribution. Hercules and a giant seems a more probable interpretation.

Bibliography: Espérandieu, *Gaule*, 7:275-76 no. 5731 (Mainz). Espérandieu, *Germanie*, pp. 152-53 no. 231 (Darmstadt). Brommer, *Denk*, 1:36 (Mainz) and 1:8 no. C 4 (Darmstadt), both as questionable.

APPENDIX III
MARSYAS IN THE FORUM

Notes on Use

1. This is not a catalogue, like Appendices I and II, but a list of all the extant sources pertaining to Marsyas in the Forum. The Appendix is divided into four sections: (A) Literary Sources; (B) Representations from Rome and Italy; (C) Imperial Coins; and (D) Imperial Inscriptions. In Sections A and B the items are arranged chronologically, but in C and D geographically. Each entry is assigned a number within its own section, e.g. III A 1.
2. Since the scholarship is enormous for certain pieces, such as B 2 and 3, only a selected bibliography is given. For Section C, the Imperial Coins, an attempt has been made to cite a published photograph for each coin.
3. Each section, as necessary, contains individual notes on use.

A. Literary Sources

Notes

1. All dates are from *OCD²*.
2. Only references that specifically mention the Marsyas in the Forum are included; others appear in the text and notes to Chapter IV.
3. Only the texts are given here; translations appear in Chapter IV.

1. Horace, *Satires* 1.6.119-21:

> . . . mihi quod cras
> surgendum sit mane, obeundus Marsya, qui se
> Voltum ferre negat Noviorum posse minoris.

30s B.C.

2. Seneca, *De Beneficiis* 6.32.1:

Divus Augustus filiam ultra impudicitiae maledictum impudicam relegavit et flagitia principalis domus in publicum emisit: admissos gregatim adulteros, pererratam nocturnis comissationibus civitatem, forum ipsum ac rostra, ex quibus pater legem de adulteriis tulerat, filiae in stupra placuisse, cotidianum ad Marsyam concursum, cum ex adultera in quaesturariam versa ius omnis licentiae sub ignoto adultero peteret.

50s A.D.

3. Pliny, *Historia Naturalis* 21.6 (8-9):

P. Munatius cum demptam Marsuae coronam e floribus capiti suo inposuisset atque ob id duci cum in vincula triumviri iussissent, appellavit tr. pl., nec intercessere illi . . . apud nos exemplum licentiae huius non est aliud quam filia divi Augusti, cuius luxuria noctibus coronatum Marsuam litterae illius dei gemunt.

70s A.D.

4. Martial, *Epigrams* 2.64.7-8:

> . . . fora litibus omnia fervent,
> ipse potest fieri Marsua causidicus.

86 A.D.

5. Acron *ad* Horace, *Satires* 1.6.120-21:

120. *obeundus Marsya.* Marsya dicitur locus [statua] in rostris, in quo solebant esse accusatores, quia ibi antea causae agebantur. [Statua in rostris erat, ad quam solebant homines convenire illi, qui inter se lites atque negotia conponebant]; nam [et a] ex statua nomen locus acceperat [, in quo solebant esse accusatores.].

121. *Vultum ferre negat Noviorum po. minoris.* Id est, minimi fratris Noviorum, cuiusdam feneratoris et ligatoris. Fratres Novii, [fuerunt], quorum minor ad locum, qui adpellatur 'Ad Marsyam', [fenerari] consueverat opsonari. Hi autem Novii fuerunt acerrimi feneratores, et iocatur de hac re Horatius. Ideo ait: puto Marsyam erectam unam manum habere, quoniam illorum feneratorum inpudentiam non potest sustinere; deinde quod ad statuam Marsyae vadimonium statuebatur.

Second century A.D.

MARSYAS IN THE FORUM

6. Charax (of Pergamon), *Etymologicon Magnum*:

ΚΟΛΩ'ΝΕΙΑ· κτητικὸς τύπος εἰς ἰδιότητα ἀναπέμπεται.

Φασὶ γάρ ποτε τὸν Διόνυσον ⟨μετὰ⟩ τὸν ἐπὶ Τυρσηνοὺς ἀπιόντα πόλεμον τοὺς γεγηρακότας τῶν Σειληνῶν μετὰ τῆς ἀχρήστου ἡλικίας ἐν Ἰταλίᾳ καταλιπεῖν· τοὺς δὲ τραπῆναι ἐπὶ ἀμπέλων ἐπιμέλειαν, καὶ εὔοινον γενέσθαι τὴν Ἰταλίαν· τοὺς δὲ γεωργοὺς οἱ Ἰταλοὶ κολώνους ἐκάλουν· ὡς καὶ ἱδρύσασθαι τοιαῦτα ἀγάλματα οἰνοφοροῦντα ἐν ἀσκοῖς.

Ἐσπούδαζον δὲ καὶ ἃς ᾤκουν πόλεις οἱ Ἰταλοὶ τιμὴν ταύταις παρέχειν, ἀνιστάντες δαίμονά τινα ὡς πρεσβύτην ὅμοιον Σειληνῷ, ἵνα καὶ τῇ κοινωνίᾳ τῶν ἱερῶν συγκραθῶσιν. Αἱ δὲ πέδαι περιτιθέμεναι δηλοῦσι τὸ ὑπήκοον, τῷ συνδεδέσθαι αὐτοῖς τὰς πόλεις τὰς ἐχούσας τὰ τοιαῦτα ἀγάλματα.

Ταῦτα εἴρηται Χάρακι ἱστοριογράφῳ.

Antonine, Second century A.D.

(The text is from Veyne, "Marsyas" 89, with translation, commentary, and references on 88-92.)

7. Porphyrion *ad* Horace, *Satires* 1.6.120-21:

120. 121. *qui se Vultum f. neg. Noviorum po. minoris.* Duo Novii fratres illo tempore fuerunt, quorum minor tumultuosus foenerator fuisse traditur. Satirice autem et eleganter hoc dictum, quasi ideo manum levet Marsyas, quod sustinere in Foro non possit hunc Novium. *Obeundus* autem *Marsyas*, quia in Foro vadimonium sistendum apud signum Marsyae sit.

Early third century A.D.

8. Servius *ad Aeneidem* 3.20:

quod autem de Libero diximus, haec causa est, ut signum sit liberae civitatis. nam apud maiores aut stipendiariae erant, aut foederatae, aut liberae. sed in liberis civitatibus simulacrum Marsyae erat, qui in tutela Liberi patris est.

Late fourth century A.D.

Virtually the same as 11 infra.

9. Servius *ad Aeneidem* 4.58:

    LYAEO dictus 'Lyaeus' ἀπὸ τοῦ λύειν, quod nimio vino membra solvantur; qui, ut supra (III 20) diximus, apte urbibus libertatis est deus; unde etiam Marsyas, minister eius, per civitates in foro positus vel libertatis indicium est, qui erecta manu testatur nihil urbi deesse.

    PATRIQUE LYAEO qui, ut supra (III 20) diximus, apte urbibus libertatis est deus; unde etiam Marsyas, eius minister, est in civitatibus libertatis indicium.

    Late fourth century A.D.

    Virtually the same as 10 below.

10. *Mythographi Vaticani* 3.9.13:

    Lyaeo, id est Baccho, qui, ut in sequentibus docebimus, apte urbibus libertatis est deus. Unde et Marsyas, eius minister, est in civitatibus libertatis indicium.

    Medieval.

    Virtually the same as 9 above.

11. *Mythographi Vaticani* 3.12.1:

    Civitates enim aut stipendiariae erant, aut foederatae, aut liberae. In liberis autem civitatibus in signum libertatis simulacrum Marsyae erat, qui in tutela Liberi patris est.

    Medieval.

    Virtually the same as 8 above.

12. Macrobius, *Saturnalia* 3.12:

    Lyaeus vero, id est Liber, urbibus liberatis est deus, unde Marsyas eius minister in civitatibus libertatis est indicium.

MARSYAS IN THE FORUM

Late fourth century A.D.

Virtually the same as 9 above.

B. Representations from Rome and Italy

NOTE: Because the statue of Marsyas in the Forum Romanum has not survived, it is not included in this list. The scholarship on it is cited in Chapter IV n. 9 and *passim*.

No representations, except on coins, have been preserved from areas outside of Italy.

1. Anaglypha Traiani, also known as the Plutei Traiani. Figs. 22-23

   Rome, now in the Curia, Forum Romanum. Found in the central area of the Forum Romanum between the Comitium and the Column of Phocas in 1872. See Plan 4b.
   Pair of marble reliefs.
   Hadrianic.

   Bibliography: *TDAR*, pp. 453-55, s.v. "Rostra Augusti." Dudley, p. 89 and pls. 23-25. *PDAR*, 2:176-77 (with extensive bibliography), figs. 902 (left panel) and 905 (right panel); p. 399 fig. 1190 (left panel, detail).

2. Denarius. Figs. 24-25b, d, e, f
   Lucius Marcius Censorinus. Mint-Rome.
   82 B.C. (Crawford).

   Bibliography: Crawford, *RRC*, pp. 377-78 no. 363, pl. XLVII.11.

3. Paestum, Museo Archeologico, from the Forum in Paestum. Fig. 27
   Bronze statuette. Height 1.035 m.
   Third-second century B.C.

   Bibliography: Brendel, "Funde," cols. 639-42, 641-42 figs. 25-26. Piganiol, "Marsyas," pp. 118-26. Sestieri, pp. 177, 182 n. 8 (dates to second or first century B.C.). Colonna, pp. 269, 271 fig. 66 (dates to second century B.C.). Zancani Montuoro, pp. 837-38 (dates to 100-50 B.C.). Bianchi-Bandinelli and Giuliano, p. 246 fig. 283 and 412 (dates to third-second century B.C.). *EAA* 4:271 fig. 320.

4. Once Dorpat, private—G. Loeschke. Now?   Fig. 28
From Rome.
Marble statuette, fragmentary (head and torso only). Preserved height 0.023 m.
Date: ? I have seen this statuette only in the Jordan drawing.

Bibliography: Loeschke, *BdI*, pp. 72-73. Jordan, *Marsyas*, pp. 8-9, pl. III C. Loeschke, *AA*, col. 14-15.

C. Imperial Coins

Notes

1. Several lists of the cities minting coins with the Marsyas in the Forum have been compiled—the later the date of publication the more complete the list. Generally they name the cities producing such coins with no further information; hence this section. The major lists are: Kornemann, pp. 580-81. Paoli, "Marsyas," pp. 101-111 (with previous bibliography). Veyne continues Paoli's numbering in "Marsyas," p. 93 n. 1 and p. 94 n. 2. L. Robert, *MAT*, pp. 55-56. Krzyżanowska, Table 13 (a chart displaying the issues with colonial types by emperor and city for Asia Minor). Bernhart, pp. 161-70.

2. The cities are listed according to numismatic conventions—geographically as in Head, *HN²*, rather than alphabetically as in Paoli, "Marsyas." The emperors and their relatives, whose portraits appear on the obverses, are collated in a chronological chart at the end of this section; because certain issues have not been thoroughly studied, there may be some gaps. Some issues were autonomous, and are so noted on the chart.

3. Unless otherwise noted, the coins are bronzes and the Marsyas appears alone on the reverses. Because of the number of variations even within an individual city's coinage, the surrounding devices, when they are used, will be described on select coins only to give an idea of the range of types. An analysis of the coins as a whole with all the devices and types considered lies beyond the present scope.

4. Unless otherwise qualified, the Marsyas on these coins stands with his right hand raised in an *adlocutio* and with his left hand holding a winesack balanced on his left shoulder. He generally has a slight bend at the knees. He is a silenus—old, with a receding hairline, full beard, slight paunch, and a tail. He wears boots. Any variations in these particular details indicate that another silenus is portrayed; that is, not all sileni carrying winesacks are Marsyas, much less the Marsyas in the Forum.[1] On the other hand, the

---

[1] Three cities are sometimes cited as striking coins with the Marsyas in the Forum, but the addition or substitution of different attributes and the absence of boots make all the identifications questionable. The cities are: (a) *Patras* (Peloponnese). Paoli ("Marsyas," pp. 110-11), as well as Veyne ("Marsyas," p. 94 n. 1), question this attribution. Only one example of this coin of disputed provenance has survived with the Marsyas on the reverse. While the piece may be dated without difficulty to Ha-

Marsyas may be depicted in left or right profile or more rarely to front, as shall be noted.

5. I have visited the following coin cabinets, and shall note with abbreviations given here in parentheses which issues of theirs I have studied: London, British Museum (BM); New York, American Numismatic Society (ANS); Oxford, the Ashmolean Museum (Ash); and Paris, Cabinet des Médailles (CM). I have not personally examined coins from nos. 1, 12, and 16; in all three cases the published photographs and/or the coins are poor and/or extremely worn, but they do appear to fit the rest of the series.

6. Not included in the list is a separate group of four cities (Athens, Germe in Lydia, Apamea-Celaenae in Phrygia, and Alexandria in Egypt) which struck coins with Marsyas the satyr of the musical contest with Apollo. These cities minted no coins with the Marsyas in the Forum and vice versa. In other words, there was a clear separation between the two Marsyae.

1. THESSALONIKI (Macedonia). Colony.
   Small Marsyas on left, to right, facing Janus.

   Bibliography: Veyne, "Marsyas," no. 24, and p. 96 where he compares this issue to the inscription from El Ust (here App. III D 3). Gäbler, p. 130 no. 67, pl. XXIV.27.

2. COELA in the Chersonese (Thrace). Municipium.
   Marsyas to right.
   Museums: Ash. BM. CM.

   Bibliography: Paoli, "Marsyas," p. 102 no. 7. Bernhart, nos. 1393-1401. Kraft, p. 155, pl. 50 no. 15. *BMC the Tauric Chersonese, Sarmatia, Dacia, Moesia, Thrace, etc.*, p. 192 no. 7 (Philip Sr.) and p. 193 no. 16 (Gallienus).

3. DEULTUM (Develtos) (Thrace). Colony.
   Marsyas to right or to left.
   Museums: Ash. CM.

   Bibliography: Paoli, "Marsyas," p. 104 no. 10. Veyne, "Marsyas," fig. 2. Bernhart, nos. 1387-92. Jurukova, pp. 5, 11-12, 22-23, 35; nos. 5, 33, 41,

---

drian, the inscription on the reverse, Col. A. Patr., is not among the abbreviations generally used for Patras. It is listed as Bernhart, no. 1402. (b) *Bizya* (Thrace): a silenus, standing to left, wears a diazoma and carries a kantharos, in addition to the askos. See *BMC The Tauric Chersonese, Samartia, Dacia, etc.*, p. 88 nos. 1-2; Bernhart, no. 1386. (c) *Parlais* (Pisidia): standing, bearded silenus to left, raises his right hand and holds a krater in his left hand. Veyne, "Marsyas," p. 93 n. 1 no. 25. Imhoof-Blumer, *AGM*, pp. 92-93 no. 264 (with question mark as Marsyas), pl. IV.1. Aulock, "Parlais," p. 18 no. 34, pl. 2.34.

MARSYAS IN THE FORUM

70, 143, 196, 214, 256, 293, 340, 362, 365, 407-408, 421, 446-47, 476-77, 497; all are illustrated except nos. 70, 446, and 477.

4. APAMEA (Myrlea) (Bithynia). Colony.
    Marsyas to right.
    Museums: BM.

    Bibliography: Paoli, "Marsyas," p. 102 no. 4. Bernhart, no. 1407a. *BMC Pontus, Paphlagonia, Bithynia, and the Kingdom of Bosporus*, p. 113 no. 31 (Julia Domna).

5. PARIUM (Mysia). Colony.
    Marsyas to left, with right foot raised slightly.
    Museums: BM.

    Bibliography: Paoli, "Marsyas," p. 106 no. 17. Bernhart, no. 1407.

6. ALEXANDRIA TROAS (Troas, Asia Minor).   Fig. 26a
    Colony.
    Marsyas to left or to right, sometimes on a high base.
    Museums: ANS. BM. CM.

    Bibliography: Paoli, "Marsyas," p. 101 no. 1. Bernhart, nos. 1408-17a, pl. X.33 (no. 1416). Jordan, *Marsyas*, pl. III B. Bellinger, pp. 46-47 nos. 57-58, pl. XI. Salmon, fig. 60. *BMC Troas, Aeolis, and Lesbos*, p. 19 nos. 78-79 (Commodus), pl. V.9; p. 23 no. 109 (Caracalla); p. 27 no. 146 (Trebonius Gallus), pl. VI.8; p. 28 no. 147 (Trebonius Gallus); p. 31 no. 182 (Gallienus).

7. ANTIOCH (Pisidia). Colony.
    Marsyas to left, sometimes on base.
    Museums: CM.

    Bibliography: Paoli, "Marsyas," p. 102 no. 3. Bernhart, no. 1418, pl. X.36. Krzyżanowska, pp. 29 (type struck only under Marcus Aurelius), pp. 119, 139, pl. IV Table 7 fig. 6.

8. CREMNA (Pisidia). Colony.
    Marsyas in three-quarter view to left, and to front.
    Museums: BM.

    Bibliography: Paoli, "Marsyas," p. 103 no. 8. Kubitschek, "Statue," pp. 151-54. Kubitschek, "Marsyas," pp. 198-200 (with five examples illustrated).

9. ICONION (Konia) (Lycaonia). Colony.
Marsyas to left.
Museums: BM.

Bibliography: L. Robert, *MAT*, pp. 55-56. Bernhart, no. 1419. Aulock, *Lykaoniens*, p. 90 nos. 483-84 (Gallienus).

10. MALLOS (Cilicia). Colony.
Obverse: In the center the founder of the city in military garb delivers a statuette of the Marsyas (to right) on his outstretched right hand to the Tyche of the city, standing on the left, to right. On the far right, a colonist crowns the founder with his right hand; sometimes with two quadrupeds standing to right in front of him.
Museums: BM.

Bibliography: Veyne, "Marsyas," no. 27, fig. 4. Cesano, "Medagliere," pp. 206-208, pl. X.9. Cesano, "Bronzo," pp. 53-55.

11. NINICA CLAUDIOPOLIS (Cilicia). Colony.
Marsyas sometimes almost to front, with right foot slightly raised; sometimes to left.
Museums: BM. CM.

Bibliography: Paoli, "Marsyas," pp. 105-106 no. 14. Bernhart, nos. 1421-22. Kubitschek, "Ninica," pp. 12, 19 no. 12 (pl. 2.15), and p. 24 no. 26. *BMC Lycaonia, Isauria, and Cilicia*, p. 117 no. 7 (Maximinus), pl. XXI.4.

12. PALMYRA (Syria). Colony.
Marsyas to left before a column on the left.

Bibliography: Paoli, "Marsyas," p. 106 no. 16. Le comte du Mesnil du Buisson, pl. XCII no. 3; XCIII-XCIV nos. 3, 5, and 6 (all examples illustrated here are extraordinarily worn).

13. LAODICEA ad mare (Syria). Free city.
Marsyas sometimes alone to left or to right. Under Caracalla and Elagabalus sometimes Marsyas stands on the left, facing toward or away from Tyche seated on the right, to left.
Museums: BM. CM.

Bibliography: Paoli, "Marsyas," p. 105 no. 12. Veyne, "Marsyas," fig. 3 (Marsyas alone). Bernhart, nos. 1424-29. *BMC Galatia, Cappadocia, and Syria*, p. 261 no. 104 (Elagabalus, with Tyche), pl. XXXI.3.

14. DAMASCUS (Syria). Colony.   Fig. 26d
   Obverse: Philip Senior; Reverse: Marsyas to right before a tree, on the right.
   Obverse: Octacilia; Reverse: Marsyas, to left, within a shrine above a river god reclining to the left in a grotto.
   Museums: BM. CM.

   Bibliography: Paoli, "Marsyas," p. 103 no. 9. Bernhart, nos. 1430-34. Price and Trell, p. 210 fig. 433.

15. BERYTOS (Phoenicia). Colony.   Figs. 26i, j
   Within a gate, topped by horned altars, Marsyas stands to left or to right on a high base; above, Dionysos on a panther, to right.
   Museums: ANS. BM. CM.

   Bibliography: Paoli, "Marsyas," p. 102 no. 5. Bernhart, nos. 1435-38, pl. X.39 (no. 1438). Trell, figs. 50-52. Price and Trell, p. 155 fig. 276. *BMC Phoenicia*, pp. 56-57 nos. 27-38 (without heads of emperors, and Marsyas alone, to left or right, on obverses), pl. VIII.1-4 (nos. 27, 31, 35, 36 respectively); pp. 81-83 nos. 191-205 (Elagabalus), pl. X.9-11 (nos. 194, 197, 204 respectively).

16. CAESAREA (Phoenicia). Colony.
   Within a temple, on the left Astarte with left foot on river god and male figure, on right, crowning her; below, in exergue Marsyas(?) to left.

   Bibliography: L. Robert, *MAT*, pp. 55-56. Bernhart, no. 1439. *BMC Phoenicia*, p. 110 no. 8 (Elagabalus), pl. XIII.9.

17. AKKO (Ace) PTOLEMAIS (Phoenicia). Colony.
   Sometimes with thunderbolt on left, Marsyas to right, caduceus on right (Philip Junior); sometimes with Tyche and Nike (Salonina).
   Museums: Ash.

   Bibliography: L. Robert, *MAT*, pp. 55-56. Kadman, pp. 78-79, 124 no. 163 (Elagabalus); p. 136 no. 223 (Philip Jr.), p. 142 no. 252 (Gallienus); p. 144 no. 262 (Salonina); p. 201 no. 103 (Philip Jr.)—all are illustrated except no. 103.

18. SIDON (Phoenicia). Colony.   Figs. 26e, f
   Several elaborate types:
   (a) Obverse: Elagabalus. Reverse: Within a temple of Astarte,

diminutive Marsyas on left, to right; Astarte in center, to front; Nike on column, on right, crowning Astarte.

(b) Obverse: Elagabalus. Reverse: Same three figures as "a," but without the temple structure.

(c) Obverse: Julia Paula. Reverse: Same as "b," but with two palm trees added.

(d) Obverse: Elagabalus. Reverse: Within a sanctuary of Astarte/Europa a small Marsyas in center, to left, and flanked by two statues on pillars; in pediment above, Europa on the bull, to right.

Museums: BM. CM.

Bibliography: Paoli, "Marsyas," pp. 106-107 no. 18. Bernhart, no. 1440. Trell, figs. 2, 4, 8, 101-104. Price and Trell, opposite p. 13 (color) and p. 157 fig. 277 ("d" above). *BMC Phoenicia*, p. 184 no. 243, pl. XXIV.4 ("a" above); p. 184 no. 242, pl. XXIV.3 ("b" above,); and p. 192 no. 289, pl. XXV.2 ("c" above); p. 192 no. 290, pl. XXV.3 ("a" above).

19. TYRE (Phoenicia). Colony. Figs. 26g, h
    Several types:

(a) Obverse: Julia Domna. Reverse: Very similar to Sidon (no. 18) Type "b"; from left to right—trophy; tiny Marsyas, to right; Astarte, to front; Nike on a column.

(b) Obverse: Philip Senior. Reverse: Top, same as "a"; below, four women (cities) performing a sacrifice with an altar in the middle.

(c) Obverse: Alexander Severus. Reverse: Marsyas, to right; a prow?; palm tree.

Museums: ANS. BM. CM.

Bibliography: Paoli, "Marsyas," pp. 107-109 no. 20. Bernhart, nos. 1441-47, 1456 d and e; pl. X.34 (no. 1444) and 37 (no. 1442). Trell, fig. 96. *BMC Phoenicia*, p. 269 no. 369, pl. XXXII.7 ("a" above); p. 270 nos. 372-73; pp. 273-74 nos. 385, 388-93, pl. XXXIII.1 (no. 389); p. 279 no. 419; p. 280 no. 423; p. 282 nos. 431-33, pl. XXXIV.1 (no. 433—"b" above); pp. 283-84 nos. 436, 438; p. 286 nos. 449-51, pl. XXXIV.7 (no. 449); p. 291 nos. 474-75.

20. NEAPOLIS (Samaria). Colony. Figs. 26b, c

Marsyas, on the left, to right, with a hill (Mt. Gerizim) and an eagle with outspread wings on the right. The two groups of figures can be reversed. A Victory may be substituted for the eagle, or two city goddesses may flank Marsyas with Mt. Gerizim above.

MARSYAS IN THE FORUM

Marsyas may stand alone.
Museums: BM. CM.

Bibliography: Paoli, "Marsyas," p. 105 no. 13. Bernhart, nos. 1448-54, pl. X.35 (no. 1449) and 41 (no. 1451). *BMC Palestine*, p. 64 nos. 117-21 (Philip Senior), pl. VI.17 (no. 119) and VI.18 (no. 120); p. 67 no. 132 (Philip Senior and Junior)—with Victory; p. 68 no. 137 (Octacilia Severa), pl. VII.8 (two city goddesses); p. 69 no. 144 (Philip Junior); p. 74 nos. 166-67 (Volusianus).

21. BOSTRA (Arabia). Colony.
    Marsyas to right.
    Museums: ANS. BM.

Bibliography: Paoli, "Marsyas," p. 102 no. 6. Bernhart, nos. 1455-56. Kubitschek, "Bostra," p. 187. *BMC Arabia, Mesopotamia and Persia*, pp. 21-22 nos. 28-30 (Alexander Severus), pl. IV.8 (no. 29).

D. Imperial Inscriptions

NOTE
1. The inscriptions, like the coins, are arranged geographically.
2. Except for one questionable inscription,[2] all those extant come from North Africa. None of these sites appear to have struck any coins with the Marsyas as a device.

[2] An inscription from Olbasa in Pisidia, a colony, has been interpreted by Kubitschek ("Marsyas," pp. 199-200) as referring to the statue of Marsyas. This identification has been accepted by Paoli ("Marsyas," p. 106 no. 15) and Veyne ("Marsyas," p. 94 n. 1). The inscription, on a round base, is as follows:

AVREL NICO DVo uir col. sta
TVAM DEI MARONIS dul
CISSIMAE PAtriae de suo

ΑΥΡΗΛΙΟC ΝΙΚΩΝ ΔΥΑΝδρι
ΚΟC ΤΗC ΚΟΛ· ΤΟΝ ΑΝΔΡΙ
ΑΝΤΑ ΤΟΥ ΜΑΡΩΝΟC ΤΗ ΓΛΥ
ΚΥΤΑΤΗ ΠΑΤΡΙΔΙ ΕΚ ΤΩΝ
ΙΔΙΩΝ

[*CIL* III:6888.]
I question Kubitschek's equation of Maron with Marsyas for two reasons. (1) Nonnus in Book 19 of his *Dionysiaca* clearly distinguishes the two as separate figures, for after the contest proper between Maron and Seilenos (a third character here) Marsyas's story is told belatedly as a moral for Maron. This passage begins, "νήπιε [Μάρων], τίς σε δίδαξεν ἀρειοτέροισιν ἐρίζειν;/Σειληνὸς πάλιν ἄλλος, . . ." (19.316-18). Nonnus's "Σειληνὸς . . . ἄλλος" neatly explains my position. (2) Since there was more than one silenus and nothing in the inscription itself indicates that the statue stood in the forum, there seem to be no grounds to assume that the statue in Olbasa was of Marsyas.

Distribution and Date of Greek Imperial Coins with Marsyas in the Forum

Cities	Hadrian	Antoninus Pius	Marcus Aurelius	Commodus	Septimius Severus	Julia Domna	Geta	Caracalla	Macrinus	Diadumenianus	Elagabalus	Julia Maesa	Julia Paula	Alexander Severus	Julia Mamaea	Maximinus	Gordian III	Tranquillina	Philip Senior	Otacilia Severa	Philip Junior	Trajan Decius	Trebonius Gallus	Volusianus	Valerian	Gallienus	Salonina	Claudius II	Aurelian	Autonomous
1 Thessaloniki																						•								
2 Coela								•			•						•		•				•	•		•				
3 Deultum						•			•	•				•		•	•	•	•		•									
4 Apamea						•																								
5 Parion			•	•										•		•									•	•	•			•
6 Alexandria Troas			•	•																					•	•	•			•
7 Antioch			•																							•				
8 Cremna	•	•	•	•	•	•	•	•	•	•	•	•	•	•	•	•	•	•	•	•	•	•	•	•	•	•	•	•	•	
9 Iconium																										•				
10 Mallos														•	•		•													•
11 Nimca Claud					•									•		•														
12 Palmyra																							•							
13 Laodicea					•	•		•	•		•			•									•							
14 Damascus								•	•	•	•								•		•		•							
15 Berytos											•																			
16 Caesarea											•																			
17 Akko Ptolemais											•										•									
18 Sidon												•	•														•			
19 Tyre						•	•	•		•	•						•		•	•	•		•	•	•	•				
20 Neapolis																			•	•	•			•						
21 Bostra															•				•											

MARSYAS IN THE FORUM

1. FURNI (Proconsular Africa). Municipium.
   On a base:

   [. Ge]ntius Proculus Rogatia-|nus, f(lamen) p(erpetuus), L. Genti Zebuciani | f(laminis) p(erpetui) fil(ius), signum Marsuae ex|[hs] VII mil(ibus) [dedi]t, ob cujus de-|dicationem ludos scaeni-|cos biduo edidit et epu-|lum decurionibus et cu-|riis omnibus dedit. L(oco) d(ato) d(ecreto) d(ecurionum).

   Bibliography: Text from Veyne, "Marsyas," pp. 92-93 (his no. 28). G.-C. Picard, "Séance," pp. 85-88 (with comments of others).

2. ALTHIBUROS (Medeina), Tunisia (Proconsular Africa). Municipium.
   On a base, found in the middle of the Forum:

   ```
     C · IVLIVS · Q · F · FELIX
     AVRVNCVLEIANVS · AED ·
     OB · HONOREM · AEDILITATIS · SIGNVM ·
     MARSYAE · QVOD · EX · HS · ĪĪCCCC · Ñ · CVM ·
   5 LEGITIMA · SVM · TAXAVERAT · ADIECT ·
     AMPLIVS · PEC · POSVIT ET DEDIC ·
     D · D · IDEMQ · PRIMVS · LVDOS · DEDIT ·
   ```

   Bibliography: Text from *CIL* VIII:27771. Paoli, "Marsyas," p. 101 no. 2.

3. EL UST, Tunisia (Proconsular Africa).

   [pro s]alute imp. Caes. M. Aureli Comm[odi] Antonini Pii Fel[icis Aug.] Ger[manici Sarmatici Britannici pontif.] max. trib. potest XIII imp. VIII cos. V. p. p. C. Ortius L. f. Corn. Luciscus pra[ef.? i. d. sacerdos Cer]erum qq. sacerdos publicus deae Caelestis et Aesculapi arcum quem suo et C. O[rt]i O . . . . . [fili sui] [nomine p]ro praecipua erga sanctissimum numen relig(ione) proque perpetus patriae amore pro[miserat, sua pec(unia) fecit; a]mplius statua(m) Iano patri perfecit et dedicavit; statuam quoque in foro Mar[sya]e . . . . . . [constituit; o]b cuius dedicatione(m) ludos [sc]aenico s[et] epulum curiis et Caerealicis ex(h)ibuer[unt] . . .

   Bibliography: Restoration of text from *CIL* VIII:16417, dated to 188 A.D. Paoli, "Marsyas," p. 110 no. 22. Veyne, "Marsyas," p. 94 n. 1, p. 96 n. 1 (compares it to the coin from Thessaloniki, C 1 above).

MARSYAS IN THE FORUM

4. LAMBAESIS, Algeria. Municipium or Colony.

    a. PGEMINIVS ROGAT
       ANVS FL PP EX DEC AL
       FL IS VI N INLATA ET
       A M SVM LEG IS XI
       N ET AD OPVS CV
       RIAE IS X N ITEM

    b. STATVAM MARŠAE
       QVE · FLL B · PP
       AVREIS SIN
       GVLIS ET HO
       NOR FVNCTS
       DVPLIS ET

    c. COND SED
       ET CVRIAL
       SPORTVLIS
       DATIS POSV
       IT

Bibliography: Text from *L'Année Epigraphique* (1914):7 no. 40. Paoli, "Marsyas," pp. 104-105 no. 11. Veyne, "Marsyas," pp. 94-95.

5. TIMGAD (Thamugadi), Algeria (Numidia). Colony.
On a six-sided column:

     PRO SALVTE ET VC
     TORIA IMP · NER
     VAE TRAIAN CAES
  5 AVG GERMANICI
     DACICI · CONDITO
     RIS COL·T·FLAVIVS
     FELIX CONDVCTOR
     QVINTARVM · MAR
 10 SYAN SPFID

Bibliography: Text from *CIL* VIII:17841. Paoli, "Marsyas," p. 107 no. 19 (notes that the inscription is Trajanic).

6. VERECUNDA (Markouna), Algeria. Municipium.
On a cippus:

PRO SA	C IVLI	PROM
LVTE	VS VIC	SERAT
ET IN	TORI	SVAPE

MARSYAS IN THE FORUM

	COLV	NVS	CVNIA
5	MITA	AEDI	FECIT
	TE DD	LIS STa	ET DE
	NN VA	TVAM	DICA
	LERIA	MAR	VIT 🌿
	NI ET	SYAE	
10	GALLI	QVM	
	ENI	Ob ho	
	AVGG	noREM	
		aeDIL	
		iTAt	

Bibliography: Text from *CIL* VIII:4219. Paoli, "Marsyas," pp. 109-110 no. 21. Veyne, "Marsyas," pp. 94-95.

ABBREVIATIONS AND SELECTED BIBLIOGRAPHY

ABBREVIATIONS for journals and basic references follow those listed in the *American Journal of Archaeology* 82 (1978):5-10 and 84 (1980):3-4.

ABV	J. D. Beazley. *Attic Black-Figure Vase-Painters*. Oxford, 1956.
Alföldi, "Apollo"	A. Alföldi. "Redeunt Saturnia regna, IV: Apollo und die Sibylle in der Epoche der Bürgerkriege." *Chiron* 5 (1975):165-92.
Alföldi, "Aspects"	———. "The Main Aspects of Political Propaganda on the Coinage of the Roman Republic." *Essays in Roman Coinage Presented to Harold Mattingly*, pp. 63-95. Oxford, 1956.
Alföldi, *ERL*	———. *Early Rome and the Latins*. Ann Arbor, 1963.
Alföldi, *SVR*	———. *Die Struktur des voretruskischen Römerstaates*. Heidelberg, 1974.
Alföldi, *Vater*	———. *Der Vater des Vaterlandes im römischen Denken*. Darmstadt, 1971.
Allen and Greenough	J. B. Greenough; G. L. Kittredge; A. A. Howard; and B. L. D'Ooge, eds. *Allen and Greenough's New Latin Grammar*. Boston, 1931.
Altheim, *Religion*	F. Altheim. *A History of Roman Religion*. London, 1938.
Andrén, "Dionysius"	A. Andrén. "Dionysius of Halicarnassus on Roman Monuments." *Hommages à Léon Herrmann*, pp. 88-104. *CollLat* 44. Brussels, 1960.
ANF	J. Donaldson, and A. Roberts, eds. *The Anti-Nicene Fathers*. Vol. VII. Translated by A. C. Coxe. Reprint. Grand Rapids, Mich., n.d.
ANRW	H. Temporini, ed. *Aufstieg und Niedergang der römischen Welt*. Berlin and New York, 1972-.
APS	A. Cambitoglou, and A. D. Trendall. *Apulian Red-Figured Vase-Painters of the Plain Style*. Tokyo, 1961.
*ARV*²	J. D. Beazley. *Attic Red-Figure Vase-Painters*. 2nd ed. Oxford, 1963.
Aulock, *Lykaoniens*	Hans von Aulock. *Münzen und Städte Lykaoniens*. *IstMitt-BH* 16 (Tübingen, 1976).
Aulock, "Parlais"	———. "Kleinasiatische Münzstätten X. Parlais in Pisidien." *JfNG* 23 (1973):7-18.

BIBLIOGRAPHY

Bartoli	A. Bartoli. "Marsia e Apollo sul Palatino." *BdA* 37-38 (1952-53):1-8.
Basanoff, *Pomerium*	V. Basanoff. *Pomerium Palatinum*. MemLinc ser. 6, vol. 9, fasc. 1 (Rome, 1939).
Bayet, "Arcadisme"	J. Bayet. "Les origines de l'arcadisme romain." *MélRome* 38 (1920):62-143.
Bayet, "Funéraire"	———. "Hercule Funéraire." *MélRome* 39 (1921-22): 219-266; 40 (1923):19-102.
Bayet, *Herclé*	———. *Herclé*. Paris, 1926.
Bayet, *Hercule*	———. *Les origines de l'Hercule romain*. BEFAR 132. Paris, 1926.
Bayet and Baillet *Tite-Live*	———, and G. Baillet. *Tite-Live Histoire romaine*. Vol. 5, bk. 5 (Paris, 1954).
Becker	C. Becker. "Der Schild des Aeneas." *WS* 77 (1964):111-27.
BEFAR	Bibliothèque des Écoles Françaises d'Athènes et de Rome.
Bellen	H. Bellen. "*Adventus Dei*. Der Gegenwartsbezug in Vergils Darstellung der Geschichte von Cacus und Hercules (Aen. VIII 184-275)." *RhM* 106 (1963):23-30.
Bellinger	A. R. Bellinger. "The Late Bronze of Alexandria Troas." *ANSMN* 8 (1958):25-53.
Berger	A. Berger. *Encyclopedic Dictionary of Roman Law*. TAPS n.s. vol. 43, pt. 2 (Philadelphia 1953).
Bernhart	M. Bernhart. *Dionysos und seine Familie auf griechischen Münzen. Numismatischer Beiträg zur Ikonographie des Dionysos*. *JfNG* 1 (Munich, 1949).
Bianchi-Bandinelli, "Caratteri"	R. Bianchi-Bandinelli. "I caratteri della scultura etrusca a Chiusi." *Dedalo* 6 (1925):5-31.
Bianchi-Bandinelli, *Center*	———. *Rome—The Center of Power*. Translated by P. Green. New York, 1970.
Bianchi-Bandinelli, "Clusium"	———. "Clusium. Ricerche archeologiche e topografiche su Chiusi e il suo territorio in età etrusca." *MonAnt* 30 (1925):209-578.
Bianchi-Bandinelli and Giuliano	———, and A. Giuliano. *Etruschi e italici prima del dominio di Roma*. 2nd ed. Milan, 1976.
Binder	G. Binder. *Aeneas und Augustus: Interpretationem zum 8. Buch der Aeneis. Beiträge zur Klassischen Philologie*. Vol. 38 (Meisenheim am Glan, 1971).
Bisi	A. Bisi. "Orfeo." *EAA* V:744-47.
Blatter	R. Blatter. "Hermes, der Rinderdieb." *AntK* 14 (1971):128-29.

BIBLIOGRAPHY

Bloch, *Prodiges*	R. Bloch. *Les prodiges dans l'antiquité classique*. Paris, 1963.
BMC and Area	*British Museum Catalogue of Greek Coins*. 29 volumes. London, 1873-1927.
Bömer, *Komm*	F. Bömer. *P. Ovidius Naso. Die Fasten*. Heidelberg, 1957-1958.
Bömer, "Studien"	———. "Studien zum VIII. Buche der Aeneis." *RhM* 92 (1944):319-69.
Bolchazy	L. Bolchazy. *Hospitality in Early Rome. Livy's Concept of Its Humanizing Force*. Chicago, 1977.
Bouché-Leclerq	A. Bouché-Leclerq. *Histoire de la divination dans l'antiquité. IV—Divination italique*. Paris, 1882.
Bréal	M. Bréal. *Mélanges de mythologie et de linguistique*. 2nd ed. Paris, 1882.
Brelich, *Tre*	A. Brelich. *Tre variazione romane sul tema delle origini*. Rome, 1956.
Brendel, *EtrArt*	O. Brendel. *Etruscan Art*. New York, 1978.
Brendel, "Funde"	———. "Archaeologische Funde in Italien, Tripolitanien, der Kyrenaika und Albanien von Oktober 1932 bis Oktober 1933. Regio III Lucania, Bruttii, Paestum." *AA* 48 (1933):cols. 639-42.
Brendel, "Persian"	———. "A Kneeling Persian: Migration of a Motif." *Essays in the History of Art Presented to Rudolf Wittkower*, pp. 62-70. London, 1967.
Brilliant, *Gesture*	R. Brilliant. *Gesture and Rank in Roman Art*. Memoirs of the Connecticut Academy of Arts and Sciences 14 (New Haven, 1963).
BrK	H. Brunn, and G. Körte. *I rilievi delle urne etrusche*. 3 vols. Berlin, 1870-1916.
Brommer, "Caco"	F. Brommer. "Caco." *EAA* 2:247-48.
Brommer, *Denk*	———. *Denkmälerlisten zur griechischen Heldensage*. 4 vols. Marburg, 1971-1976.
Brommer, *Vasen*[3]	———. *Vasenlisten zur griechischen Heldensage*. 3rd ed. Marburg, 1973.
Brown, *Hermes*	N. O. Brown. *Hermes the Thief*. New York, 1969.
Buchheit	V. Buchheit. *Vergil über die Sendung Roms. Untersuchungen zum Bellum Poenicum und zur Aeneis*. Gymnasium Supplement 3. Heidelberg, 1963.
Camps IV	W. W. Camps. *Propertius Elegies Book IV*. Cambridge, 1965.
Capovilla	G. Capovilla. *Eracle in Sicilia e nella Magna Grecia*. Milan, 1925.
Carcopino, *Passion*	J. Carcopino. *Passion et politique chez les Césars*. Paris, 1958.

BIBLIOGRAPHY

Carettoni, "Problemi"	G. Carettoni. "I problemi della zona augustea del Palatino alla luce dei recenti scavi." *RendPontAcc* 39 (1966-67):55-75.
Carpenter, *MAAR*	R. Carpenter. *Observations on Familiar Statuary in Rome.* *MAAR* 18. Rome, 1941.
Catalano	P. Catalano, *Contributi allo studio del diretto augurale.* I. Torino, 1960.
Catalano, "Aspetti"	———. "Aspetti spaziali del sistema giuridico-religioso romano. Mundus, templum, urbs, ager, Latium, Italia." *ANRW* Pt. II, vol. 16, pt. 1 (1978):440-553.
Cesano, "Bronzo"	S. L. Cesano. "Un bronzo coloniale di Giulia Mammaea per Mallus di Cilicia." *Transactions of the International Numismatic Congress (London 1936)*, edited by J. Allan, H. Mattingly, and E.S.G. Robinson, pp. 53-55. London, 1938.
Cesano, "Medagliere"	———. "Il medagliere del Museo Nazionale Romano. Seconda relazione." *Atti e Memorie dell' Istituto Italiano di Numismatica, Rome* 8 (1934):206-208.
Clairmont	C. W. Clairmont. "Studies in Greek Mythology and Vase-Painting: Apollo and Marsyas." *YCS* 15 (1957):161-78.
Clifford	H. R. Clifford. "Two Etruscan Funerary Urns in the New York University Archaeological Museum." *AJA* 41 (1937):300-314.
Coarelli, "Ara"	F. Coarelli. "Ara Saturni, Mundus, Senaculum." *DialAr* 9-10 (1976-77):346-77.
Coarelli, "Comizio"	———. "Il Comizio dalle origine alla fine della Repubblica: cronologia e topografia." *ParPass* 32, fasc. 174 (1977):166-238.
Coarelli, *Guida*	———. *Guida archeologica di Roma.* Verona, 1974.
Colini	A. M. Colini. *Storia e topografia del Celio nell' antichità.* *MemPontAcc* ser. 3, vol. 7 (1944).
CollLat	*Collection Latomus*
Colonna	G. Colonna. "Italica, Arte." *EAA* 4:251-74.
Le comte du Mesnil du Buisson	Le comte du Mesnil du Buisson. *Tessères et monnaies de Palmyre.* Paris, 1944.
Cook, *Zeus*	A. D. Cook. *Zeus.* Vol. III. Cambridge, 1940.
Crawford, *RRC*	M. Crawford. *Roman Republican Coinage.* 2 vols. Cambridge, 1974.
Cristofani, *Etrusco*	M. Cristofani. *Introduzione allo studio dell' etrusco.* Florence, 1973.
Cristofani, "Vulci"	———. "Ricerche sulle pitture della Tomba François di Vulci. I fregi decorativi." *DialAr* 1 (1967):186-219.

BIBLIOGRAPHY

Croft	P. Croft. *All Color Book of Roman Mythology*. London, 1974.
Crook	J. Crook. *Law and Life of Rome*. Ithaca, 1967.
CUE	M. Cristofani, et al. *Corpus delle urne etrusche di età ellenistica*. Vols. I-II pt. 1. Florence, 1975-1977.
P. C. Davies	P. C. Davies, trans. *Macrobius—The Saturnalia*. New York and London, 1969.
Del Chiaro, *EVP Caere*	M. Del Chiaro. *Etruscan Red-Figured Vase-Painting at Caere*. Berkeley and Los Angeles, 1975.
Del Chiaro, "Gasp"	———. "Etruscan Red-Figure's Dying Gasp." *RömMitt* 84 (1977):261-66.
De Ruyt, *Charun*	F. De Ruyt. *Charun, démon étrusque de la mort*. Brussels, 1934.
De Simone	C. De Simone. *Die griechischen Entlehnungen im Etruskischen*. 2 vols. Wiesbaden, 1968, 1970.
DKP	*Der Kleine Pauly*. Ed. K. Ziegler, W. Sontheimer, and H. Gärtner. 5 volumes. Munich, 1964-1975.
Dudley	D. R. Dudley. *Urbs Roma*. Aberdeen, 1967.
Dumézil, *ARR*	G. Dumézil. *Archaic Roman Religion*. Translated by P. Krapp. Chicago and London, 1970.
Dumézil, *Horace*	———. *Horace et les Curiaces*. Paris, 1942.
Eckhart	L. Eckhart. "Zum 'Torso vom Belvedere.' " *XI International Congress of Classical Archaeology*, pp. 69-70 (Abstract). London, 1978.
Eckhel	J. Eckhel. *Doctrina numorum veterum*. 8 vols. Vienna, 1792-1798.
Eden	P. T. Eden. *A Commentary on Virgil: Aeneid VIII*. Supplement 35: *Mnemosyne*. Leiden, 1975.
Ellis	R. S. Ellis. *Foundation Deposits in Ancient Mesopotamia*. New Haven, 1968.
ES	E. Gerhard. *Etruskische Spiegel*. 5 vols. Berlin, 1840-1897.
Espérandieu, *Gaule*	É. Espérandieu, and R. Lantier. *Recueil général des bas-reliefs de la Gaule romaine*. 15 vols. Paris, 1907-1966.
Espérandieu, *Germanie*	———. *Recueil générale des bas-reliefs de la Germanie romaine*. Paris, 1931.
EVP	J. D. Beazley. *Etruscan Vase-Painting*. Oxford, 1947.
Fauth	W. Fauth. "Hestia." *DKP* II 1118-19.
Flacelière, "Plutarque"	R. Flacelière. "Quelques passages des vies de Plutarque. 1. Thésée-Romulus." *REG* 61 (1948):67-103.
Flinck	E. Flinck. *Auguralia und Verwandtes*. Annales Academiae Scientiarum Fennicae, ser. B XI 10. Helsingfors, 1921.

BIBLIOGRAPHY

Fontenrose, *Python*	J. Fontenrose. *Python*. Berkeley and Los Angeles, 1959.
Fowler, *Festivals*	W. W. Fowler. *The Roman Festivals of the Period of the Republic*. London, 1925.
Frazer, *Fasti* II	J. G. Frazer. *The Fasti of Ovid*. Vol. II. London, 1929.
Froning	H. Froning. *Dithyrambos und Vasenmalerei in Athen*. Würzburg, 1971.
Gäbler	H. Gäbler. *Die antiken Münzen Nord-Griechenlands*. Vol. III, pt. 2. Berlin, 1935.
Gagé, *Apollon*	J. Gagé. *Apollon romain*. BEFAR 182. Paris, 1952.
Gagé, *Chute*	———. *La chute des Tarquins et les débuts de la République romaine*. Paris, 1976.
Gagé, "Dieu"	———. "Le dieu 'Inventor' et les Minucii." *MélRome* 78 (1966):79-122.
Gagé, "Diplomates"	———. "Diplomates inviolables ou magiciens de la trêve? Les règles de l'hospitium et l'assistance aux jeux sacrés dans la Rome primitive." *Cahiers Internationaux de Sociologie* 51 (1971):237-76. Reprinted in Gagé, *Enquêtes*, pp. 443-83.
Gagé, *Enquêtes*	———. *Enquêtes sur les structures sociales et religieuses de la Rome primitive*. CollLat 152. Brussels, 1977.
Gagé, "Mégalès"	———. "Mégalès ou Attus Navius? À propos du *ritus comitialis* étrusque et des symboles du *Comitium* romain." *Études offertes à Jean Macqueron*, pp. 331-39. Aix-en-Provence, 1970. Reprinted in Gagé, *Enquêtes*, pp. 119-34.
Gagé, "Tarquinies"	———. "De Tarquinies à Vulci: Les guerres entre Rome et Tarquinies au IVe siècle avant J.-C. et les fresques de la 'Tombe François.' " *MélRome* 74 (1962):79-122.
Gagé, "Rom."	———. "Romulus-Augustus." *MélRome* 47 (1930):138-81.
Galinsky, "Cacus"	G. K. Galinsky. "The Hercules-Cacus Episode in Aeneid VIII." *AJP* 87 (1966):18-51.
Galinsky, *Herakles*	———. *The Herakles Theme*. Totowa, New Jersey. 1972.
Galli	E. Galli. "Marsia sileno." *MemLinc* ser. 5, vol. 16 (1920):4-54.
Gantz, "Tarquin"	T. N. Gantz. "The Tarquin Dynasty." *Historia* 24 (1975):539-54.
Gardner, "Cacus"	P. Gardner. "Cacus on a Black-Figured Vase." *JHS* 13 (1893):70-76.
Gardthausen	V. Gardthausen. *Mastarna oder Servius Tullius*. Leipzig, 1882.

BIBLIOGRAPHY

Gauthier	P. Gauthier. "Notes sur l'étranger et l'hospitalité en Grèce et à Rome." *Ancient Society* 4 (1973):1-21.
Gelsomino	R. Gelsomino. *Varrone e i sette colli di Roma*. Università degli Studi di Siena. Collana di Studi e Testi 1. Rome, 1975.
Giglioli, *Arte*	G. Q. Giglioli. *L'Arte etrusca*. Milan, 1935.
Gilmartin	K. Gilmartin. "Hercules in the *Aeneid*." *Vergilius* 14 (1968):41-47.
Gioffredi	C. Gioffredi. "I tribunali del Foro." *Studia et Documenta Historiae et Juris* 9 (1943):227-82.
Gjerstad, *ER*	E. Gjerstad. *Early Rome*. 6 vols. Lund, 1953-1973.
Goidanich	P. G. Goidanich. "Rapporti culturali e linguistici fra Roma e gl' Italici: del dipinto vulcente di Vel Saties e Arnza." *StEtr* 9 (1935):107-118.
Gransden	K. W. Gransden. *Aeneid Book VIII*. Cambridge, 1976.
Guarducci, "Enea"	M. Guarducci. "Enea e Vesta." *RömMitt* 78 (1971):73-118.
Hackens and Van den Driessche	T. Hackens, and B. van den Driessche. *Antiquités italiques, étrusques et romaines. Choix de documents graphiques*. Vol. I: *L'Italie de la protohistoire à l'époque républicaine*. Louvain Document de Travail 7. Louvain, 1977.
Hamburg, *Urnas*	L. Hamburg. *Observations Hermeneuticae in Urnas Etruscas*. Berlin, 1916.
Hampe, "Dädalus"	R. Hampe. "Dädalus und Icarus auf spätrömischer Sigillatakanne." *Mansel 'E Armağan. Mélanges Mansel*, 1:25-30. Ankara, 1974.
Harris, *Rome*	W. V. Harris. *Rome in Etruria and Umbria*. Oxford, 1971.
Hauser	F. Hauser. "Zu den Institutsschriften." *AA* 5 (1890):68-69.
Haynes, *Utensils*	S. Haynes. *Etruscan Bronze Utensils*. London, 1965.
Head, *HN*[2]	B. V. Head. *Historia Numorum*. 2nd ed. Oxford, 1911.
Heichelheim, "Nymphai"	F. Heichelheim. "Nymphai (Kultstätten) C." *RE* XVII:1592-96.
Heisterbergk	B. Heisterbergk. "Zum ius Italicum. II. Die Marsyasstatuen." *Philologus* 50 (1891):639-47.
Helbig, *BdI*	W. Helbig. *BdI* 40 (1868):216.
Hermon	E. Hermon. "Réflexions sur la propriété à l'époque royale." *MélRome* 90 (1978):7-31.
Heurgon, "Coupe"	J. Heurgon. "La coupe d'Aulus Vibenna." *Mélanges d'archéologie, d'épigraphie et d' histoire offerts à J. Carcopino*, pp. 515-28. Paris, 1966.
Heurgon, *Rome*	———. *The Rise of Rome to 264 B.C.* London, 1973.
Heurgon, "Vegoia"	———. "The Date of Vegoia's Prophecy." *JRS* 49 (1959):41-46.

BIBLIOGRAPHY

Heurgon, *Vie*	J. Heurgon. *La vie quotidienne chez les étrusques.* Paris, 1961.
Hill	P. V. Hill. "The Temples and Statues of Apollo in Rome." *NC* ser. 7, vol. 2 (1962):125–42.
Hiltbrunner	O. Hiltbrunner. "Hostis und ΞΕΝΟΣ." *Festschrift für Friedrich Karl Dörmer*, pp. 424–46. Leiden, 1978.
Höfer, "Tarvos"	E. Höfer. "Tarvos Trigaranos." *ML* 5:128-32.
Holland, *Janus*	L. A. Holland. *Janus and the Bridge.* PAAR 21. Rome, 1961.
Hommel, "Vesta"	H. Hommel. "Vesta und die frührömische Religion." *ANRW* I.2. 397-420.
Hubaux	J. Hubaux. "L'aruspice et la sentinelle." *Mélanges Joseph Hombert. Phoibos* 5 (1950-51):73-85.
Huls, "Urne"	Y. Huls. "Urne funéraire inédite du Musée de Pérouse." *Bulletin de l'Institut Historique Belge de Rome* 27 (1952):133-40.
Hus, *Statuaire*	A. Hus. *Recherches sur la statuaire en pierre étrusque archaïque.* BEFAR 98. Paris, 1961.
Hus, *Vulci*	———. *Vulci étrusque et étrusco-romaine.* Paris, 1971.
Imhoof-Blumer, *AGM*	F. Imhoof-Blumer. *Antike griechische Münzen.* Geneva, 1913.
Jannot	J. R. Jannot. "La lyre et la cithare: Les instruments à cordes de la musique étrusque." *AntCl* 48 (1979):469-507.
Johannovsky	W. Johannovsky. "L'occupazione etrusca di Campania." In Alföldi, *ERL*, pp. 420-23.
Johnson, *Tribunal*	H. D. Johnson. *The Roman Tribunal.* Baltimore, 1927.
Jolowicz and Nicholas	H. F. Jolowicz, and B. Nicholas. *Historical Introduction to the Study of Roman Law.* 3rd ed. Cambridge, 1972.
Jordan, *Marsyas*	H. Jordan. *Marsyas auf dem Forum in Rom.* Berlin, 1883.
Jurukova	J. Jurukova. *Griechisches Münzwerk. Die Münzprägung von Deultem.* Schriften zur Geschichte und Kultur der Antike 8. East Berlin, 1973.
Kadman	L. Kadman. *The Coins of Akko Ptolemais.* Corpus Nummorum Palaestinensium, vol. I, pt. 4. Jerusalem, 1961.
Kapossy	G. Kapossy. "Marsyas und die Politik der Populares." *Gazette Numismatique Suisse* 15 (1965):74-79.
Körte, "Wandgemälde"	G. Körte. "Ein Wandgemälde von Vulci als Document zur römischen Königsgeschichte." *JdI* 12 (1897):57-80.
Kornemann	E. Kornemann. "Colonia." *RE* IV:510-88.
Kraft	K. Kraft. *Das System der kaiserzeitlichen Münzprägung in Kleinasien.* Berlin, 1972.

BIBLIOGRAPHY

Krauskopf	I. Krauskopf. *Der thebanische Sagenkreis und andere griechische Sagen in der etruskischen Kunst.* Mainz am Rhein, 1974.
Kroll	J. Kroll. *Gott und Hölle: Der Mythos vom Descensuskampfe.* Studien zur Bibliothek Warburg 20. Leipzig and Berlin, 1932.
Krzyżanowska	A. Krzyżanowska. *Monnaies coloniales d'Antioche de Pisidie.* Travaux du Centres d'Archéologie Méditerranéenne de l'Académie Polonaise des Sciences 7. Warsaw, 1970.
Kubitschek, "Bostra"	W. Kubitschek. "Bostra." *NZ* n.s. 9 (1916):182-94.
Kubitschek, "Marsyas"	———. "Marsyas und Maron in Kremne (Pisidien)." *Festschrift für Otto Benndorf*, pp. 198-200. Vienna, 1898.
Kubitschek, "Ninica"	———. "Ninica Claudiopolis." *NZ* 34 (1902 [1903]):1-28.
Kubitschek, "Statue"	———. "Eine Marsyas-Statue in Cremna (Pisidien)." *AEM* 20 (1897):151-54.
Lambrechts	P. Lambrechts. "La politique apollinienne d'Auguste et le culte impérial." *NouvClio* 5 (1953):65-82.
Latte, *RRG*	K. Latte. *Römische Religiongeschichte.* Handbuch der Altertumswissenschaft. Abt. 5, vol. 4. Munich, 1960.
Laviosa, *Scultura*	C. Laviosa. *Scultura tardo-etrusca di Volterra.* Milan 1965.
LAW	*Lexikon der Alten Welt.* Edited by C. Andresen et al. Munich, 1965.
LCL	*Loeb Classical Library.* Cambridge and London.
LCS	A. D. Trendall. *The Red-Figured Vases of Lucania, Campania and Sicily.* Oxford, 1967.
Le Bonniec, "Hercules"	H. Le Bonniec. "Hercules." In *dtv-Lexikon der Antike, II Religion, Mythologie.* Reprint of *LAW.* 1:302-303. Munich, 1970.
Le Gall	J. Le Gall. "Rites de fondation." *Studi sulla città antica. Atti del Convegno di Studi sulla Città Etrusca e Italica. Preromana*, pp. 59-65. Bologna, 1970.
Le Gall, "Rites"	———. "Les rites de fondation des villes romaines." *BAntFr* 1970 (1972):292-307.
Letta	C. Letta. *I Marsi e il Fucino nell' Antichità.* Milan, 1972.
Levi, "Chiusi"	D. Levi. "Regione VII (Etruria). III. Chiusi—La Tomba della Pellegrina." *NSc* ser. 6, vol. 7 (1931):474-505.
Levi, "Pellegrina"	———. "La Tomba della Pellegrina a Chiusi." *RivIstArch* 4 (1932-33):7-60, 101-144.
Lewis and Short	C. T. Lewis, and C. Short. *A Latin Dictionary.* Oxford, 1879.

BIBLIOGRAPHY

Lincoln	B. Lincoln. "The Indo-European Cattle-Raiding Myth." *History of Religions* 16 (1976):42-65.
Lintott	A. W. Lintott. *Violence in Republican Rome*. Oxford, 1968.
Loeschke, *AA*	G. Loeschke. "Erwerbungsberichte der Deutschen Universitätssammlungen Bonn." *AA* (1891):14-20.
Loeschke, *BdI*	———. "I. Adunanze dell' Instituto." *BdI* 50 (1878):72-73.
LSJ	H. G. Liddell; R. Scott; H. S. Jones; and R. McKenzie. *A Greek-English Lexicon*. 9th ed. Oxford, 1940.
Luce	T. J. Luce. "Political Propaganda on Roman Republican Coins: circa 92-82 B.C." *AJA* 72 (1968):25-39.
Lugli, *FTVUR*	G. Lugli. *Fontes ad topographiam veteris urbis Romae pertinentes*. 7 vols. Rome, 1952-1969.
Lyngby	H. Lyngby. "Ricerche sulla Porta Trigemina." *OpusRom* 6 (1963):75-96.
Magdelain, "*Auguraculum*"	A. Magdelain. "L'*Auguraculum* de l'*Arx* à Rome et dans d'autres villes." *REL* 47 (1969):253-69.
Magdelain, "Inauguration"	———. "L'inauguration de l'*urbs* et l'*imperium*." *MélRome* 89 (1977):11-29.
Magdelain, "Pomerium"	———. "Le pomerium archaïque et le mundus." *REL* 54 (1976):71-109.
Mannsperger	D. Mannsperger. "Apollon gegen Dionysos. Numismatische Beiträge zu Octavians Rolle als Vindex Libertatis." *Gymnasium* 20 (1973):381-404.
Marchese, "Mito"	L. Marchese. "Il mito di Amico nell' arte figurata." *StEtr* 18 (1944):45-81.
Marshall, "Library"	A. J. Marshall. "Library Resources and Creative Writing at Rome." *Phoenix* 30 (1976):252-64.
Martin, "Héraclès"	P. M. Martin. "Héraclès en Italie d'après Denys d'Halicarnasse A. R. I, 34-44." *Athenaeum* 56 (1972):252-75.
McCracken	G. E. McCracken, trans. *Arnobius of Sicca: The Case against the Pagans*. Westminster, Md., 1949.
Merlin	A. Merlin. *L'Aventin dans l'antiquité*. BEFAR 97. Paris, 1906.
Messerschmidt, "Probleme"	F. Messerschmidt. "Probleme der etruskischen Malerei des Hellenismus." *JdI* 45 (1930):62-90.
Messerschmidt, *Vulci*	———. *Nekropolen von Vulci*. JdI-EH 12. Berlin, 1930.
Metzger, *Rep*	H. Metzger. *Les représentations dans la céramique attique du IVe siècle*. BEFAR 172. Paris, 1951.
Michaelis, "Marsyas"	A. Michaelis. "Marsyas." *AZ* 27 (1869):41-50.
ML	W. H. Roscher. *Ausführliches Lexikon der griechischen und römischen Mythologie*. Leipzig, 1884-1937.

BIBLIOGRAPHY

Momigliano	A. Momigliano. *Claudius—The Emperor and His Achievement*. Translated by W. D. Hogarth. Oxford, 1934.
Morgan, "Heph II"	C. H. Morgan. "The Sculptures of the Hephaisteion II." *Hesperia* 31 (1962):221-35.
Müller-Deecke	K. O. Müller, and W. Deecke. *Die Etrusker*. 2 vols. Stuttgart, 1877. Revised by A. J. Pfiffig. Graz, 1963.
Müller-Karpe	H. Müller-Karpe. *Vom Anfang Roms*. RömMitt-EH 5. Heidelberg, 1959.
Münzer, *Cacus*	F. Münzer. *Cacus der Rinderdieb*. Basel, 1911.
Münzer, "Marcius"	———, et al. "Marcius." *RE* XIV:1535-1608.
Münzer, "Vibenna"	———. "Caeles Vibenna und Mastarna." *RhM* 53 (1898):596-620.
Neumann, *Gesten*	G. Neumann. *Gesten und Gebärden in der griechischen Kunst*. Berlin, 1965.
Ninck	M. Ninck. *Die Bedeutung des Wassers im Kulte und Leben der Alten*. Philologus Supplement 14.2. Leipzig, 1921.
OCD^2	N.G.L. Hammond, and H. H. Scullard, eds. *The Oxford Classical Dictionary*. 2nd ed. Oxford, 1973.
Ogilvie, *Comm*	R. M. Ogilvie. *A Commentary on Livy Books 1-5*. Oxford, 1970.
OGR	F. Pichlmayr, and R. Gruendel, eds. *Origo gentis romanae*. Leipzig, 1961.
Opelt, "Roma"	I. Opelt. "Roma=ΡΩΜΗ und Rom als Idee." *Philologus* 109 (1965):47-56.
Overbeck, *Gallerie*	J. Overbeck. *Gallerie heroischer Bildwerke*. Brunswick and Stuttgart, 1853 and 1857.
Pairault, *Recherches*	F.-H. Pairault. *Recherches sur quelques séries d'urnes de Volterra à représentations mythologiques*. Collection de l'École Française de Rome 12. Rome, 1972.
Pallottino, *Etr*	M. Pallottino. *Etruscologia*. 6th ed. Milan, 1968.
Pallottino, *EtrP*	———. *Etruscan Painting*. Geneva, 1952.
Pallottino, *Etruscans*	———. *The Etruscans*. Translated by J. Cremona. Edited by D. Ridgway. Bloomington and London, 1975.
Pallottino, "Iscrizione"	———. "A proposito della iscrizione veiente di Avile Vipiennas." *StEtr* 15 (1941):399.
Pallottino, "Specchio"	———. "Uno specchio di Tuscania e la leggenda etrusca di Tarchon." *RendLinc* ser. 6, vol. 6 (1930):49-87.
Palmer, *ACR*	R.E.A. Palmer. *The Archaic Community of the Romans*. Cambridge, 1970.
Palmer, *Religion*	———. *Roman Religion and Roman Empire. Five Essays*. Philadelphia, 1974.

BIBLIOGRAPHY

Paoli, "Marsyas"	J. Paoli. "Marsyas et le 'ius italicum.' " *MélRome* 55 (1938):96-130.
Paoli, "Statue"	———. "La statue de Marsyas au 'Forum Romanum.' " *REL* 23 (1945):150-67.
Para	J. D. Beazley. *Paralipomena*. Oxford, 1971.
Paratore	E. Paratore. "Hercule et Cacus chez Virgile et Tite-Live." *Vergiliana—Recherches sur Virgile*, edited by H. Bardon and R. Verdière, pp. 260-82. Leiden, 1971.
Parke, *Oracles*	H. W. Parke. *Greek Oracles*. London, 1967.
PDAR	E. Nash. *Pictorial Dictionary of Ancient Rome*. 2nd ed. 2 vols. New York and Washington, 1968.
Pease, *Comm*	A. S. Pease, ed. *M. Tulli Ciceronis de Divinatione*. University of Illinois Studies in Language and Literature 6 and 8. Urbana, 1920, 1923. Reprint Darmstadt, 1977.
PECS	R. Stillwell; W. L. MacDonald; and A. H. McAllister, eds. *The Princeton Encyclopedia of Classical Sites*. Princeton, 1976.
Peter, *HRR*[2]	H. Peter. *Historicum Romanorum Reliquiae*. Vol. I. 2nd ed. Leipzig, 1914.
Petersen, "Vibenna"	E. Petersen. "Caele Vibenna und Mastarna." *JdI* 14 (1899):43-49.
Pfiffig, "Prophezeiung"	A. J. Pfiffig. "Eine etruskische Prophezeiung." *Gymnasium* 68 (1961):55-64.
Pfiffig, *Religio*	———. *Religio Etrusca*. Graz, 1975.
Philippart	H. Philippart. "Iconographie de l' "Iphigénie en Tauride" d'Euripide." *RBPhil* 4 (1925):5-33.
G.-C. Picard	G.-C. Picard. "II. Le temple d'Apollon Palatin et la Maison d'Auguste." *REL* 51 (1973):349-51.
G.-C. Picard, "Séance"	———. "15 Décembre 1958. Séance de la Commission de l'Afrique du Nord." *BAC* (1958):85-88.
Piccaluga, *Terminus*	G. Piccaluga. *Terminus*. Studi e Materiali di Storia delle Religioni Quaderni 9. Rome, 1974.
Piganiol, "Hercule"	A. Piganiol. "Les origines d'Hercule." *Hommages à A. Grenier*, pp. 1261-64. *CollLat* 58. Brussels, 1962.
Piganiol, *Jeux*	———. *Recherches sur les jeux romains*. Strasbourg, 1923.
Piganiol, "Marsyas"	———. "Le Marsyas de Paestum et le roi Faunus." *RA* 22 (1944):118-26.
Platner, *TMAR*	S. B. Platner. *The Topography and Monuments of Ancient Rome*. Boston and New York, 1911.
Posner, *Archives*	E. Posner. *Archives in the Ancient World*. Cambridge, 1972.
Poucet, "Pictor"	J. Poucet. "Fabius Pictor et Denys d' Halicarnasse: Les enfances de Romulus et Remus." *Historia* 25 (1976):201-16.

BIBLIOGRAPHY

Poucet, *Sabine*	——. *Recherches sur la légende sabine des origines de Rome.* Université de Louvain. Recueil de Travaux d'Histoire et de Philologie, ser. 4, fasc. 37. Louvain, 1967.
Poulsen, *BildEtr*	F. Poulsen. *Bildertafeln des etruskischen Museums der Ny Carlsberg Glyptotek.* Copenhagen, 1928.
Poulsen, *Kat*	——. *Katalog des etruskischen Museums (Helbig Museum) der Ny Carlsberg Glyptotek.* Copenhagen, 1927.
V. Poulsen, *EtrSam*	V. Poulsen. *Ny Carlsberg Glyptotek: Den etruskiske Samling.* Copenhagen, 1966.
Preller-Robert	L. Preller, and C. Robert. *Griechische Mythologie.* 2 vols. 4th ed. Berlin, 1887-1926.
Preuner	A. Preuner. *Hestia-Vesta.* Tübingen, 1864.
Price and Trell	M. J. Price, and B. Trell. *Coins and Their Cities.* London and Detroit, 1977.
Radke, "Etrurien"	G. Radke. "Etrurien—Ein Produkt politischer sozialer und kultureller Spannungen." *Klio* 56 (1954):29-53.
Radke, *Götter*	——. *Die Götter Altitaliens.* Fontes et Commentationes 3. Münster, 1965.
Radke, *Viae*	——. *Viae publicae romanae. RE* Supplement XIII. Stuttgart, 1971.
Radke, "Vibenna"	——. "Vibenna." *RE* ser. 2, vol. VIII.2. (1958):2454-57.
Radke, "XVviri"	——. "Quindecemviri sacris faciundis, Libri Sibyllini." *RE* XXIV.1. (1963):1114-48.
Raubitschek, *Hearst*	I. K. Raubitschek. *The Hearst Hillsborough Vases.* Mainz, 1969.
Rawson, "Annalists"	E. Rawson. "The First Latin Annalists." *Latomus* 35 (1976):689-717.
Rawson, "Caesar"	——. "Caesar, Etruria and the *Disciplina Etrusca*." *JRS* 68 (1978):132-52.
Rawson, "Religion"	——. "Religion and Politics in the Late Second Century B.C. at Rome." *Phoenix* 28 (1974):193-212.
Rebuffat, "Tombe"	D. and R. Rebuffat. "De Sidoine Apollinaire à la tombe François." *Latomus* 37 (1978):88-104.
Reeker	H.-D. Reeker. *Die Landschaft in der Aeneis.* Spudasmata 27. Hildesheim and New York, 1971.
A. Reinach, "Marsyas"	A. Reinach. "L'Origine du Marsyas du Forum." *Klio* 14 (1914):321-37.
S. Reinach, *RépStat*	S. Reinach. *Répertoire de la statuaire grecque et romaine.* 4 vols. Paris, 1897-1930.
E. Richardson, *Etruscans*	E. Richardson. *The Etruscans.* Chicago and London, 1964.
E. Richardson, "Gods"	——. "The Gods Arrive." *ArchNews* 5 (1976):125-33.

BIBLIOGRAPHY

Richter, *SSG*   G.M.A. Richter. *The Sculptures and Sculptors of the Greeks.* 4th ed. New Haven and London, 1970.

Ridley, "Enigma"   R. T. Ridley. "The Enigma of Servius Tullius." *Klio* 57 (1975):147-77.

Robert, "Cacus"   C. Robert. "Cacus auf etruskischen Bildwerken." *Festgabe Hugo Blümner*, pp. 75-85. Zurich, 1914.

L. Robert, *MAT*   L. Robert. *Monnaies antiques en Troade.* Hautes Études Numismatiques 1. Geneva and Paris, 1966.

Romanelli, "Scavo"   P. Romanelli. "Lo scavo al tempio della Magna Mater sul Palatino e nelle sue adiacenze." *MonAnt* 46 (1963):201-338.

Ronzitti-Orsolini   G. Ronzitti-Orsolini. *Il mito dei Sette a Tebe nelle urne volterrane.* Studi dell' Ateneo Pisano 2. Florence, 1971.

Rose, *Handbook*   H. J. Rose. *A Handbook of Greek Mythology.* New York, 1959.

Roux   G. Roux. "Meurtre dans un sanctuaire sur l' amphore de Panagurište." *AntK* 7 (1964):30-41.

Ruch, "Devin"   M. Ruch. "La capture du devin (Tite-Live, V, 15)." *REL* 44 (1966):333-50.

Rumpf, *Kat*   A. Rumpf. *Staatliches Museum zu Berlin. Katalog der etruskischen Skulpturen.* Berlin, 1928.

RVA I   A. D. Trendall, and A. Cambitoglou. *The Red-Figured Vases of Apulia.* Vol. I: *Early and Middle Apulian.* Oxford, 1978.

Rykwert   J. Rykwert. *The Idea of a Town.* Princeton, 1976.

Salmon   E. T. Salmon. *Roman Colonisation under the Republic.* Ithaca, 1970.

Santoro   A. Santoro. *I problemi della composizione dell' Eneide. Livio fonte di Virgilio.* Altamura, 1938; Naples, 1947.

Sanz Ramos   J. Sanz Ramos. "La leyenda de Hércules y Caco en Virgilio y en Livio." *Congresso Español Estudios Clássicos. Actas* III.2 (1967-68):389-400.

Sbordone   F. Sbordone. "Il ciclo italico di Eracle." *Athenaeum di Pavia* n.s. 19 (1941):72-96 and 149-80.

Schaewen   R. von Schaewen. *Römische Opfergeräte.* Archäologische Studien I. Berlin, 1940.

Schauenburg, "Achilleus"   K. Schauenburg. "Achilleus in der unteritalischen Vasenmalerei." *BonnJBB* 161 (1961):215-35.

Schauenburg, "Bes. Marsyas"   ———. "Der besorgte Marsyas." *RömMitt* 79 (1972): 317-22.

Schauenburg, "Marsyas"   ———. "Marsyas." *RömMitt* 65 (1958):42-66.

Schefold, *DWP*   K. Schefold. *Die Wände Pompejis.* Berlin, 1957.

Schlie   F. Schlie. *Die Darstellungen des troischen Sagenkreises auf etruskischen Aschenkisten.* Stuttgart, 1868.

BIBLIOGRAPHY

Schneider	A. Schneider. "Aus Roms Frühzeit." *RömMitt* 10 (1895):160-78.
Schnepf	H. Schnepf. "Das Herculesabenteuer in Virgils Aeneis (VIII 184ff.)." *Gymnasium* 66 (1959):250-68.
Schoeller	F. M. Schoeller. "Darstellungen des Orpheus in der Antike." Ph.D. dissertation, Freiburg, 1969.
Scott, "ERTrad"	I. G. Scott. "Early Roman Traditions in the Light of Archaeology." *MAAR* 7 (1929):7-118.
Scullard, *Cities*	H. H. Scullard. *The Etruscan Cities and Rome.* London, 1967.
Sestieri	P. C. Sestieri. "Il Nuovo Museo di Paestum." *BdA* ser. 4, vol. 38 (1953):176-82.
Seston	W. Seston. "Les 'Anaglypha Traiani' du Forum Romain et la politique d'Hadrien en 118." *MélRome* 44 (1927):154-83.
Sherwin-White[2]	A. N. Sherwin-White. *The Roman Citizenship.* 2nd ed. Oxford, 1973.
Sichtermann, *SlgJatta*	H. Sichtermann. *Griechische Vasen in Unteritalien aus der Sammlung Jatta in Ruvo.* Tübingen, 1966.
Simon, "Apollo"	E. Simon. "Apollo in Rom." *JdI* 93 (1978):202-227.
Skutsch, "Enniana"	O. Skutsch. "Enniana IV: 'Condendae urbis auspicia.' " *CQ* 11 (1961):252-67.
Small, "Aeneas"	J. P. Small. "Aeneas and Turnus on Late Etruscan Funerary Urns." *AJA* 78 (1974):49-54.
Small, "Cacu Imprisoned"	———. "Cacu Imprisoned." *Adaptation et transformation de la mythologie gréco-romaine dans les régions limitrophes de l'empire romain.* Colloques internationaux du C.N.R.S. No. 593. (Paris, 1981):29-35.
Small, "Lucretia"	———. "The Death of Lucretia." *AJA* 80 (1976):349-60.
Small, "Matricide"	———. "The Matricide of Alcmaeon." *RömMitt* 83 (1976):113-44.
Small, "Models"	———. "Greek Models and Etruscan Legends: Cacu and the Vibennae." *Bronzes hellénistiques et romains—Tradition et renouveau. Actes du colloque international sur les bronzes antiques Lausanne, 8-13 Mai 1978,* pp. 133-39. Cahiers d'Archéologie Romande 17. Lausanne, 1979.
Small, *Studies*	———. *Studies Related to the Theban Cycle on Late Etruscan Funerary Urns.* Ph.D. dissertation, Princeton University, 1972. Rome, 1981.
Smith	R. E. Smith. "The Use of Force in Passing Legislation in the Late Republic." *Athenaeum* 55 (1977):150-74.
Stambaugh	J. E. Stambaugh. "The Functions of Roman Temples." *ANRW* Pt. II, vol. 16, pt. 1. 554-608.

BIBLIOGRAPHY

E. Strong, *Scultura*	E. Strong. *La scultura romano da Augusto a Costantino.* Florence, 1923.
Sutherland	C.H.V. Sutherland. *Roman Coins.* New York, 1974.
Sutton	D. F. Sutton. "The Greek Origins of the Cacus Myth." *CQ* 27 (1977):391-93.
Tanner	R. G. Tanner. "Some Problems in *Aeneid* 7-12." *Proceedings of the Virgil Society* 10 (1970-71):37-44.
Taylor, *Divinity*	L. R. Taylor. *The Divinity of the Roman Emperor.* Middleton, 1931.
Taylor, *Politics*	———. *Party Politics in the Age of Caesar.* Berkeley, Los Angeles, and London, 1971.
TDAR	S. B. Platner, and T. Ashby. *A Topographical Dictionary of Ancient Rome.* London, 1929.
Thimme I	J. Thimme. "Chiusinische Aschenkisten und Sarkophage der hellenistischen Zeit." *StEtr* 23 (1954):25-147.
Thimme II	———. "Chiusinische Aschenkisten und Sarkophage der hellenistischen Zeit." *StEtr* 25 (1957):87-160.
Thomas, *Mythos*	E. Thomas. *Mythos und Geschichte.* Cologne, 1976.
Thuillier	J.-P. Thuillier. "La frise gravée de lébès Barone de Capoue." *Mélanges offerts à Jacques Heurgon,* pp. 981-89. Rome, 1976.
Thulin, *Script*	C. Thulin. *Scriptorum Disciplinae Etruscae Fragmenta.* Berlin, 1906.
Tibiletti	G. Tibiletti. "Marsyas, die Sklaven und die Marser." *Studi in onore di E. Betti,* pp. 349-60. Milan, 1962.
Torelli, "CIL"	M. Torelli. "Contributi al supplemento del CIL IX." *RendLinc* 24 (1969):9-48.
Torelli, *Elogia*	———. *Elogia Tarquiniensia.* Florence, 1975.
Torelli, "Templum"	———. "Un 'templum' augurale d'età repubblicana a Bantia." *RendLinc* 21 (1966):293-315.
Touchefeu-Meynier	O. Touchefeu-Meynier. *Thèmes odysséens dans l'art antique.* Paris, 1968.
Trell	B. L. Trell. "Architectura Numismatica Orientalis. A Short Guide to the Numismatic Formulae of Roman Syrian Die-Makers." *NC* ser. 7, vol. 10 (1970):29-50.
Trendall, *Early*	A. D. Trendall. *Early South Italian Vase-Painting.* Mainz, 1974.
Trendall, "Felton"	———. "The Felton Painter and a Newly Acquired Apulian Comic Vase by His Hand." *In Honour of Daryl Lindsay. Essays and Studies,* pp. 45-52. Melbourne, 1964.
Trendall, *Indigeni*	———. *Gli indigeni nella pittura italiota.* Taranto, 1971.
Trendall, "Post-Script"	———. "Paestan Post-Script." *BSR* 21 (1953):160-67.

BIBLIOGRAPHY

Trendall-Webster	———, and T.B.L. Webster. *Illustrations of Greek Drama*. London, 1971.
Turcan	R. Turcan, "Encore la prophétie de Vegoia." *Mélanges offerts à Jacques Heurgon*, pp. 1009-1019. Rome, 1976.
Verzar	M. Verzar. "L'Umbilicus Urbis—Il Mundus in età tardo-repubblicana." *DialAr* 9-10 (1976-77):378-98.
Veyne, "Marsyas"	P. Veyne. "Le Marsyas colonial et l'indépendence des cités." *RevPhil* 35 (1961):87-98.
Wagenvoort, *Dynamism*	H. Wagenvoort. *Roman Dynamism*. Oxford, 1947.
Walters, *CatBr*	H. B. Walters. *Catalogue of the Bronzes, Greek, Roman, and Etruscan, in the Department of Greek and Roman Antiquities, British Museum*. London, 1899.
Waser	O. Waser. "Flussgötter." *RE* VI (1909):2774-2815.
Weiler	I. Weiler. *Der Agon im Mythos. Zur Einstellung der Griechen zum Wettkampf*. Darmstadt, 1974.
Weinstock, "Mundus"	S. Weinstock. "Mundus patet." *RömMitt* 45 (1930):111-23.
Weinstock, "Templum"	———. "Templum." *RömMitt* 47 (1932):95-121.
Weinstock, "Vegoia"	———. "Vegoia." *RE* ser. 2, vol. XIV (1930):577-81.
Weis, "Cista"	H. A. Weis. "The Ficoroni Cista and Amykos 'religatus.'" *Abstracts—A.I.A. 79th General Meetings, December 28-30, 1977*, p. 3.
Welin	E. Welin. *Studien zur Topographie des Forum Romanum. Acta Institutis Romani Regni Sueciae*. Lund, 1953.
Winter	J. G. Winter. "The Myth of Hercules at Rome." *University of Michigan Studies* 4, pp. 171-273. New York, 1910.
Wissowa, "Cacus"	G. Wissowa. "Cacus." *RE* ser. 1, vol. III (1899):1165-69.
Wissowa, *Religion*	———. *Religion und Kultus der Römer. Handbuch der Altertumswissenschaft*. Vol. V, pt. 4. 2nd ed. Munich, 1912.
Wolters	P. Wolters. "II. Darstellungen auf anderen Bildwerken." In Münzer, *Cacus*, pp. 121-31.
Yalouris	N. Yalouris. "Ἑρμῆς βοῦκλεψ." *ArchEph* (1953/54): Pt. II, pp. 162-84.
Zancani Montuoro	P. Zancani Montuoro. "Paestum." *EAA* 5:829-40.
Zanker, *Forum*	P. Zanker. *Forum Romanum. Die Neugestaltung durch Augustus*. Monumenta Artis Antiquae 5. Tübingen, 1972.
Zarker	J. W. Zarker. "The Hercules Theme in the Aeneid." *Vergilius* 18 (1972):34-48.

BIBLIOGRAPHY

Zmigryder-Konopka Zmigryder-Konopka. "Marsyas italski. Auspicia i libertas w strukturze państwowości rzymskiej. (Marsia italico. Auspicia e libertas nella struttura dello Stato romano.)" *Przegląd klasyczny* (1939):585-603.

INDEX

Actium, 34n
adlocutio, 71-74, 77, 82-83, 84n, 92
Aeneas, 22-23, 74, 77n
Albula, 26n
Albunea, 21, 33
Aliunea, 125-26
ambush, 4, 12, 20, 42-43, 50, 58, 106, 110
Amphiaraus, 46
Amycus, 66n
Anchises, 23
Annalists, 7, 9, 14-15, 20n, 49, 56. *See also* individual writers
Apamea-Celaenae, 76n, 81n, 84n, 133
Apollo, 68-69, 85, 87-88, 92, 105-106, 108, 133; Medicus, 98; Palatinus, 98-104; Tortor, 98n. *See also* musical contest
aposkopein, 72n
Arcadians, 8, 22. *See also* Evander
Archippe, 48, 76
Argei, 21n
Aricia, battle of, 41-42, 44-47, 54
Aristodemus, 44, 46-47, 50
Arnobius, *Adv. Nat.* 6-7, 13-14
Arnth, 40-41, 55
Arruns, *see* Arnth: Porsenna, Arruns; Veltymnus, Arruns
Artemis, 51
Artile, *see* Porsenna, Arruns
Athena, and Marsyas, 68
attribute, 58
Attus Navius, *see* Navius, Attus
augurs, xv, 74-75, 79
augury, xv, 16-17, 20-22, 48-50, 74-77, 86, 93-105, 107n, 110. *See also* birds and specific practices
Augustine, St., *De civ. D.* 19.12, 9n
Augustus, 31, 34, 97-104, 108-109
Aulocrene, 76n

birds in augury, 30, 75, 77-79, 94-95, 97, 101-102, 110
Bolsena, 40n
Bona Dea, 29, 31n, 106n
boots, 77, 85

Caca, 32-34, 54, 62
Cacius, 10n
Cacu(s), Chapters I-III, V-VI, *passim*. *See also* specific deeds, such as ambush, cattle-stealing
Caeculus, 33n
Campania, Etruscans in, 15-16, 44-47, 49
caput Olus, 13-14, 48n. *See also* Vibennae
carmina Marciana, 87-88, 90-91
Cassius Dio, 54.17.12, 100
Cassius Hemina, *apud OGR* 7.6-7, 6, 25-26
cattle-stealing, 3, 10-12, 21, 24-29, 32, 33n, 124
cave, 11, 33-34, 107
Celaenae, *see* Apamea-Celaenae
cena δωδεκάθεος, 98
Censorinus coins, 85-92, 108-110
centaur, 6
Chiusi, 40, 43, 53, 55-56
choice of moment, pictorial, 40n, 52, 58, 66n
Cicero: *Div.* 1.41.42, 42; *Leg.* 2.12.31, 93
CIL VI 37068, 81
Claudius, 15
coins: Greek imperials, 73-74, 82; Roman Republican, 71-72. *See also* Censorinus coins
column, 86, 88-89
composition, pictorial, 55n, 57, 60, 88
Cumae, 44-47
Cumeresa, 55

Dante, 6n
decemviri, 87, 90-91
Derkyllos, 22-23
Diodorus Siculus, 1.4.1-2, 20n; 3.58.3, 69; 4.21, 10n, 19-20, 24, 106, 124n
Diomedes, 23n
Dionysius of Halicarnassus, *Ant. rom.* 1.32.2, 8-9, 19; 1.79.4ff, 7n, 25; 4.62.1-5, 95-96; 4.62.5-6, 90; 5.36, 44-45, 47-50; 7.1.4, 49; 7.3.2-4, 45-46
diptych, 39n, 51-53

161

INDEX

disciplina etrusca, 43, 53
divination, xv, 4-5, 12, 20-22, 33-34, 38-44, 47-50, 53, 54n, 85, 97, 106, 109-110; public vs. private, 12, 93n, 102-103. *See also* specific types and uses
duumviri, 96

education, 42, 110
Etruscan inscriptions, 4, 15, 41, 55
Etruscans, 38-44
Etrusco-Roman, xiv
euhemerization, 24, 34n, 85
Euripides, *IT*, 50-52
Evander, 7-9, 21-26, 29, 31, 46. *See also* Arcadians
evocatio, 78n
exauguration, 77-79, 84, 92, 102-103, 105-106, 109
exorcism, 79n

Fabius Pictor, 7n
Faunus, 12, 21-25, 29-30, 33, 106n
Festus, *Romam* (L 328), 20n
fig trees, *see* Rome, *city, fici*
fillet, 86
flutes, 68-69
Forum, 81n, 83, 84n
foundations, 8, 17
François Tomb, *see* Vulci, François Tomb

Garanus, 27
Gellius, Gnaeus, 5-6, 12, 15, 23-24, 40n, 44-50, 53-54, 56, 67-68, 76-77, 81n, 84, 86, 105-106, 108-109
Geryjon, 3, 25, 27-29
gesture, 57
Glaukos, 23n
guest-friendship, *see ius hospitii*

haruspicy, xv, 94-95
Helen, 52n
hepatoscopy, 93-95, 102
Hercules, 3, 5, 21n, 22-23, 25, 27-31, 45-47, 50, 105-106
Hermes, 10-12
Herodotus, 7.26, 68n, 76n, 81n
Homeric Hymn to Hermes, 11
Horace, 70-71

indicium libertatis, see libertas
Iphigenia, 50-52
italic, xiv-xv, 35-36
ius hospitii, 22-26, 29, 105

ius hostium, 105-106
ius Italicum, 74n, 82

Jupiter Capitolinus, 98n, 100, 102n. *See also* Rome, *city*, temple of
Juturna, 32-33n

κακός, 7-9, 32, 33n
knife, 60-61

Lactantius, *Div. Inst.* 1.20.36, 32
landscape, *see* setting
Lars Porsenna, *see* Porsenna, Lars
Larth, 41, 55
lectisternium, 98n
legatus, 12, 23, 49, 86, 105-106
legend-making, xiii-xiv, 3, 5, 8, 28-29, 31, 37, 42, 92, 108
leges Aelia et Fufia, 97
letter, 51-53
Liber, 72, 79n, 82n
liberatio, see exauguration
libertas, 72-74, 77-82, 85-86, 102, 109; *indicium libertatis*, 77-83, 85
libri, 38, 43, 87, 89, 99-100
limitatio, 43, 102
Livy, 1.6.4-7.2, 30; 1.7.5, 6; 1.18.7, 79n; 1.36.3-7, 95; 2.15, 110; 5.15.7-11, 38; 25.12, 87, 90, 91n
ludi Apollinares, 87-88, 90-91
Lupa Romana, 82n
Lydians, 48, 76n

machaira, 61n
Marcii, 86-92
Marcius *vates*, 87-88
Marius, 85-86
marketplace, *see* Forum
Maron, 138n
Marsi, 76
Marsyas, 48-50, 105-111; and Augustus, 102-103; Chapters III-IV, *passim*. *See also* musical contest
Mastarna, 15
Megales, 48-50, 53-54, 61, 81n, 86, 105-106, 110
Midas, 12, 69n, 107n
models, pictorial, 108; Chapter III, *passim*
monster, 6
mourning, pictorial, 53-54, 65
musical contest between Apollo and Marsyas, 58-64, 66-67, 84-85, 91-92, 103, 105-106, 133
Myron, Athena and Marsyas, 68n

INDEX

Navius, Attus, 48, 80-81n, 94-96
Nereus, 75-76
Nonnus, *Dion.* 19, 138n
nudity, 52-53n
Numa, 12, 30, 33-34

obnuntiatio, 97
Olympus, 60, 62
omen, 38, 46, 48, 77-78, 94
Orestes, in Tauris, 50-52, 54n
Orpheus, prophesying head of, 125-26
Ovid, *Fasti* 4.949-54, 35n, 102

Pallas, 8
Paris, recognition of, 63
patronage, artistic, 55, 109
Phrygians, 48, 76-77
Picus, 12
Pinarii, 28
Pliny, *HN* 34.11 (20, 22), 88-89; 34.39 (139), 41n
Plutarch: *Vit. Publicola* 18-19, 47n; *Vit. Sulla* 27.6, 91
pomerium, 31, 34, 98
Populares, 85-86
Porsenna, Arruns, 4, 39-44, 47-50, 53-55, 68, 109-110; pictorial, 58-66
Porsenna, Lars, 40-43, 45-50, 109-110
Potitii, 28
prisoners, 50-55, 62-63
prodigy, *see* omen
Propertius 4.9.7, 24, 31n
prophecy, *see* divination
Proteus, 12, 75-76
Punic Wars, 87-88
Purni, 55
Pylades, 50-52, 54n

Quintilian, *Inst.* 11.3.112, 72; 11.3.120, 72n

Recaranus, 25-27
Remus, 25, 30
rivalry, 22, 24, 30. *See also* musical contest
river gods, 75-76, 81n
Rome, *city*: Ara Iuppiter Inventor, 29n; Ara Maxima, 26, 28-29, 31n; auguratorium, 17n; Aventine, 21, 29-32, 34; Caelian, 13; casa Caci, 19-21, 109; casa Romuli, 16-18; Comitium, 80-81n; cornel tree, 18; curia Saliorum, 17, 18n; *fici*, 80-81; ficus Ruminalis, 35n; fig, olive, and vine, 80; Forum Romanum, 80-82, 88-89, 92, 102, 106, 109; Lacus Curtius, 81n, 82n; mundus, 17n; Palatine, 8, 16-22, 24, 29-34, 41, 98-103, 105-106; Porta Trigemina, 29-31; *regia*, 35n, 101; *Roma quadrata*, 17n, 47; rostra, 79-80, 88-89; Scalae Caci, 10n, 18-21, 32, 103, 109; temple of Apollo Palatinus, 34. *See also* Augustus; temple of Jupiter Capitolinus, 13-14, 77-79, 90; Tria Fata, 89; tribunal for foreign praetor, 82; Umbilicus, 17n; Vicus Tuscus, 44-45
Rome, *historical*, 16-22, 34n, 41, 110
Romulus, 16-17, 22, 25, 30, 81, 82n, 95, 99, 101

Sabines, 22n, 48, 86, 105-106, 110
sanctuary, 54n
satyr, xv, 75n
secespita, 61n
seers, xv, 12, 38, 41-44, 46-50. *See also* Veii
Sentinate, 55
servant, 51, 54n
Servius, *ad Aen.* 8.190, 7, 32; 8.203, 27; 8.269, 23; 8.345, 23n; 11.34, 47
Servius Tullius, 15
servum noxae dedit, 26
setting, 10, 12, 65
Severans, 82-83
shepherd, 6, 25-27, 107
Sibyl, 88-91, 95-96, 98n, 100, 109; Cumaean, 34
Sibylline Books, 34, 43, 48, 89-91, 95-96, 99-100, 102
silenus, xv, 12, 71, 76n, 84-85, 86n, 106, 107n, 132, 138n
sleeping figures, 40n
Social Wars, 85-92, 97, 109
socius, 48
Solinus, 5-6
style, artistic, 57
Suetonius, *Aug.* 29.3, 99; 31.1, 99; 70, 98n
Sulla, 85, 88, 91
Surdinus, L. N., 81-82

Tacitus: *Ann.* 4.65, 13; *Hist.* 3.72.1, 41n
Tages, 47, 93-95
Tarchon, 23, 40n, 47-50, 53-54, 93-95, 105
Tarquinia, 37
Tarquinius Priscus, 48, 94-96
Tarquinius Superbus, 47-49, 53, 78, 95-96

INDEX

Tarquins, 93-97, 98n, 104
Tauris, *see* Orestes
templum, 79, 81
Theseus, 112n
Tiber, 26n
Timaios, 19n
trickster, 10
Turnus, 32-33n, 108
types, pictorial, *see* individually; stock, 62n, 63-64
Tyrannicides, 58

urns, 6, 37-67, 109; Chiusi, 63; footed, 117n; local styles, 64; workshops, 55, 109, 117n

vase painting: Apulian, 51-52, 58-59; Attic, 60; Faliscan, 59; Lucanian, 60-61, 84; Paestan, 62; South Italian, 57-67
Vegoia, 43, 102

Veii, war with Rome, 38
Vel Satıe, 75n
Veltymnus, Arruns, 41n, 43
Vergil, 29, 31, 108, 112n; *Aen.* 8.184-305, 3, 6, 23n, 27, 31-34, 103, 107-108; *Ecl.* 6.19, 86n
Vesta, 32, 34, 35n, 101-102
Vestal Virgins, 32
Vibennae, 4, 13-16, 37, 39-43, 49n, 52n, 54, 56, 58-59, 61, 63, 110, 124. *See also caput Olus*: Vulci, François Tomb
Victory, 88
Volturnus, 45-46
Vulcan, 32-33n
Vulci, François Tomb, 14-15, 37, 43n, 52n, 55, 63, 75n, 109, 124

winesack, 106

xenia, see *ius hospitii*

Library of Congress Cataloging in Publication Data

Small, Jocelyn Penny, 1945-
Cacus and Marsyas in Etrusco-Roman legend.
(Princeton monographs in art and archaeology; 44)
Bibliography: p.
Includes index.
1. Cacus (Roman deity) 2. Marsyas (Greek deity)
3. Etruscans—Religion. 4. Rome—Religion. I. Title.
II. Series.
BL820.C127S6   292'.211   82-47614
ISBN 0-691-03562-8   AACR2

Jocelyn Penny Small is the Director of the U.S. Center of the Lexicon Iconographicum Mythologiae Classicae at Rutgers University. She is the author of *Studies Related to the Theban Cycle on Late Etruscan Urns* (Giorgio Bretschneider, 1981) and has contributed to other volumes, including *The Princeton Encyclopedia of Classical Sites*, as well as writing many reviews and articles for journals both in the United States and abroad.

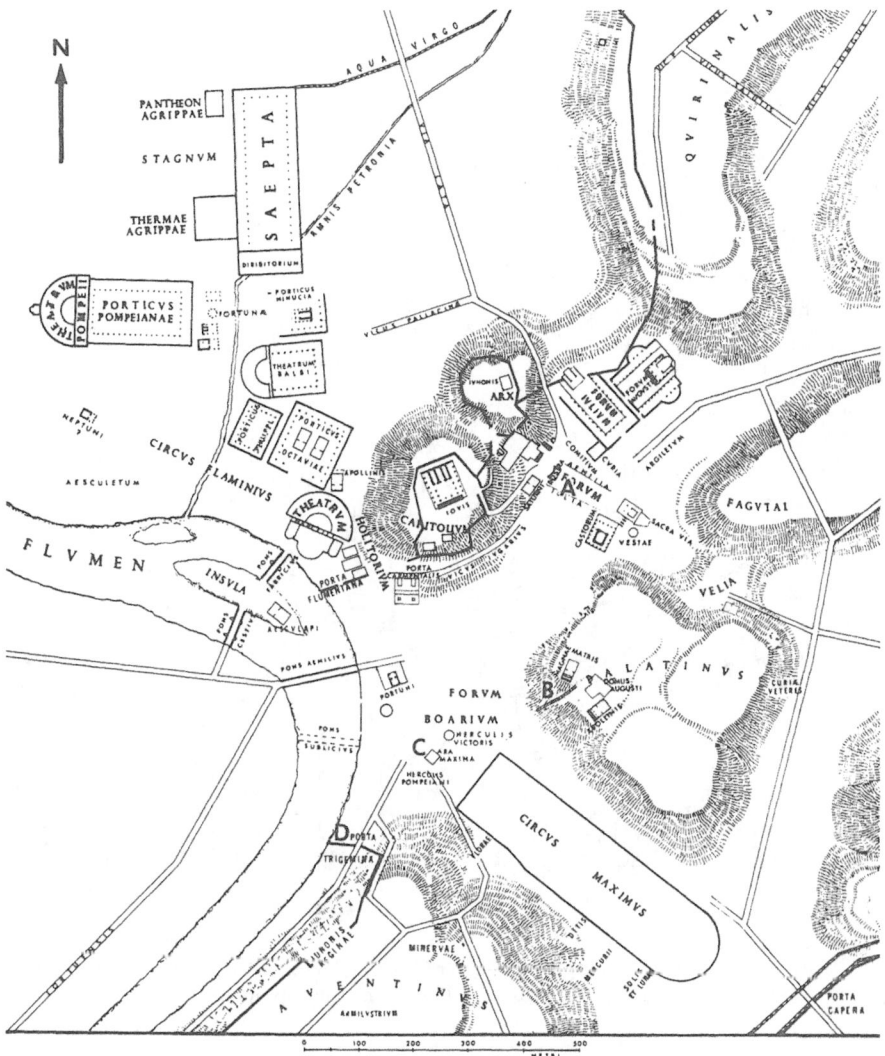

Plan 1. Rome, Augustan Era. (A) Marsyas in the Forum; (B) Scalae Caci; (C) Ara Maxima; (D) Porta Trigemina

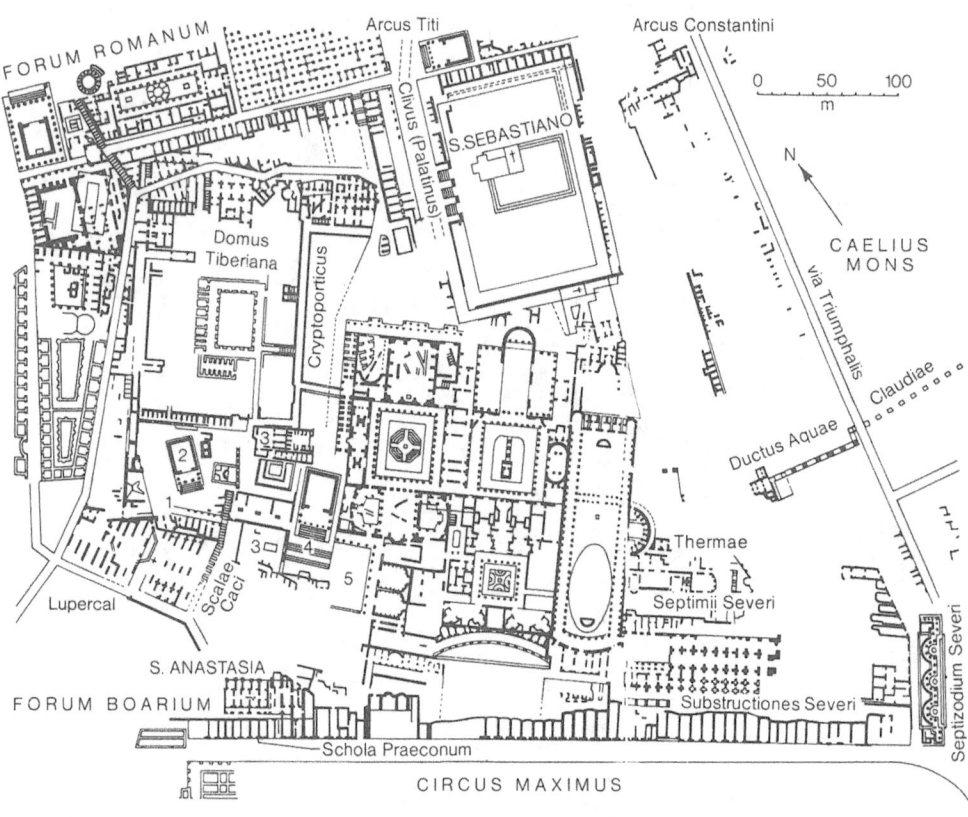

Plan 2. Palatine. (1) Huts; (2) Temple of Magna Mater; (3) House of Livia and Augustus; (4) Temple of Apollo Palatinus; (5) Portico of the Library

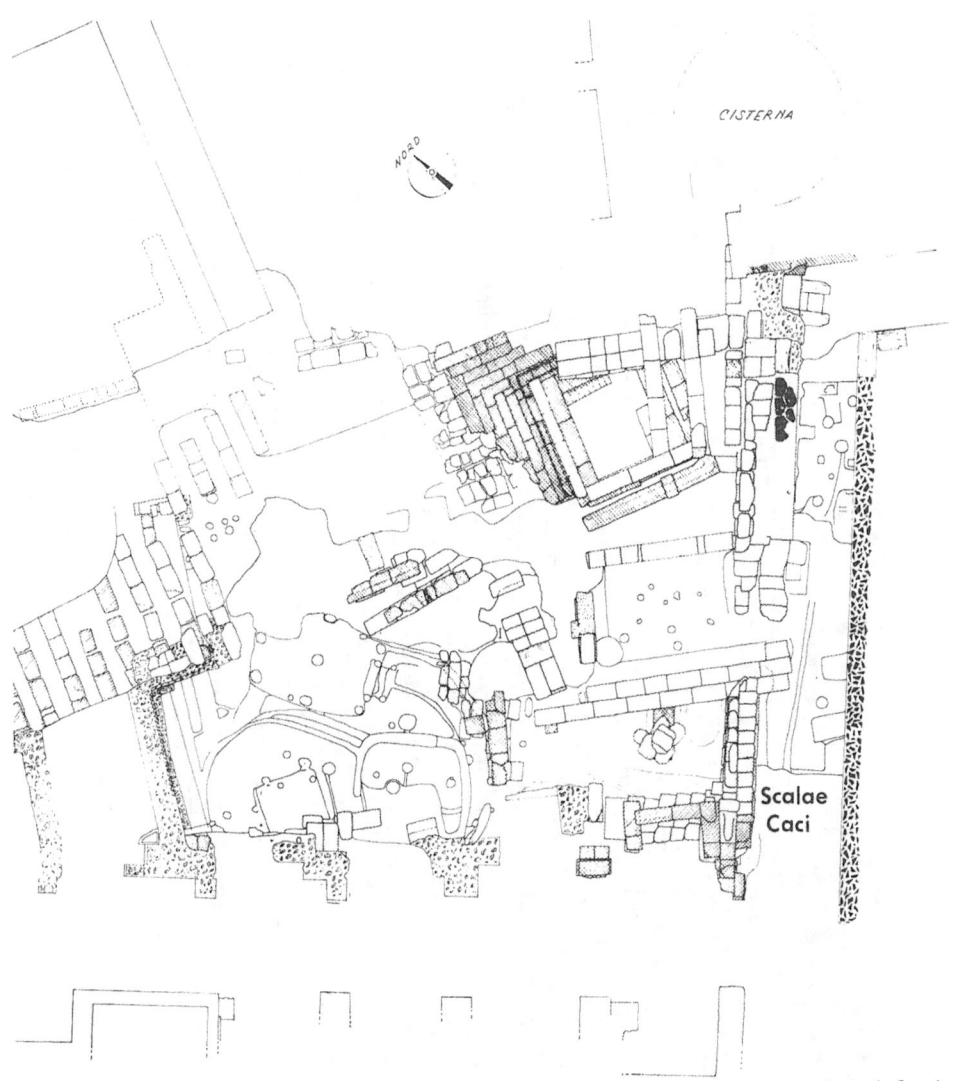

Plan 3. Palatine, Scalae Caci and Area.

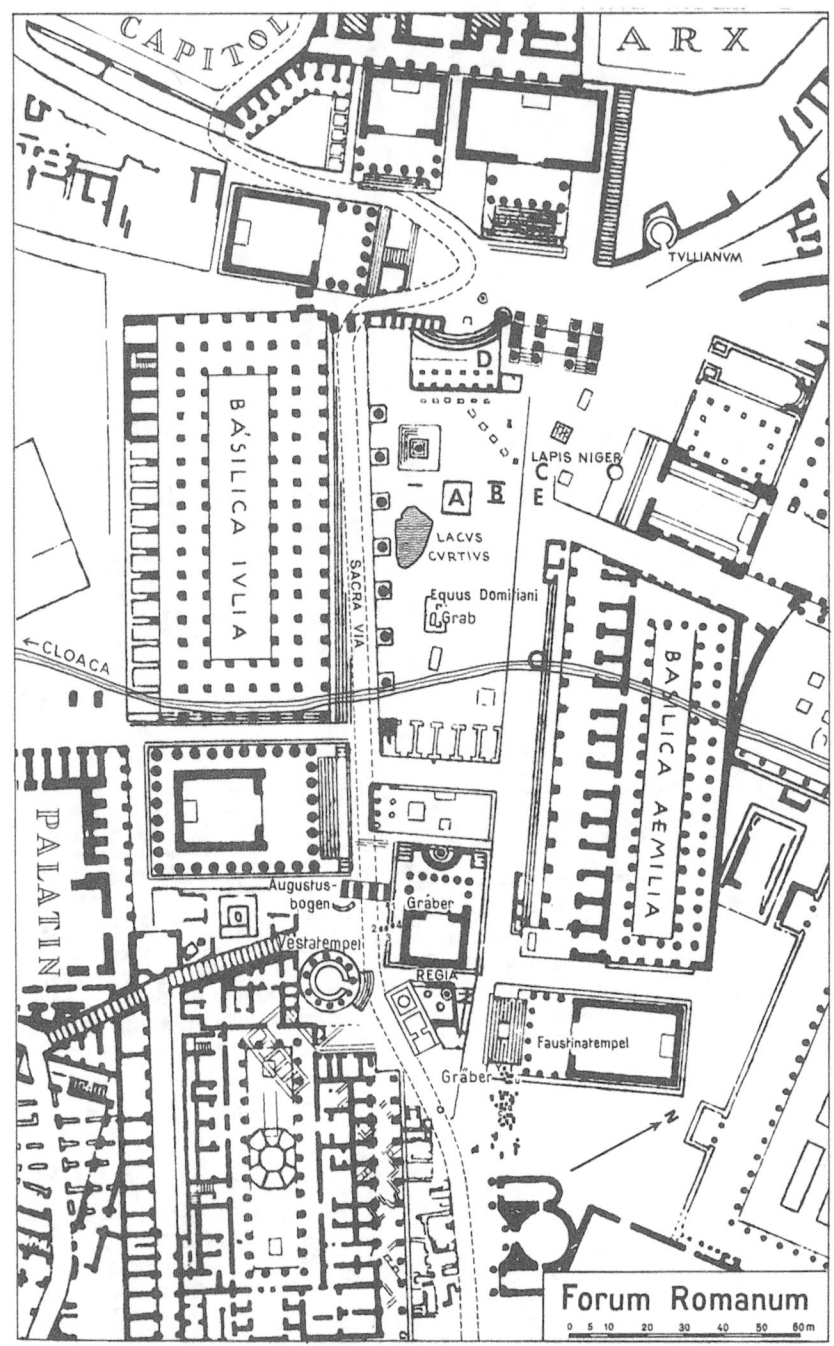

Plan 4. Forum Romanum. (A) Marsyas in the Forum; Fig, Olive, and Vine; (B) Anaglypha Traiani; (C) Old Rostra; (D) Augustan Rostra; (E) Statues of the Sibyl

Fig. 1. Cacu and the Vibennae
(App. I, no. 1)

Fig. 2. Cacu and the Vibennae
(App. I, no. 1)

Fig. 3. Cacu and the Vibennae
(App. I, no. 2)

Fig. 4. Cacu and the Vibennae
(App. I, no. 3)

Fig. 5. Cacu and the Vibennae
(App. I, no. 4)

Fig. 6. Cacu and the Vibennae
(App. I, no. 5)

Fig. 7. Cacu (?) the Prisoner
(App. I, no. 6)

Fig. 8. Cacu (?) the Prisoner
(App. I, no. 7)

Fig. 9. Cacu (?) the Prisoner
(App. I, no. 8)

Fig. 10. Cacu (?) the Prisoner
(App. I, no. 8)

Fig. 11. Cacu (?) the Prisoner
(App. I, no. 9)

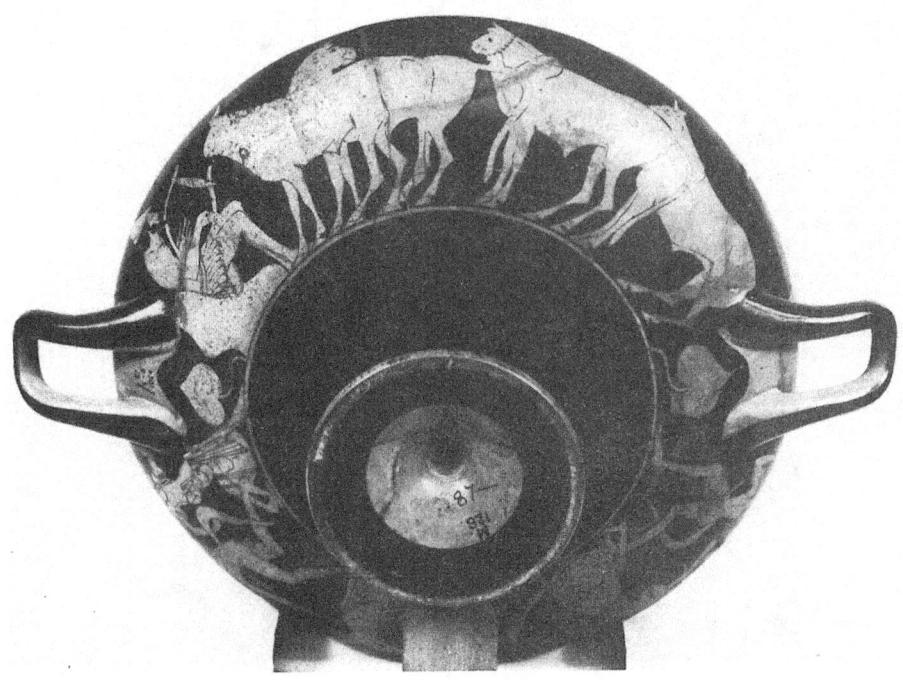

Fig. 12. Hermes and Cattle

Fig. 13. Orestes and Pylades in Tauris

Fig. 15. Musical Contest between Apollo and Marsyas

Fig. 14. Musical Contest between Apollo and Marsyas

Fig. 17. Musical Contest between Apollo and Marsyas

Fig. 16. Musical Contest between Apollo and Marsyas

Fig. 18. Musical Contest between Apollo and Marsyas

Fig. 19. Musical Contest between Apollo and Marsyas

Fig. 20. Apollo and Marsyas

Fig. 21. Marsyas? Bound

Fig. 22. Detail of Right Panel of Anaglypha Traiani (App. III, B 1)

Fig. 23. Detail of Left Panel of Anaglypha Traiani (App. III, B 1)

Fig. 24. Denarii of L. Marcius Censorinus (App. III, B 2), Obverse—Apollo, Reverse—Marsyas

Fig. 25: (a) Aureus of A. Manlius, Reverse—Sulla; (b), (d), (e), (f) Denarii of L. Marcius Censorinus, Reverse—Marsyas; (c) Denarius Serratus of A. Postumius Albinus, Reverse—Togate Figure

Fig. 26. Imperial Bronzes with Marsyas (App. III, C): (a) no. 6—Alexandria Troas; (b,c) no. 20—Neapolis; (d) no. 14—Damascus; (e,f) no. 18—Sidon; (g,h) no. 19—Tyre; (i,j) no. 15—Berytus

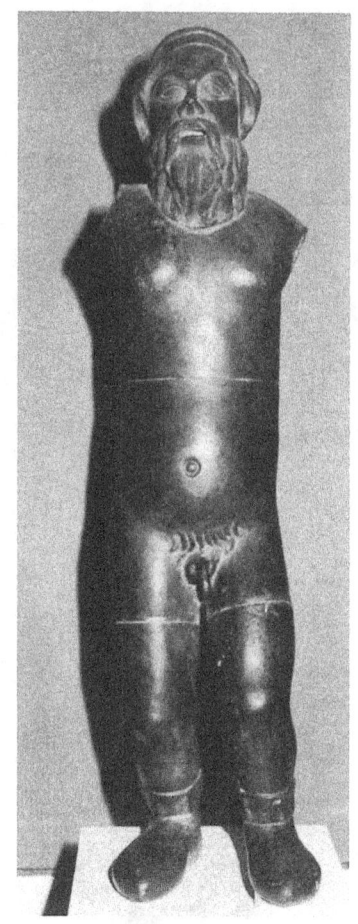

Fig. 27. Marsyas (App. III, B 3)

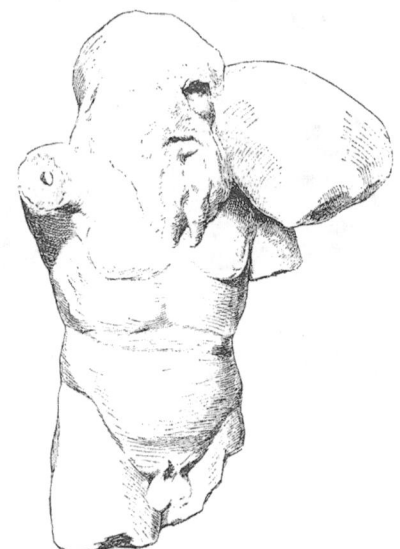

Fig. 28. Marsyas (App. III, B 4)

Fig. 29. Forum Romanum—View from the Palatine

Fig. 30. Forum Romanum—View from Curia

GPSR Authorized Representative: Easy Access System Europe - Mustamäe tee 50, 10621 Tallinn, Estonia, gpsr.requests@easproject.com

www.ingramcontent.com/pod-product-compliance
Lightning Source LLC
Chambersburg PA
CBHW060512300426
44112CB00017B/2638